W9-CLH-559

Euclid Public Library
631 E. 222nd Street
Euclid, Ohio 44123
216-261-5300

PUTIN

AND THE

RISE OF RUSSIA

PUTIN
AND THE
RISE OF
RUSSIA

MICHAEL STUERMER

PEGASUS BOOKS
NEW YORK

PUTIN AND THE RISE OF RUSSIA

Pegasus Books LLC
80 Broad Street, 5th Floor
New York, NY 10004

Copyright © 2009 by Michael Stuermer

First Pegasus Books edition 2009

All rights reserved. No part of this book may be reproduced in whole or in part
without written permission from the publisher, except by reviewers who may quote
brief excerpts in connection with a review in a newspaper, magazine, or electronic
publication; nor may any part of this book be reproduced, stored in a retrieval system,
or transmitted in any form or by any means electronic, mechanical, photocopying,
recording, or other, without written permission from the publisher.

Library of Congress Cataloging-in-Publication Data is available.

ISBN: 978-1-60598-062-1

10 9 8 7 6 5 4 3 2 1

Printed in the United States of America
Distributed by W. W. Norton & Company, Inc.
www.pegasusbooks.us

CONTENTS

ACKNOWLEDGEMENTS

The author is indebted to many people who have, through their ideas, expertise and advice, contributed to the concept of this book. First and foremost I wish to thank Ms Katja Machotina from St Petersburg, Russia and Munich, Germany who has given me invaluable help and advice, asking questions and providing answers, and checking much of the detail.

Many diplomats, active and retired, have given advice, some have provided information and also source material otherwise difficult to obtain. Among them the late Dr Otto von der Gablenz, Dr Ernst-Georg von Studnitz, Dr Hans von Ploetz, Dr Michael Libal, Dr Hermann Freiherr von Richthofen, Dr Eberhard von Puttkamer, and last but not least Dr Hans-Georg Wieck who, as the head of Bundesnachrichtendienst in Pullach, was my neighbour in Ebenhausen while I was director of Stiftung Wissenschaft and Politik. I should also like to acknowledge the help received from Russia's ambassador to Berlin Wladimir Kotenew. I recall many conversations with the Italian ambassador to Berlin Antonio Puri Purini. Ambassador (ret.) Robert Blackwill (ex NSC), Washington and now with the RAND-Corporation Santa Monica, with General (ret.) Klaus Naumann, with Professor Lothar Ruehl, State Secretary MoD (ret.), Bonn, with the Finnish Ambassador to Berlin René Nyberg, and also with John Kornblum, former US ambassador to Germany and now with Lazard Frères.

Dr Regina von Flemming has given me many insights on what it means to do business in Russia, as has Dr Axel Lebahn, formerly of Deutsche Bank, Göttingen.

Dr Alexander Rahr, DGAP, Berlin, has contributed much expertise on personalities and problems. Professor Sergei Karaganow, Moscow, has opened many doors for me. Dmitri Trenin, Carnegie Endowment, Moscow, has been a constant source of inspiration, and likewise Harvard Professor Marshall Goldman. Important advice on financial matters was given by Kurt Viermetz, Chairman of the Overseeing

Board, Deutsche Borse AG, Frankfurt. Dr Gerhard Saoebathil, a Euro-crat of the best kind, formerly in Berlin and now Brussels, has con-tributed his vast experience on EU–Russian relations.

Dmitry Tulchinsky, RIA Novosty, Berlin, has been helpful in arran-ging various excursions to Russia. Dr Klaus Joachim Herrmann, Neues Deutschland, Berlin, has helped with some of the pictures.

Of course, the economic aspects of Russia's standing in the global market place are of crucial importance, and I wish to thank, among others, Dr Klaus Mangold and Dr Oliver Wieck from Ost-Ausschuss der Deutschen Wirtschaft, Berlin. Prof. Dr Klaus-Ewald Holst, CEO, Verbundnetz Gas AG (VNG) Leipzig, has provided many insights into the working of the energy industry.

I have also profited immensely from conversations with Russian experts such as Lilia Shevtsova, Carnegie Endowment, Moscow; Vlad-imir Ryshkow, Member of Duma; Vyacheslav Nikonov, Editor in Chief of Strategija Rossii, Moscow; Alexei Arbatov, Member of Duma, Moscow.

I would also like to acknowledge the insights provided over many years by friends like Ivar Tangen, Secretary General, The Norwegian Energy Foundation, Oslo; Dr Ulrich Schlie, MoD, Berlin; and last but by no means least, Dr Peter Scholl-Latour, Berlin and Paris.

Finally I feel very much indebted to the late George F. Kennan who, while at the Institute for Advanced Study in Princeton many years ago, through conversation and writing, gave me many insights into the historical forces at work inside the Soviet Union and Russia.

While I thank all of those who have accompanied, wittingly or unwittingly, the writing of this book over many years, the responsibility for what I offer the reader in terms of information and judgement is, of course, entirely mine.

Michael Stuermer

Putin in 1994: 'What happens to ethnic Russians beyond our borders is for us an existential question.'

Ethnic Russians in the Newly Independent States

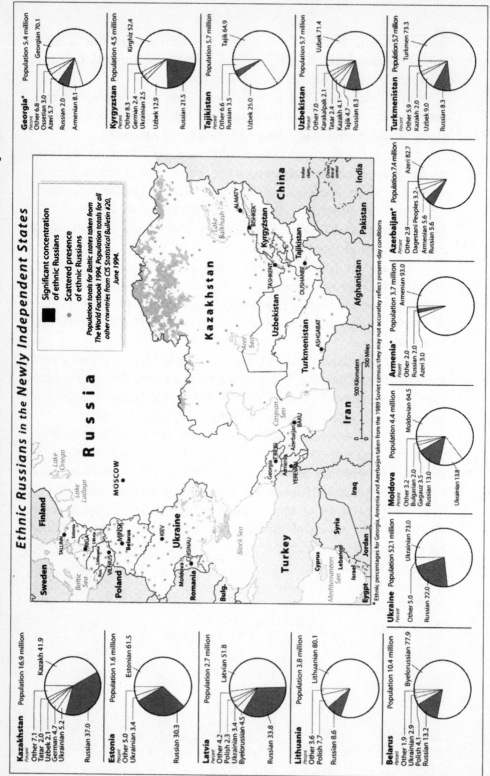

Kazakhstan Population 16.9 million
Percent
Kazakh 41.9
Other 7.1
Tatar 2.0
Uzbek 2.1
German 4.7
Ukrainian 5.2
Russian 37.0

Estonia Population 1.6 million
Percent
Estonian 61.5
Other 5.0
Ukrainian 3.4
Russian 30.3

Latvia Population 2.7 million
Percent
Latvian 51.8
Other 4.2
Polish 2.3
Ukrainian 3.4
Byelorussian 4.5
Russian 33.8

Lithuania Population 3.8 million
Percent
Lithuanian 80.1
Other 3.6
Polish 7.7
Russian 8.6

Belarus Population 10.4 million
Percent
Byelorussian 77.9
Other 1.9
Ukrainian 2.9
Polish 4.1
Russian 13.2

Ukraine Population 52.1 million
Percent
Ukrainian 73.0
Other 5.0
Russian 22.0

Moldova Population 4.4 million
Percent
Moldovian 64.5
Other 3.2
Bulgarian 2.0
Gagauz 3.5
Russian 13.0
Ukrainian 13.8

Armenia* Population 3.7 million
Percent
Armenian 93.0
Other 2.0
Russian 2.0
Azeri 3.0

Azerbaijan* Population 7.4 million
Percent
Azeri 82.7
Other 2.9
Dagestani Peoples 3.2
Armenian 5.6
Russian 5.6

Georgia* Population 5.4 million
Percent
Georgian 70.1
Other 6.8
Ossetian 3.0
Azeri 5.7
Russian 2.0
Armenian 8.1

Kyrgyzstan Population 4.5 million
Percent
Kirghiz 52.4
Other 8.3
German 2.4
Ukrainian 2.5
Uzbek 12.9
Russian 21.5

Tajikistan Population 5.7 million
Percent
Tajik 64.9
Other 6.6
Russian 3.5
Uzbek 25.0

Uzbekistan Population 5.7 million
Percent
Uzbek 71.4
Other 7.0
Tatar 2.1
Karakalpok 2.1
Kazakh 4.1
Tajik 4.7
Russian 8.3

Turkmenistan Population 5.7 million
Percent
Turkmen 73.3
Other 5.9
Kazakh 2.0
Uzbek 9.0
Russian 8.3

■ Significant concentration
of ethnic Russians
• Scattered presence
of ethnic Russians

*Population totals for Baltic states taken from
The World Factbook 1994. Population totals for all
other countries from CIS Statistical Bulletin #20,
June 1994.*

*Ethnic percentages for Georgia, Armenia and Azerbaijan taken from the 1989 Soviet census; they may not accurately reflect present-day conditions

The new currencies of power: Gas and pipelines for the empire. Targeting the European market.

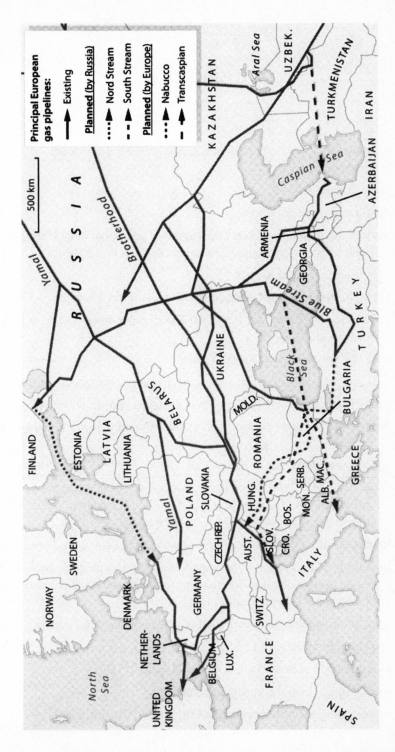

Principal European gas pipelines:

— Existing

Planned (by Russia)
······ Nord Stream
– – – South Stream

Planned (by Europe)
······ Nabucco
– – – Transcaspian

500 km

CHRONOLOGY

7 October 1952: Putin born in Leningrad, growing up in rough neighbourhood

1953: Stalin dies

1973/74: first oil price hike

1975: Putin graduates at Law Department of Leningrad State University (while also working for the Leningrad Directorate of KGB)

1975: Helsinki Final Act

1978/79: second oil price hike, crisis thoughout the West

July 1982: in Lebanon war Israeli Air Force shoots down 70 Syrian MIGS, shock in Moscow

1982/83: Juri Andropov Kremlin Chief

1985: oil price breaks down, a boost for the West, catastrophe for Russia

1986: Chernobyl burnout, Gorbachev demands perestroika and glasnost

1987: sweeping arms control agreements between USSR and USA (INF Treaty)

9 November 1989: fall of Berlin Wall

1990: 'Two plus Four' negotiations, Nato offers 'brotherly hand', German unification: Putin adviser to Mayor Anatoli Sobchak on international affairs after KGB work in Dresden, DDR from 1985

June 1991–96: Putin head of administration of St Petersburg Mayor's Office

June 1996–March 1997: Putin joins Russian presidential administration, deputy to chief of Main Control Directorate, Presidential Property Management Department

1998: Putin appointed deputy chief of presidential administration

1998/99: Putin head of FSB

Summer 1998: financial crisis in Russia, oil at USD 10

August 1998: financial collapse and default

September 1998: Yeltsin appoints Evgeny Primakov prime minister

1999: Nato widening includes ex-Warsaw Pact countries

Spring 1999: tense political situation in Russia. Kremlin loses control over events

1999: Putin appointed Secretary of the Security Council

August 1999: Chechen fighters headed by Shamil Basayev invade Northern Republic of Daghestan

August 1999: Duma confirms appointment of Putin as Premier

September 1999: second Chechen War starts

31 December 1999: Yeltsin nominates Putin his successor

March 2000: Putin elected President of Russia

August 2000: Submarine *Kursk* lost at sea, crisis of Putin's leadership

November 2000: clampdown on independent media

March 2001: Sergei Ivanov appointed defence minister

Spring 2001: proclamation of 'managed democracy', aka 'sovereign democracy'

June 2001: creation of Shanghai Cooperation Organization (China, Russia, Kazakhstan, Kyrgyzstan, Tajikistan, Uzbekistan)

Fall 2001: Russia cooperates with US in war against Taliban in Afghanistan

December 2001: United States withdraws from ABM Treaty

October 2002: terrorist action at Dubrovka theatre in Moscow. Rescue attempt by federal forces leaves 120 dead

November 2002: EU-Russia summit in Brussels

March 2003: second Iraq War

May 2003: EU–Russia Summit in St Petersburg: definition of four 'common spaces' for cooperation Russia–EU

October 2003: Mikhail Khodorkovsky, CEO of YUKOS, taken into custody, sentenced for alleged tax fraud to eight years in prison

November 2003: Georgia's 'Rose Revolution' and chagrin in Moscow

February 2004: Putin dismisses premier Mikhail Kasianov

September 2004: terrorists attack Beslan school, Ingushetia, North Caucasus

November–December 2004: 'Orange Revolution' in Ukraine, souring of relations between Russia and the Yushchenko-team

January 2005: street protests against intended reform of 'monetization' of social benefits

December 2005: Gazprom raises gas price for Ukraine, briefly cutting off supply

July 2006: G-8 summit in St Petersburg

August 2006: ethnic clashes in the town of Kondopoga in Karelia

October 2006: Anna Politkovskaya, independent-minded columnist for *Novaya Gazeta*, murdered

10 February 2007: Munich Security Conference, Putin speaks out

30 November 2007: Shvartsman in interview with *Kommersant* spills the Kremlin beans

2nd December 2007: elections for Duma

12th December 2007: Putin endorses Dmitry Medvedev as successor

2nd March 2008: Medvedev elected president

7th May 2008: inauguration of Medvedev

ABBREVIATIONS

ABM – Anti-Ballistic Missile (Treaty)
BTC Pipeline – Baku-Tiflis-Ceyhun Pipeline
CEO – Chief Executive Officer
CFE – Conventional Forces in Europe (Treaty)
CIS – Commonwealth of Independent States
CSCE – Conference for Security and Cooperation in Europe
EU – European Union
FSB – Federal'naya Sluzhba Beszopasnosti – Federal Security Service
IAEA – International Atomic Energy Agency, Vienna
ICBM – Intercontinental Ballistic Missile
IPO – Initial Public Offering
KGB – Komitet Gosudarstvennoy Bezopasnosti – Committee for State
  Security
LNG – Liquified Natural Gas
NAFTA – North American Free Trade Association
NATO – North Atlantic Treaty Organization
NGO – Non-Governmental Organization
NPT – Non-Proliferation Treaty
OECD – Organisation for Economic Cooperation and Development
OSCE – Organisation for Security and Cooperation in Europe
PCA – Partnership and Cooperation Agreement EU–Russia
PRC – People's Republic of China
ROC – Russian Orthodox Church
SALT – Strategic Arms Limitation Treaty
SCO – Shanghai Cooperation Organization
SEC – Securities and Exchange Commission (US)
START – Strategic Arms Reduction Treaty
UN – United Nations
USD – US Dollar
WTO – World Trade Organisation

PREFACE

For the time being and for some time to come the world is living under the sign of the global crisis that, for some months, did not dare to give its name: Depression. Russia cannot claim much of an exception, but finds itself in the middle of a double predicament.

On the one hand the global slump that began its infernal course in the depths of the US financial markets, turned into a crisis of trust and confidence among banks worldwide, led to a global deflation of consumer prices, made millions redundant, provoked massive government intervention and gave the social climate a distinctly nasty turn – the London Economist of April 4, 2009, carried a dossier entitled "Get the Rich", illustrated with the famous Delacroix painting celebrating the revolution marching over dead bodies.

On the other hand, Russia learnt that a petrostate cannot dissociate itself from the ups and downs of the world market, that a return to the old Soviet ways of self-sufficiency and insulation is impossible, that the Promised Land of the science based economy is still far away and very costly to attain, possibly requiring nothing short of a revolution from above. Just sitting out the crisis would be dangerous to the social equilibrium and, in fact, to the distribution of power and wealth and, in fact, to the regime.

The reaction from the Kremlin was, at first glance, a question: Crisis? What crisis? After a while, Putin decreed that TV and newspapers should avoid mentioning the unpleasantness which, anyway, was nothing but a problem of the West. Had not Mother Russia put aside enough Petrodollars for a rainy day in foreign currency reserves and, if need be, the stabilization fund? Little did the men in the Kremlin understand that, if growth throughout the industrial world turned into recession, the demand for oil and gas would plummet and the all important oil price, having corrected its excesses at USD 147 in summer of 2008, might well slide to a miserable USD 40 or even less.

No question that Russia's state budget for 2009, based on an average oil price of USD 71, had become pie in the sky. The reserves, stabilization fund or no, were thrown into battle and, after about eight months of fighting, were reduced to half the strength they had mustered before the lean years started. Moscow's building boom has come to a grinding halt. Cranes are idle, turning in the wind. Luxury boutiques are looking for well-healed customers who won't show up. Hundreds of thousands of people are made redundant across the country. Imports of premium cars from Germany and even machine tools, until 2008 on a steep upward curve, were cut back sharply.

Worst of all, investment in energy, whether oil or gas, dwindled, thus preparing, out of today's chokepoints, tomorrow's oil and gas shortages – plus the ensuing price hikes. When this turn-around will happen – somewhere between one year and three years – is impossible to predict with any precision. It depends not only on the downward curve of production but also on the upward curve of demand. But happen it will, and by that time Russia's worst troubles will be over. Does that mean a return to business as usual? Probably not.

Under Mr. Putin's presidency the bargain between Russia's rulers and Russia's masses was simple: The people accepted an increasingly autocratic regime while the Kremlin delivered rising living standards – as never before. Annual economic growth, fuelled by rising oil prices and cheap credit thundered forward at an immodest 7 to 8 percent. In 2009, however, it is reckoned that low oil prices plus the world recession will result in a fall in Russian GDP of six percent. Predictions out of London are that hundreds of Russian banks will disappear. Incoming foreign investment, in 2008 still running at 28 billion USD, is drying up. Both Russian stockmarkets have lost, after their peak in 2008, around two thirds of their sum total. The rubel is on a downward slide. Unemployment will rise, while inflation will remain high at close to 12 percent.

In most Western countries such a situation would unhinge the social contract, and trouble would ensue. The same can happen in Russia, and some signs are fairly ominous already at the time of writing. However, Russia is not a Western style industrial democracy. The country has hidden reserves and stabilizers that will allow Kremlin rulers to control their worries – if they have any. Russian power will not disappear, nor will Russian self-confidence dissipate.

Russian power is based first if all on its vast geography. It can project power towards most or all of the "Near Abroad", and the rest of the world can do very little about it. At home, the Kremlin uses an iron fist to control public sentiment and to nip social unrest in the bud. The security services have by now re-infiltrated almost every aspect of Russian public life. Lack of stability in most of the post-Soviet states allows Russian intelligence to operate with impunity.

The social system is based on the tradition that the survival of the state is more important than the well-being of the people – and so far the people accept this time-honoured state of affairs. Through all those collapses, Weimar style, that haunted the country since 1985, Russia continued to function. Mass protests in Russia? So far they are an alien notion. Moscow can count on a stable population.

Russia can also draw on a wealth of natural resources. The markets may play havoc with prices, but in the end the fundamentals will prevail, and the world will, once again, buy buy buy. Russia will not only sell its natural wealth to the highest bidder but also use it to project power: No need to specifically mention natural gas and Europe's dependence on it.

The Russian military, underpaid and underequipped, is restructuring and reconstituting its war fighting capability. The mixed evaluation of the Georgia war resulted in a massive upgrading of military equipment. Above all, Russia, through a renewed effort at arms control, is trying to establish parity with the US.

In intelligence the Russians continue to be second to none. The KGB instills fear into hearts around the world – and certainly into Russian hearts. The FSB and other Russian intelligence agencies have infiltrated most former Soviet republics and satellite states, and it is said that their reach extends to Latin America and the US. Russian intelligence has access to military and industrial realms worldwide: The Russians wrote the book on the subject, and have not forgotten. The most intense focus is on the "Near Abroad" where Russia claims, as President Medvedev put it, "privileged interests".

While oil prices, for the time being, are low and the financial sector is torn apart, the hard core of Russia's power is not affected. The Soviet Union was never as strong as it looked, nor is Russia as weak as it appears. By Western standards Russia is in crisis. By Russian standards, Russia continues to be a dominant power and claims a place in the world second to none. This is the time for a new realpolitik.

PUTIN

AND THE

RISE OF RUSSIA

INTRODUCTION

'On entering the country of the Russians, you see at a glance that the social order as arranged by them can serve for their use only. You have to be Russian to live in Russia, although on the surface everything proceeds much as elsewhere. The difference is in fundamentals.'
Marquis de Custine, *Journey for Our Time*

When, on a recent visit to Russia, I was hurrying through Moscow's Kazan railway station, my eye caught sight of a tiny gold coin. On stopping to pick it up, I discovered that it was too light to be the real thing, only ten copecks, a mere nothing. But it was a carefully struck piece, with St George on horseback slaying the dragon. No more hammer and sickle to frighten the world, no more red stars to enlighten the world – orthodox Russia had reasserted itself, and the hallowed image of the saintly victor is now everywhere, adorning every uniform, even Mr Putin's malachite inkwell, shielding the presidential palaces against intruders and signalling, in the guise of a return to the past, a journey into the unknown. One wonders what Lenin, his giant bronze statue in the central square of Tatarstan's capital Kazan (he came from a place not far away called Uljanowsk) – still preaching to the invisible masses, or his giant profile in Berlin's Behrenstrasse, once guarding the KGB headquarters in the now extinct German Democratic Republic, would have made of the return of St George to Russia.

It is not for the first time in the last two centuries that Russia leaves the world wondering about its destiny. Russia is, notwithstanding the losses incurred when the Soviet empire imploded upon itself, still the enormous country of eleven time zones from Kaliningrad Oblast on the Baltic Sea to the far eastern island of Sakhalin, a land of vast empty spaces full of promise, with a population of more than 140 million of whom 20 million are Muslim, looking at the crescent rising rather than the cross and the stars, suspecting that St George might not be their friend and protector. It is a power with vast military resources, among them more than 10,000 nuclear weapons in various configurations, an energy giant whose oil reserves will last, at present rates of exploit-ation, for more than thirty years, with enough natural gases for more than 180 years.

There is also the old Russian cultural and geopolitical ambiguity between Europe and Asia, and the new oscillation between weak elem-ents of democracy and, invariably, strong elements of autocracy.

When it comes to world affairs, the question may well be asked whether Russia forms part of an emerging multipolar balance or is striving to have a say and, in particular, a veto in all major affairs around the globe, especially in Eastern Europe, the Caucasus, the Greater Middle East and Central Asia. Can Russia be persuaded from outside, beyond its manifest interests, to support those elements of the Pax Americana that continue to be regulators of globalization, like the World Trade Organization, the World Bank, the International Mon-etary Fund? Will Russia support what is left of world order after the demise of the Cold War and the accompanying global, nuclear and bipolar system that is no more? In a nutshell: Will yesterday's revolu-tionary power become tomorrow's stabilizer of the industrial and post-industrial world from, as envisaged after the fall of the Soviet Union, Vancouver to Vladivostok? Russia clearly has the potential to act one way or the other, to be a force for stability or a force for turmoil. So far it seems that the leaders of Russia have not yet decided. Which way they go depends, in no small degree, on the West, its cohesion, statecraft and understanding of Russia.

We are back to the question that, in the grim winter of 1940, was asked in Britain while the European continent belonged to the dictators, when Sir Winston Churchill famously said on BBC radio: 'I cannot forecast to you the action of Russia. It is a riddle, wrapped in a mystery, inside an enigma.' And then the British PM added, almost as an afterthought: 'The only key is the national interest of Russia.'

So the question remains as to what today constitutes Russia's national interest, and who is the man, or the power elite around him, to define and implement it. When Putin's second term was about to end, it was not only the Russians who feared, after eight years of rising oil and gas revenues that brought modest gains for many and vast riches for a few, instability and insecurity. But the outside world, too, kept wondering who and what would follow after Putin: possibly, after a while, Putin himself, in a different incarnation? Whatever the answer,

Russia is going, for better or for worse, through a defining moment. What are the implications for the rest of the world?

In the post-1989 world the greatest of all challenges for the former antagonists was to create together an equitable and fair system, in which Russia would be part of a new world order – as promised by the elder Bush in the aftermath of the 1990–91 Gulf War. This opportunity was missed during the decade when the West was strong and Russia was weak. Do we have today the Russia we deserve? To be torn between a resurgent Russia and a declining Pax Americana would be divisive, indeed fatal, for today's Europe and an enormous burden on the Atlantic alliance.

It is late, but perhaps not too late, to think big and try once more. After all, the rise and rise of China in the Far East – which is not so far away when seen from Siberia, where much of Europe's oil and gas comes from – poses vast challenges. So does the threat of radical Islam in the Middle East, be it the Iranians' nuclear ambitions, be it terrorist disruption. For good measure one can add accelerating climate change and the spread – and eventual containment – of weapons of mass destruction, of terrorism and failed states, of cyberwar and organized crime. All those spectres haunting the world are of equal concern both to Russia and to Western nations.

History is on the move again. But it is not an inexorable fate that we face but an open and challenging future. In all of this, Russia, for better and for worse, will have a key role to play.

I

A moment of truth

'The Tsar of Russia is the military chief, and each of his days is a day of battle.'

Marquis de Custine *Journey for Our Time*

The date was 10 February 2007, in the middle of Munich's popular carnival season. The venue was the Bayerischer Hof, a five-star hotel where traditionally the annual Wehrkunde Conference of Cold War times and now the post-Cold War 'Munich Security Conference' meets for a high-level, two-day event. This get-together of the strategic community was initiated by Ewald von Kleist, a man from the history books who supported Count Stauffenberg in the July 1944 attempt to blow up the German dictator. His successor in the chair was Horst Teltschik, for many years Chancellor Kohl's most trusted foreign policy adviser. In 2007 he had invited the Russian leader to give a key-note speech. Little did those wearing insiders' badges or, for that matter, the scores of journalists following the proceedings from adjacent rooms, know that they were in for a defining moment in Russia's relations with America and the West. Indeed, after that Munich meeting some red lines, hitherto blurred by arrogance, ignorance and wishful thinking, were clearly discernible – lines which the master of the Kremlin wanted to be respected, in Eastern Europe, in the Balkans and throughout Central Asia.

On that first morning of the conference, German chancellor Angela Merkel was holding forth. Meanwhile, those who sat near him could observe how Russian president Vladimir Putin was busy making changes to the manuscript that his staff had given him, striking out entire paragraphs and putting in new ones, scribbling notes in the margins, from time to time shaking his head as if in anger, and paying little or no attention to what the German Number One had to tell the world leaders, defence experts and political analysts assembled in the air-conditioned, brightly lit ballroom. It was clear beyond the slightest doubt that Putin, sitting in the front row, did not have to ask any one for approval of the speech he was to deliver, let alone for permission to outline the future course of Russia's relations with the West in general and the United States in particular. Putin was clearly in control – not only of the next thirty or so minutes but of Russia's foreign and security affairs.

When Putin mounted the rostrum, he showed no emotion except cold resolve. He spoke in a low-key voice, with sparse body language, his emotions carefully disciplined and controlled. Of course he spoke in Russian. The conference's tradition, he warned his listeners with a whiff of sarcasm, 'allows me to avoid excessive politeness'.

The bear growls

What he had to say to the 200 or so experts assembled, live into the world's TV cameras, did indeed not amount to a lesson in diplomatic finesse. He made no secret of the fact that he felt, like all of Russia, that the West had unilaterally and unfairly exploited the period of troubles that the heirs to the Soviet Union had recently experienced. That instead of offering compensation for Russian losses the West had done everything in its power to secure geopolitical advantage throughout Eastern Europe and most of Central Asia. That the relationship with Nato was tenuous at best. That the Russians felt encircled from their front garden on the Baltic to their backyard in Uzbekistan. That he resented Nato's recent 'expansion' to Eastern Europe – referring to Poland, the Czech Republic, Hungary and Slovakia, formerly Soviet satellites in the Warsaw Pact, and also to the Baltic states that were formerly part of the Soviet Union. That the US had not honoured the cheque of goodwill expressed in the agreements on Germany winding up the Cold War or the military support offered – and obtained – after 9/11. That the West had no idea what was at stake in Chechnya – though Putin did not name the troubled province. The bottom line: the bear had left his den, and things would have to change.

While the Europeans were seen as minor offenders, and the former satellite countries of the Soviet Empire a mere irritant, the United States came in for a targeted attack, the aspiring great power pitted against the declining global power. There was disappointment in his tone and manner about being excluded from Europe. Putin felt let down by the West, accusing Western nations of 'ideological stereotypes, double standards and other typical aspects of Cold War thinking'. But his wrath was reserved for the United States. Was he merely irritated at being constantly lectured by George W. Bush et al on democracy and Russia's civil society deficits? Or did he want to deepen the rift between Europe and the US? Or was he angry at having been largely ignored at the UN and elsewhere, and not acknowledged as a global player and essential partner by the US?

Putin spoke like a professor of political theory, but not without visible contradiction. While stating that 'the unipolar world proposed after the Cold War' had not materialized, he proceeded to take on the United States precisely for aspiring to this kind of world order, run from Washington: 'What is a unipolar world? However one might embellish the term, at the end of the day it refers to one type of situation, namely one centre of authority, one centre of force, one centre of decision-making.'

Russia wants to be respected

The leader of a crashed empire was warning the US that the unipolar order of post-Cold War dreams was beyond their reach: 'It is a world in which there is one master, one sovereign. And at the end of the day this is pernicious for all those within this system, but also for the sovereign because it destroys itself from within.'

Was this the lesson the former intelligence officer, who as a KGB resident in Dresden, East Germany, had seen imperial control vanish from close-up, was handing down to the US and all those nations who trusted the US as security lender of last resort? The message was clear: do not trust the US as it is going, sooner or later, the way of all empires.

The verdict was as clear as the warning: 'The unipolar model is not only unacceptable but also impossible in today's world. ... Unilateral and frequently illegitimate actions have not resolved any problems.' Putin then proceeded to put Russia forward as the champion of international law against the US: 'What we are seeing is ever greater disdain for the principles of international law. And independent legal norms are, as a matter of fact, coming increasingly closer to one state's legal system. One state, first and foremost the United States, has overstepped its national borders in every way.' What Putin disliked was not only US hard power but also US soft power in all its dimensions, which Russia could never hope to match: 'This is visible in the economic, political, cultural and educational policies it imposes on other nations.'

While warning against 'militarization' of outer space, especially placing weaponry into orbit – something that for the foreseeable future only the US is capable of undertaking – Putin also made it clear that Russia and the US shared interests in world security, and nowhere more so than in the field of non-proliferation. To preserve the nuclear oligarchy expressed in the Non-Proliferation Treaty of 1968 had been the guiding principle for the superpowers during the Cold War, and Putin was certainly not willing to part, for short-term gain, with this essential strategy. Without specifically mentioning North Korea, Iran or other potential offenders, he made it clear that Russia and the US still had strategic interests in common.

Conflict and competition

But conflict and competition were the leitmotif, not the unavoidable strategic bargains of the future, dictated by technology and necessity. In particular, Putin made it clear that separating the future of Kosovo from Serbia would meet with fierce resistance from Russia. The Kremlin would use its veto in the UN Security Council, thus dealing a deadly blow to the UN-sponsored Ahtisaari Plan, presented only a few days before at the Security Council, for a controlled and peaceful settlement under the formula of 'supervised sovereignty'. He certainly did not attach much importance to the remaining attempts of the Kosovo trio, consisting of US, Russian and EU diplomats, to deactivate the bomb ticking, once again, in the Balkans. Putin made it clear that Nato's military intervention and air war in the spring of 1999 to stop Slobodan Milosevic's ethnic cleansing of Kosovo Albanians had not been forgotten, let alone forgiven.

Not that Russia had a better or more sustainable formula to offer for Balkan stability, but Kosovo was one of the items on the global agenda where Putin wanted to make it clear, beyond any doubt, that little or nothing could be achieved against Russia. Serbia, traditionally the overlord of the Kosovo Albanians, was an old ally and protégé of

Russia since the wars of the tsars against the Ottoman Empire and the rivalries with Austria – Belgrade was seen as Russian turf where Western nations should tread carefully. At a later stage, at the G8 meeting in the upmarket seaside resort of Heiligendamm in the summer of 2007, Putin even warned Western nations that to allow Kosovo separation from Serbia would mean defeat for 'Christianity' in its epic struggle against Islam – recalling the age-old protector role that Russia had traditionally claimed over orthodox lands.

With this timely warning on Kosovo the Tsar's anger was not yet exhausted. What followed was an attack on the US project of missile defence against future Iranian nuclear-tipped Intercontinental Ballistic Missiles. The giant radar to be placed, controversially, somewhere south of Prague in the Czech Republic to control the flightpath of future Iranian intercontinental missiles across Europe to the US was anathema to Putin, as was the proposal for complementary missile positions further north in Poland to shoot down whatever threat came from Southern shores. Putin claimed that these future US deployments were nothing but a thinly veiled threat against Russia. He linked the plan to the recent US renunciation of the Anti-Ballistic Missile Treaty of 1973, banning major anti-missile deployments between the superpowers, that the Bush administration had indeed cancelled not so long ago – much to the anger and annoyance of the Russians. But the Russian president must have known from his military intelligence sources that the new project, still in its infancy, would not have the capacity, nor be in a location to upset the largely abstract balance of nuclear-tipped missiles between the US and Russia.

Shooting down the anti-missile missiles

So why did Putin raise the issue of the anti-missile missiles? There seemed to be three principal reasons. First, Russia wanted to be consulted and was not, neither in the Nato–Russia Council nor in high-level meetings – and Putin knew of course that the White House had not made much effort to refer the divisive issue to the councils of Nato but had chosen the bilateral route with the East European countries concerned. Second, placing anti-missile installations into former satellite countries was, in Russian eyes, a clear breach if not in the letter then certainly in the spirit of the Two plus Four Agreement on Germany and Nato deployments. Third, Putin must have sensed that the project would invite massive protest throughout Europe against US deployments, especially in Germany among those middle-aged social democrats and greens who wanted to relive their youth and re-enact the INF (Intermediate Nuclear Forces) crisis of the late 1970s and early 1980s. That had been the last major Cold War confrontation, provoking to no small extent not only the rise of the German greens but also the downfall of the lib-lab Schmidt–Genscher government in the autumn of 1982 and the rise of Chancellor Helmut Kohl. Why not use the issue to sow discord among Nato countries and between the US and the rest?

This may have been a short-lived tactical consideration, accentuated, however, by a Russian general's boastful announcement that those irritating sites in Eastern Europe would be high on the list of potential targets for Russia's missiles. Tactical, because after that Munich confrontation it took only a few months for the Kremlin to offer the US the use of a former Soviet radar site in Azerbaijan, a few hundred miles north of the Iranian border. The Pentagon's experts, dispatched to examine the place, found the installation in a derelict state, the data-processing different from American systems and the area too close to the potential source of trouble to provide much reassurance. But after a while other US experts saw much virtue in the proposal. Moreover, the Russian offer took the steam out of the West European debate and should therefore, notwithstanding technical shortcomings, be part of any future anti-missile system.

In strategic terms, the Russians did not follow the US rationale for putting up anti-missile defences against Iran long before the Iranians had operational nuclear capacity, let alone the ability to operate and launch intercontinental missiles. No wonder, then, that the US plans created suspicion in Moscow. The Russians also continue to believe in deterrence. Why, they asked, should an Iranian regime, once it had control over nuclear weapons, risk the very existence of the country by firing nuclear missiles at the US – or, for that matter, at Israel's population centres around Tel Aviv and Haifa – and be annihilated in turn?

It was ironic that, only hours before Putin gave his speech in Munich, Russian defence minister Sergei Ivanov, at the time almost an alter ego of Putin's, had invited me to an exclusive interview on the margins of the same conference. In our conversation Ivanov stated, on the record, that whatever the Americans were planning to put into the Czech Republic and Poland, would be – 'if, God forbid, a confrontation should occur' – no match for Russia's superior missile forces. Here spoke the man responsible for Russian defence, and he was obviously out of sync with the alarmist version soon after to be promoted by the President. But Ivanov, too, wondered why, long before the Iranians had enough fissile material for a single bomb, let alone had mastered nuclear weapons technology, the US was already signalling that it had given up hope of keeping the Iranian within the restrictions of the Non-Proliferation Treaty. As far as Iranian missiles were concerned, Ivanov stated that according to Russian intelligence their maximum reach was about 1700 kilo- metres, and that intercontinental missiles would be, for a long time to come, out of reach of the Iranians. Ivanov moreover, revealed that the Russians too were worried about what the Iranian regime was up to. 'We realize that Iran with its present arsenal of missiles has the capacity to threaten not only the state of Israel but also Russian territory. This is a matter of great concern.'

If this line of thought was an implicit offer to the US to join forces and develop a common anti-missile defence in the future, it was certainly not taken up at Munich, nor any time after. Russian questions and uncertainties were never properly addressed by the White House. Nor was the issue effectively referred to Nato, as German chancellor Angela Merkel had demanded soon after the Munich conference. It is still lingering and creating bad blood not only between Russia and the US but also between the US and most Nato countries. Even in Poland the placing of the US anti-missile missiles is highly controversial, while the Czechs are not amused. But the local promoters see in it, whatever the technological merits or non-merits, the chance to make Poland or the Czech Republic an honorary 51st member state of the US. No wonder then that the Russians, too, look at the symbolic dimension – and do not like it.

Soon after that Munich meeting Brent Scowcroft, national security adviser to the elder Bush from 1988 to 2002, called the entire project premature. 'We should not have gone forward with it,' he said in his Washington office in the summer of 2007. 'It will take the Iranians many years to develop an intercontinental system, and once they are close to having one, we can still, possibly together with the Russians, instal anti-missile defences.'

Need an enemy?

In the greater scheme of things, two principal reorientations stand out, far above the tactical movements of day-to-day politics, and on both counts Putin has left a mark. One concerns China and the future Russian–Chinese relationship, the other Russia's place and role in Eurasia.

As far as China is concerned, in Munich Putin never even mentioned the Middle Kingdom, rising and rising over the vastness of Siberia. Nor did he care to describe in any detail the multipolar system that he seemed to envisage instead of US dominance. China was conspicuous by its absence from that world vision projected in Munich, though certainly not absent from any long-term Russian strategy. There was no hint at Russia's China policy of the future, except that, when it came to America-bashing, Beijing and Moscow would act in unison. In the long run, however, the US must clearly be the preferred partner in balancing the ever growing potential of mainland China – a balancer from beyond the sea.

I shall never forget what, in late 1993, those Russian generals from the Moscow Defence Ministry and the general staff who had just put the finishing touches to Russia's post-Cold War strategic doctrine told their German counterparts at the Stiftung Wissenschaft und Politik, the German government's strategy think tank in Ebenhausen. Nato? They seemed to be relaxed about the transatlantic alliance, a threat no more. At that time, long before Nato enlargement towards the East turned from a Polish and East European dream into an American policy priority, Russia, clearly an enemy of the past, was no longer a threat for the present or the foreseeable future. The real dangers, the Russian generals said, making no secret of their long-term concerns, would come from the East – they did not mean North Korea but the Middle Kingdom – and from the south, Chechnya and beyond. They were indeed traumatized by ten years of unstoppable Soviet losses in Afghanistan and the defeat of the mighty Red Army at the hands of high-tech armed jihadists.

Those Russian generals were of course painfully aware of the fact that all Russia's riches were in the East, beyond the Ural mountains. No people and all the riches on one side of the Amur and Ussuri border, and all the people and no minerals on the other side: a strategic equation unlikely to last forever, notwithstanding the assurances of friendship and cooperation towards the rulers of the Middle Kingdom, the expressions of multipolar convictions and flourishing anti-American rhetoric, the joint military manoeuvres and the more recent unfolding of the Shanghai Cooperation Organization.

Every Russian general, one of those present at Ebenhausen told me, is by heart a historian – which in this context means they are used to taking the long view. They knew enough about the Caucasus to anticipate Islamist contagion and to worry about what Russians, ever since Ivan the Terrible conquered Kazan with 60,000 soldiers, regard as the empire's soft underbelly. The south, to this present day, is a region where a border is seen as secure only when Russian soldiers keep guard on both sides. They recall the nineteenth-century 'Great Game' – to use Rudyard Kipling's oft-quoted phrase – when the armies of the Tsar and the regiments of the British Empire, not to speak of adventurers, spies and secret agents, were competing for control of Central Asia's vast spaces, Afghanistan, the Khyber Pass and access to the warm waters of the Indian Ocean. Towards the end of the twentieth century it had become increasingly clear that those lands had untapped oil and gas reserves and were strategically ideal as the location of major pipelines, but also contained rich mineral resources. Since the fall of the Soviet Union it became clear that the barren spaces of Central Asia were about to become the venue of a new Great Game, this time in a triangular configuration with the Russians, the Chinese and the Americans competing for energy, pipelines, influence and power.

We are a European nation

Even more important is Russia's place in Europe. 'We are a European nation,' Putin recently said, defiantly and pointedly, at a meeting in Sochi soon after Munich, adding that Russia insists on a global rank that is second to none. Of course he is aware of Russia's inescapable

Eurasian vocation, and he for one would never give up any of Russia's Asian possessions. The war he fought in Chechnya while aiming for the Yeltsin inheritance, putting himself in heroic pose and donning a military uniform, is a case in point. Once you let go, the reasoning goes, where would it end? In 1917, in 1941 and 1942, and in 1991 the Outer Empire fell apart, with vast repercussions throughout the Inner Empire. Putin has certainly not forgotten the early 1990s when another war in Chechnya threatened to ignite fires elsewhere, in oil-rich Tatarstan, almost 1000 kilometres north. But at the same time Putin and most of the people he has around him are natives of St Petersburg, traditionally Russia's window – and seaport – on the West. An eighteenth-century European capital on the Baltic, a dream brutally called into existence by Peter the Great, who spent his imperial apprentice years travelling throughout Europe and trying, ever since, to correct those mistakes that God had made when allotting to the Russians the icy terrain of the eastern nowhere.

By comparison, the seven giant towers that Stalin built to fence in Moscow project an image of Asian empires and the vastness of the Steppe. It is only now, when high-rise buildings begin to dwarf Stalin's brutal fantasies, that Moscow, once again, acquires an appearance in line with the architecture, and symbolism, of the West.

'Europe our common home' – this slogan had long preceded Putin. It was indeed a phrase coined by Gorbachev in 1985, during the early stages of glasnost and perestroika. Gorbachev is today, not forgotten but associated with the decline and implosion of the empire. However, his catchphrase expresses feelings deep within the Russian soul. In fact it is a key element of that Russian identity that is forever torn between the materialism and sophistication of Western Europe and the silent heroism and spirituality of the East, between the soft comforts of Baden-Baden and the icy vastness of Sakhalin.

How European will Russia be? The question is not merely academic. In the greater scheme of things, Russia's place in the world and Russia's long-term aspirations cannot be dissociated from the cultural currents now under way. Whatever anger was voiced by Putin at Munich, and whatever strategic irritation has occurred between Russia and the West over the last decade, the determining factors for the future relationship are to be found not so much in geostrategic arsenals but in the foundations of identity. On this, Putin tries to strike a Eurasian balance. 'We are a European nation, but we live both in Europe and in Asia, and we are a multicultural and multireligious society,' he tends to say. This is a political statement, politically correct and carefully equilibrated. His background may be in the intelligence system, but he seems to know that man does not live on bread alone, and that the Russia of the future needs deeper roots than the glitzy supermarkets lining Moscow's Leningradskaya Chaussee, and the fashionable boutiques now adorning the old *GUM* magazine buildings opposite the Kremlin's brick walls.

Yeltsin's and now Putin's alliance with the Russian Orthodox Church is an expression of this cultural confidence-building. The revival of the cultural roots is another one.

A vision of world order?

Driving into Moscow recently from Sheremetyevo airport, when passing the rusty monument where the Wehrmacht's advance was halted in early December 1941 I noticed a huge billboard greeting visitors from the West and displaying an old man's familiar face. It was Alexander Solzhenitsyn, once a dissident and enemy of the Soviet system, then a refugee in America and now, in a nostalgic turn-around, a refugee from America, in fact a saintly guide to a spiritual renewal based on Russia's traditional manners and mores, language and literature. Solzhenitsyn, after his long exile in the US, had finally come back to the motherland and made a kind of reluctant peace with the heirs to the Soviet system. Meanwhile, the Porsches, the BMWs and the Mercedes of the New Russians were racing by on the eight-lane motorway – how better to demonstrate the eternal ambiguity of Russia between the tortured spirituality of the East and the smart materialism of the West?

Future historians of world affairs will remember Putin's speech in Munich as the turning point from uneasy accommodation to measured defiance. In Munich, the West was put on notice as to what Putin did not want. But did Putin know what he wants instead? The Russian leader, while making it painfully clear that Russia would never be in the orbit of the US and that he resented US dominance and Russia's exclusion, failed to produce, beyond a rough sketch, a clear vision of world order beyond the post-Cold War and post- 9/11 stage. Nor did he suggest how instability and insecurity should be kept at bay in a troubled world while the sun is setting on the Pax Americana.

2

On secret service

'All Russians and all who wish to live in Russia impose on themselves unconditional silence. Here nothing is said while everything is known. Secret conversations should be very interesting; but who permits himself to indulge in them? To think, to discern is to become suspect.'
Marquis de Custine, *Journey for Our Time*

After Munich, once the shockwaves subsided, it was clear that Russia could no longer be taken for granted, nor Putin counted on as a cooperative opposite number for the leaders of the West. Once again, as in 1999 when he seemed to emerge from nowhere, first being promoted to head the vast machinery of the FSB – the Federal Intelligence Service – and then to be Yeltsin's prime minister, people wondered what talents and forces brought this man to the Kremlin and then into the unchallenged and unchallengeable position of being the new tsar.

Who is Mr Putin?

While the succession issue loomed large over Russia's political, economic and security agenda, the question was asked, inevitably: who is Vladimir Vladimirovich Putin, the man who came from almost nowhere just eight years ago and is now, at least in the triangle of power formed by domestic intelligence, state bureaucracy and oligarchs, the chief player? So much so that elections are a mere charade, a post-Soviet kabuki play enacted for the benefit of an incredulous outside world and a stunned domestic audience. KGB agents, active or retired, do not have the habit of giving anything away about themselves, let alone divulging more than the absolutely unavoidable minimum of information.

Breeding shows, and the organization follows the principle of: 'Once a Chekist always a Chekist.' This refers to the widely feared revolutionary secret police, acronym Cheka, under Felix Dzerzhinsky, the ruthless heir to the czarist Ohranak but, much more than could ever have been imagined under Russia's tsarist regime, the very heart of the Soviet system, the innermost elite with a hundred thousand eyes and ears and the means to make everybody, even the most firebrand of revolutionaries, tremble. Its empire stretched from the Lubyanka in the middle of Moscow to the deadliest of Gulag prisons in Siberia's barren north. But the KGB was also, by virtue of its almost unlimited access to untainted information, the brains of the system. This was the world which attracted the ambition, patriotism and efforts of Vladimir Putin even before he was out of school in Leningrad, today's St Petersburg. Both his home town, Russia's most European city, created by an absolutist ruler's fiat, and his early training within the secret service formed Putin's way of life, his manners and morals and his view of the world, of loyalties and of the way politics should be conducted. The secret service became his way of life, like that of the priesthood in the Roman Catholic church.

Was he a communist? The answer is yes, up to a point. But above all he grew up as a patriotic young Russian, a Russian nationalist, and when he realized that communist rule had ruined the country he loved he dissociated himself from communism old and new. Human rights, democracy, transparency, opposition? Respect for the dignity of man? If they could deliver a more powerful Russia, fine. If not, he would look for other lode stars, meaning democracy Russian-style, guided from above and controlled by an enlightened elite, what he calls 'the vertical of power'. His vision is not a Soviet renaissance but an administration that the Prussian philosopher G.F.W Hegel would recognize as akin to a rational, hierarchic system – Hegel even suggested that enlightened absolutism amounted to the end of history – and, therefore, of lasting power.

Putin's motives and visions come from further away than the inglorious Soviet past, whose rot and graft he had seen at close quarters. His dreams come from the Russian pre-Soviet past, garnished with some aspects of the West's European enlightenment. If democracy offered the magic wand to reconstruct Russia and bring back lost power and glory – so be it. If, however, democracy for Russia meant weakness, diversity and strife, then autocracy – Putin would probably call it enlightened absolutism, administered by the elite corps of the intelligence service – would fit the bill. And if the West disapproved, what would it matter? In the xenophobic atmosphere of Russia a little alienation might even recommend Putin to his fellow countrymen.

One of Putin's early biographers, Alexander Rahr, who has followed the career of Putin from childhood, observed two characteristic traits in his character. He is nothing if not a perfectionist, and he cannot stand disorder and lack of discipline. Already as a youth, 'he shunned spontaneity, risk and improvisation'.

In the sixth grade young Volodya joined the Young Pioneers, but his teachers were less than enthusiastic about his performance: too emotional, talkative and given to foul language. After eight years of standard schooling he was sent by his parents to college number 281, specializing in the training of future chemists. Their son was an assiduous pupil but by no means a model student. He seems to have been the typical 'nice boy', with a smile on his face but not given to hard work.

Outside his studies, the young student was interested in Western music. He played the guitar and gave a recital from time to time. Literature captivated him; he would read poems to his classmates, and even the banned samizdat from the political underground. The social sciences caught his interest more than the natural sciences, and he joined a political club. A dissident he never was. On the contrary, in the summer of 1970, barely seventeen years old, he knocked at the door of the local KGB headquarters. His boss in later years remembered in *Komsomolskaya Pravda* what happened: 'Putin's wish to work within the secret service goes back if not to his childhood then certainly to when he was a teenager. Immediately after finishing college he came to us in the administration and asked: "How can I become a KGB agent?"'

This was, by any standards, an exceptional application. The seasoned officer, however, advised young Putin to wait a little and first get a degree. The advice he received sent him in the direction of legal studies, which he took up in due course, after serious preparation, at the elitist Law Faculty of Leningrad University.*

* A. Rahr, *Vladimir Putin*, 2000, pp. 34–6

Joining the elite corps

Was he intent on becoming one of those faceless bureaucrats spying on their fellow-citizens, or running a small section of the vast Gulag archipelago? Alexander Rahr assumes that it was rather his ambition to be an insider to information and the power that comes with it. Putin did not have to serve his years as a conscript but took part in pre-military exercises under the auspices of the Institute for Military Affairs, finishing with the nominal rank of lieutenant. He also practised Sambo, a martial art, and became an accomplished judoka.

His life at university took an important turn when in his first year he came to know Professor Anatoli Sobchak. The professor had the reputation of being something of a dissident. His dissertation had dealt with – under Soviet rule – an eccentric subject, nothing less than the de-monopolization of state property. Thinking the unthinkable was not at a premium in Brezhnev's time and it took Sobtschak ten years to obtain his doctoral degree. In later life the professor and the student were to meet again, the older one mayor of post-Soviet St Petersburg, the younger one an administrator.

Towards the end of Putin's second year at the faculty of law his heartfelt wish was fulfilled, and he was admitted to the KGB. This was a well-paying opportunity, promising further training and wide opportunities for promotion. Some years before, the recruiting officers had invited Dr Sobchak to join the ranks but he had refused their overtures.

Putin did not rise to be a Soviet James Bond but stayed in Leningrad and became a bureaucrat in the KGB administration. In his autobiography Putin mentions that he disliked the way the KGB was employed to crush dissident art and harass the artists. He probably found this rather petty and beneath the dignity of a service that had to save the motherland from its real enemies at the secret front. Being a sports amateur and well versed in foreign languages – he speaks German, English and French – he was chosen to chaperon foreign visitors and delegations and even travel abroad with Soviet groups to protect them against enemy influence in whatever form. This may have given him a wider view on the world than what was usually available for a young Russian just out of university. But he also had more mundane jobs to do like accompanying religious processions and making sure that nothing untoward occurred. After a year of special training in Moscow, Putin was promoted to counter-intelligence. That had always been the elite unit of the KGB, mostly reserved for the offspring of the high party nomenclatura – Putin was clearly an outsider, but conscious of the privileged position offered to him. To prove his mettle he had to make a parachute-jump out of a plane, and to ensure his loyalty he had to join the CPSU. After that he had to carry out surveillance in St Petersburg, spying on fellow students and recruiting, by hook or by crook, foreign visitors to work for the KGB. It was an unappetizing task, probably not what Putin in his patriotic dreams had wished to do. He had to pressure people into spying, but he preferred softer methods of persuasion.

To Westerners visiting the Soviet Union he must have talked a great deal about the dangers of nuclear war and the attractions of peace, and how important it was that young peace-lovers should help the great cause by working for 'the organization' – which would also pay handsomely, and discreetly. In his memoirs, however, Putin makes an interesting remark about what he learned in those years: 'dealing with people' or, in one word, communication. Whether he really created a network of spies, or succeeded only in recruiting a couple of true agents – there is room for speculation. In the eighth year of his presidency he paid homage to some eminent former Soviet spies, thus paying off a moral debt to what Russians still call 'the organization'.

Dresden

It was at a time of high East–West tension over Soviet and Nato missile deployment, with dramatic repercussions in most Western countries and especially in Germany, when in 1985 Putin was sent to Dresden, the second most important city in East Germany – his excellent command of German serving as a strong argument in his favour. But it was also a time when the huge and overextended Soviet edifice showed serious signs of weariness, dysfunctional politics and the widespread resignation of the people. 'Soviet man' had not emerged and was ever more unlikely ever to make his or her appearance. It was true that sending oil and gas through giant pipelines to the West at rising prices seemed to work in favour of the Soviet system. However, disillusionment with the workers' and peasants' paradise, waste and technological backwardness, misfortune in Afghanistan and humiliation abroad and on top of all this the resilience of Western Europe in the face of the renewed Soviet threat – many factors worked together to create, the longer the 'leaden years' of the Brezhnev era lasted, a sense of looming breakdown, loss of direction, disasters waiting to happen. And, indeed, they were not long in coming.

Meanwhile, Putin was part of that elite corps that, apart from the dissidents on the other side of the political divide, was best situated to understand the threat to the Soviet system. In Dresden, he must have been aware from close observation and first-hand knowledge that even the showcase of socialism, the German Democratic Republic, was tottering towards its grave. He was in a good position to witness, half inside and half outside, the falling apart of the East German state and, with it, the beginning of the end of Soviet rule over Eastern Europe. Once the outer empire had crumbled – the fall of the Berlin wall on the night of 9 November 1989 was both in reality and symbolically the breakthrough – there was no way, except by putting up a desperate last struggle and sending in the tanks, to preserve the inner empire.

Losing an empire

This was, however, not Gorbachev's solution. He knew, and the generals knew as well, that military intervention like that of 1956 in Hungary and Poland and 1968 in Czechoslovakia could not be repeated, nor was another pincer movement against Poland a viable option. This would have ruined relations with the US, forced Russia into a new arms race and made domestic reform in Russia impossible. And, in any case, after the oil price had collapsed in 1985 there was no money to pay for military extravaganzas.

The same forces that were to tear apart the Comecon (Council for Mutual Economic Support) and the Warsaw Pact could not be prevented from tearing at the very fabric of Soviet rule at home. It is his experience in Dresden, in fact a personal trauma, that today prompts the former KGB lieutenant-colonel turned Tsar of all the Russians to refer, time and again, to the dangers of Russia falling apart.

Putin must have felt the paralysis of the Honecker regime. And of course he had been told repeatedly about the strategic role of the GDR, home to more than twenty crack Red Army divisions, for the Soviet system. Meanwhile, he was living modestly with his wife and two daughters in a small apartment in what the Germans call, with no sympathy, *Plattenbau* – the drab standard housing facilities regarded as a privileged habitat under socialism. Professionally, the many years in Dresden were devoted, with the young lieutenant-colonel's usual perfectionism and assiduousness, to such KGB business as controlling the East German Staatssicherheit, or Stasi, from afar and recruiting operatives and long-term sleepers for the Soviet cause.

Germany, even in its very modest and restricted Eastern version, was a formative experience for Putin not only in terms of presenting the end of empire but also with regards to his personal outlook on life. In the early 1980s the German Democratic Republic was often praised by its sympathizers as Comecon's model student.

A world of make-believe

It did help that a truly fantastic amount of data-laundering was going on, mostly accepted by the West. Statistically, East Germany was marching from triumph to triumph. There were two reasons: Günter Mittag, the chief of state planning, expected targets, even if they were patently absurd, to be met and norms overfulfilled. This in turn secured all kinds of benefits for managers as well as for the people on the shop floor. So statistics were not only embellished but also fabricated, and everybody learnt to live in a world of window-dressing. One would like to see the reports that Putin sent home; given his sharp eye for human weakness he must have sensed, more than most people, that the GDR was increasingly becoming a house of cards. Did he warn his superiors that trouble was brewing and that the Soviet *Titanic* was heading towards the iceberg? East Germans had a more down-to-earth way to describe the state of the state: 'We pretend to work, and they pretend to pay us.'

Strange though it sounds in retrospect, most observers in the West did not grasp what was going on, and those who did were careful not to be denounced as cold warriors out to minimize the glories of 'real existing socialism', as the official description went. Meanwhile the symptoms of decline, in fact decay and desperation, kept coming to the surface. In 1982, when the Schmidt–Genscher government was about to collapse and Helmut Kohl was preparing to take over, the GDR chiefs applied, discreetly, for a stand-by credit to the tune of one billion Deutschmarks, handled without much fuss, once Kohl was in office, via the state chancellery in Munich under the watchful eye of Franz Josef Strauss, minister-president of the state of Bavaria. This should have set off all alarm bells in the West and among Soviet German-watchers, among them Vladimir Putin. How could the East German regime ever ask the 'class enemy' to help if not in utter despair? In fact after that first financial flirtation, handled through the Bayerische Hypotheken und Wechselbank, sheer necessity pushed the East German planners even further. They began to think, sometimes aloud, about a loose confederation destined to establish an umbilical cord of credits and subsidies to the doomed East German economy – all of this in the name of peace and stability. Did Putin realize what kind of Ostpolitik was going on between the Stalinist diehards in East Berlin and the Kohl–Genscher government in Bonn? This kind of political drama was probably well above his level, and Dresden was certainly not the most important vantage point.

But if the lieutenant-colonel in Dresden ignored the writing on the wall he was certainly not alone. The GDR had developed a miraculous system of data-laundering, insisting that every East German mark – East German housewives called them, disdainfully, 'aluchips' – had to be counted as equivalent to one Deutschmark, West Germany's unassailable currency. The reality could be felt when it came to changing East German aluchips into what used to be called 'valuta' – i.e. real money, dollars or, preferably, Deutschmarks. The black market price varied, but was rarely below 6 aluchips for one real mark. *Die Geige*, the violin, was what East Germans called the green 20-Deutschmark bill that showed not only Dürer's stunningly beautiful portrait of Elsbeth Tucher of Nuremberg but also a violin. It was East German code for real money that would secure scarce services and all kinds of goods from the West not otherwise available to the man in the street.

Putin must have realized the double standards, the window-dressing, the crumbling future, the hollowness of the regime. Did he also see the mortal danger for the Soviet project? One would like to know not only what he thinks today about those tectonic shifts that took place under his eyes but also how he realized – or failed to realize – what was coming at the time. His command of German was excellent. His education in all things German would have allowed him to feel that the earth under Soviet power was trembling. The breakdown of the Soviet Union ranks for him as one of the great geopolitical catastrophes of the twentieth century, a century of breakdown and catastrophe by any standard. What happened in and around 1989 was, for Putin and his friends, a warning that turned slowly and inexorably into the Soviet endgame. The fall of the Berlin wall on 9 November 1989 meant not only uncertainty about the greater scheme of things, but also uncertainty as to the KGB officer's personal future and that of his family.

From Leningrad to St Petersburg

Always a realist, Putin did not insist on seeing Soviet rule over East Germany being wound up but requested permission to go to Leningrad. In those trying times he must have asked himself if he had backed the wrong horse. In 1990 he renewed his old acquaintance with Professor Anatoli Sobchak, who in Soviet times had been something of an outsider due to his more cosmopolitan training and style and who, when the shadows over the Soviet system grew longer and darker, was emerging as one of the natural leaders of a new Russia. In fact, although he had little administrative experience, he was elected to be mayor of Leningrad, a city of five million people affected by all the symptoms of Soviet decline: unemployment, lack of resources, breakdown of industry, shortages of everything from food to hope. Trying times indeed. Putin, a Leningrad lad who had known the city and its citizens from his early days, wasted no time in grieving for the past and turned up as an assistant to Sobchak as early as 1990, specializing in international contacts and communication, certainly helped by his command of German, French and English and the experiences he had gathered in East Germany. By ex-Soviet standards he was an expert on the outside world.

Soon he rose, under Sobchak, to be the successor to Anatoly Chubais in what Alexander Rahr in his biography described as the 'reform motor in the Neva metropolis'. In 1996, however, Sobtschak, described by foreign diplomats at the time as a charismatic personality, failed to invest in his campaign for re-election and had to retire. Putin remained in St Petersburg but set his sight on Moscow. He was in for a disappointment when Chubais, looking for a deputy at the head of the presidential administration, chose Alexei Kudrin, who had a reputation as a financial technocrat, instead of Putin with his widely praised talent for organization.

Moscow calling

But given the shortage of talent considered trustworthy by the ex-KGB political class, Putin did not have to wait too long to be offered a position in tune with his ambitions. Once installed in his new office in the ex-Politburo building near the Kremlin, within weeks Putin became expert in all financial transactions and business matters of the Kremlin administration. His most important assignment was to set up a holding company for all foreign assets of the Russian Ministry of Foreign Trade.

From his time in the St Petersburg administration Putin was well versed in handling huge sums of money, so he was charged with administering all the assets of the Russian Federation both inside and outside the country. Inside Russia the total was estimated at USD 600 billion, the assets outside Russia at USD 50 billion. Together with Pavel Borodin, Putin controlled hundreds of administrative buildings, companies, luxury hospitals and rehabilitation centres as well as Russian state property in no fewer than seventy-eight countries. Putin soon found his place in the Kremlin administration due to his personal qualities, which Alexander Rahr describes as 'loyal and trustworthy, certainly not power-obsessed, but at the same time effective'. Moreover, he was not part of the Moscow-based clans scrambling for influence and positions in the Kremlin, notably among those power-brokers the mayor of Moscow, Yuri Luzhkov.

But, inevitably, the survival of the fittest unleashed in and around the Kremlin put Putin in the thick of the battle. Who would be heir to Yeltsin? Luzhkov, or General Lebed, or Chernomyrdin, or Chubais? Putin managed to be an insider when it came to influence and control but remained an outsider when it came to corruption. This was to help him a few years later when scandal erupted in the Kremlin. He was a rare exception as, throughout those years, he was not suspected to have channelled state funds in his own direction.

In the Kremlin administration Putin was both an insider and an outsider. An outsider as he was not part of any of the established Moscow clans. And an insider, as he had made himself indispensable in his responsibilities for the Kremlin's national and international assets.

The trauma of blackout

In 1996 Yeltsin was reelected as president, but the economy went from bad to worse. Chernomyrdin, prime minister at the time, followed advice from the International Monetary Fund and tried to curb inflation, finance the country through hydrocarbon exports and rein in the powerful monopolies controlling the economy, sharpening the tools of the tax authorities, drawing down industrial subsidies and encouraging private investment and private enterprise. While all of this looked virtuous in the eyes of the West, it did not work in Russia. In early 1997 Russia's coffers were empty and the country was facing serious trouble, even upheaval. Pensions and wages could not be paid. The country was close to paralysis. To make matters worse, the price of oil began to slip and, from mid-1997, plummeted due to a slight recession in the Far East. China's rise had, ever since the early 1990s, sucked up any surplus oil in a market which provided little room for manoeuvre: a slight increase in demand would send prices up, a slight decrease would send prices down. In early 1998 prices reached rock bottom, and so did Russia's economy.

In this situation Yeltsin concentrated power around Chubais and Nemtsov, the first as prime minister and the latter as his deputy, who at the same time were to balance each other. Valentin Yumashev, a journalist and former ghostwriter for Yeltsin, became head of the Kremlin administration – his chief qualification for this key post being both his liaison with Yeltsin's daughter Tatiana and his close relationship with Berezovsky and the latter's journal *Ogonek*. Putin, by now forty-four years old and a KGB colonel on the reserve list, was promoted on the Kremlin chessboard. A presidential ukas dated 26 March 1997 made him the successor to Kudrin as deputy director of the presidential administration and head of financial controlling. By now he was one among twenty heads of department in the Kremlin's hierarchy, a lone wolf, inconspicuous, knowledgeable, indispensable, efficient and very smart. He now knew everything worth knowing about the cloak-and-dagger world inside the Kremlin, while keeping a distance from it. He seems to have been seen by the President and the 'family' as an engineer of power, but one who did not aspire to assume supreme control.

This trust in his modesty brought him a further appointment. In order to combat organized crime, and especially large-scale financial misdemeanour, Yeltsin set up a commission of the National Security Council whose powers stretched right across all branches of the state bureaucracy. The deputy secretary of the National Security Council was none other than Berezovsky. Putin was charged to look into the strange business practices of the number one arms corporation still unchanged since Soviet times. The report he produced caused one of the major storms of the second Yeltsin administration. He had found out that top managers had illegally sold weaponry to Armenia and embezzled vast sums earmarked for soldiers' pay. Putin was upset when he discovered that his top-secret report was making the rounds. Life in the struggle against organized crime became complicated, more than a little dangerous and frustrating. A few years later, Putin hinted that for a while he had considered leaving the Kremlin's service and setting up a consultancy for foreign direct investment in Russia – not a bad idea taking into account his linguistic abilities, his political connections, his St Petersburg experience and his invaluable insight into the real mechanisms of Russia's economic life. At the time a wave of privatization was set in motion. But instead of benefiting the ailing Russian state budget the controlling stakes were divided among cronies of the Kremlin, most of the beneficiaries emerging as the new race of post-Soviet oligarchs. Putin had no visible part in those transactions, but he was among the few who knew the key players and understood the rules of the game, and he did not like what he saw.

Instead of trying his luck in the rapidly expanding private sector, Putin remained within the Kremlin's high red-brick walls. While the economy was continuing on its slide, Yeltsin's health was seriously declining, due in part to his unstoppable love for vodka. The looming question for the 'family' was how to make sure that Yeltsin's concept of reform could somehow be carried on and how the family fortune could be secured against painful questions once the presidential mantle had been passed on to a successor. Neither Luzhkov, the mayor of Moscow, nor Zyuganov, the leader of the communists in the Duma, seemed to be desirable as successors to Yeltsin who, irrespective of his bouts of heavy drinking and his sometimes uncontrolled behaviour, was not only the man who had given democracy a chance in post-Soviet Russia and secured amicable relations with the West but who had also brought many men into positions of power that they did not want to lose – Putin among them.

Yeltsin appointed 35–year-old Kiriyenko to the post of prime minister, much to the approval of the people, who seem to have liked the successful, open and honest young manager – but who was, unfortunately, a stopgap and a lightweight.

Climbing the ladder

One month after Kiriyenko had formed a government, Putin moved a step higher on the ladder of power. He was appointed First Deputy Head of the presidential administration which was taking away more and more executive power from the government. Most importantly, he had to arbitrate in the miners' strike that threatened to spin out of control when the miners blocked the tracks of the Trans-Siberian railway and insisted on being paid the wages that they had not received for months. Kiriyenko, with the help of Putin, managed to calm down the furore.

Putin also had to supervise the Russian regions, eighty-nine different 'subjects of the federation' altogether, some of them aspiring to autonomy from Moscow. He built close ties with Yumashev, head of the presidential apparat and confidant of Berezovsky, and secured permanent access to Yeltsin – a key factor in a highly personalized struggle for power, with an ailing Yeltsin on one side, hungry wolves on the other. What he did was to bring his own friends as 'cadres' into key positions. Most of them were friends and colleagues whom he knew from his St Petersburg days and whom he could trust against the Moscow clans. Notable among those friends was Nikolai Patrushev, who later became the chief of the FSB. They had known each other since 1975, never lost contact and were mutually indispensable. Patrushev in the 1990s had risen to be head of counter-espionage in the

FSB. Thereafter he became chief of human resources. For Putin, Patrushev's expertise in all matters of importance for the FSB made him a trusted adviser, but also a mentor who conferred, if there was any need, the FSB mindset on the rising dark star.

Meanwhile, the oil price continued to plummet, revenue declined steeply and Russia's financial situation went from bad to worse. The overall state debt amounted to USD 200 billion, with 44 per cent of the budget going on interest payments, most of them abroad. The Central Bank offered high interest rates to stem the flood of capital leaving the country. Tax receipts remained far behind the interest due. Currency reserves shrank to no more than USD 15 billion. On the stock exchange star performers like Gazprom and Lukoil lost half their value within weeks. While the government was paying hardly any wages or pensions, the population at large paid no taxes. The tax bureaucracy took its revenge by enforcing authentic statistics, book-keeping and regular payments. Major companies were threatened with confiscation if they did not pay up. The government was struggling against financial clans as well as regional rulers. It was a desperate situation, with no rise in the oil price in sight.

At the height of the crisis on 25 July 1998 Putin was, unexpectedly for the outside world, appointed head of the FSB, the Federal Intelligence Service from which he had come and where he had his personal and ideological roots. He was now in a key position, but far from safe, and his future was anything but assured. He owed too much to Yeltsin, whose rule was visibly in decline and would in any case end soon, and with it the good fortune of all those associated with the democratic tsar. Putin, according to his own account, was not enthusiastic about his appointment. And he had good reason.

He was a mere lieutenant-colonel, on reserve since 1990, and there were many generals ahead of him who had every right to believe that they had older claims to lead the service. Every military or quasi-military organization reacts with anger and frustration, if not open obstruction, to those who are put on the fast track by political masters and bypass everybody else. Putin was enough of an experienced player not to underestimate the dangers. Nevertheless, he fired no fewer than one third of the 6000–strong top echelon, sending others to the provinces, and won respect. But for how long? Inevitably, the FSB and its newly appointed boss were drawn into the struggle for the Yeltsin succession, with no holds barred. The end – keeping Luzhkov and Zyuganov away from the levers of power – justified the means.

By late summer of 1997 the crisis was feeding the crisis. The State Duma refused to cut all social programmes no longer affordable, and the financial world offered no encouragement. The fundamental problem was, as in 1985, the breakdown of oil and gas prices. Prime minister Kiriyenko was compelled to announce a three-month moratorium for servicing the debt owed to the outside world. The population had gone through a similar experience in 1992 and in 1994, when the currency suddenly lost one third of its value and purchasing power. This time no one wanted to be caught by surprise. A run on the banks ensued. Everybody who had a chance changed roubles into dollars, causing the rouble to collapse. After a few days there was no more money, not even a banking system – only despair, disorientation and mounting debt. Shops were empty, the state was bankrupt. Inflation was rampant. The neo-capitalist system was no more. And with it foundered the hope for democratic and liberal renewal. State authority was on the wane. Putin, now head of the FSB, decided on disarming some special military units in Moscow. Obviously there were rumours of an impending coup.

At the end of August 1997 Yeltsin dismissed young Kiriyenko and asked the seasoned Chernomyrdin to head the government. General Lebed, who had become governor of Krasnoyarsk and whose reputation for both military success and diplomatic finesse should calm down hot tempers, was recalled from his Siberian fiefdom to be part of the new team. It was touch and go. The communists and their left-wing allies saw the chance to achieve now what they had failed to bring about in 1992–3: dislodging Yeltsin, reversing whatever reforms had been effected and turning Russia into a parliamentary system with communists at the levers of power. When Chernomyrdin was blocked by the Duma and Luzhkov continued to be unacceptable to Yeltsin, suddenly the 'family' had no one to put on the chessboard. The oil price, continuing at its catastrophic low, would bring no salvation. The financial crisis was grinding on, and on top of everything the political players in Moscow had lost direction. Trying times indeed for the new man at the helm of the FSB. This kind of open crisis, he might have vowed to himself, should never happen again. But he may well have concluded that only in a crisis of vast proportions would a man from nowhere have a chance to rise to the top.

Among the president's men it was Grigori Yavlinski who came up with the name of a compromise candidate. His name was Yevgeny Primakov. A heavily built Arabist and former journalist, Primakov had been a former KGB-resident in the Middle East before joining the IMEMO, in Soviet days the Kremlin's foremost think tank, and becoming its influential director. Primakov accepted his appointment but, feeling he was a mere stopgap, insisted that in order to secure safe passage through the Duma the communists should have some share in the future government.

This was not only a tactical move. It reflected, once again, the tragic truth that the majority of Russian people, much as in other post-communist countries, were willing to embrace democratic reform while refusing to accept the hardship inherent in modernization and the market economy: 'lost in transition' – to quote the title of Lilia Shevtsova's book on the Yeltsin and Putin legacy.

Crisis management

Putin's time had not yet come. Containing disaster was the programme of Primakov and his government, especially paying wages and pensions to an exasperated population. There was not much help coming from outside. Primakov put his trust in compromise, while outside trust in Russia had all but broken down and foreign direct investment became a trickle. No one could imagine that very soon oil prices would pick up and strong tailwinds would push the Russian ship of state to a better future and help the government to stay on top of affairs. Meanwhile, Primakov made two strategic mistakes. He allied himself with Moscow's top dog Luzhkov, too close for comfort in the eyes of the 'family'. And he took on Berezovsky, the Kremlin's patron, for financial misconduct and sharp practices. In so doing, Primakov fired some trustees of the financial clans from the Kremlin bureaucracy and, in good secret service tradition, put in his own people from the former foreign intelligence.

The 'family' reacted by surrounding Primakov with people not his own in order to pre-empt his move to the presidency. Nikolai Bordyuzha became Secretary of the National Security Council; Vladimir

Putin, while continuing as head of the FSB, a full member. All the power ministries were put under the direct control of the President, eating away at Primakov's power. Putin, while some members of Yeltsin's entourage were defecting in the direction of Luzhkov and others assumed to be tomorrow's masters, had finally made it to the inner circle. He was now, according to Alexander Rahr, the man to save the future of the Yeltsin 'family'. 'They trusted him, they saw in the head of the FSB their most important ally and protector of their strategic interests.' Meanwhile, Putin reorganized the service, brought more of his old friends from St Petersburg into key positions, marginalized Primakov's people and expanded the network that he had started building while in the presidential administration. General Victor Cherkesov, for example, once a fellow-student in St Petersburg and a friend from childhood days, with something of a parallel career to Putin's in the KGB, was promoted to deputy chief of the FSB with special responsibility for economic crime.

Sergei Ivanov, another former KGB general, also from St Petersburg, was made head of analysis and strategy; later on, under the Putin presidency, he was to turn up as minister of defence and, since mid-2008, first deputy prime minister.

Meanwhile, the health of Yeltsin was deteriorating and the Moscow rumour mill produced, at regular intervals, news about his impending demise. Each time Yeltsin surfaced on TV, but it was obvious that his health could not forever withstand the waves of vodka he was consuming, sometimes even in the morning. By that time, the Yeltsin 'family' had gone through most or all of the political options and consumed all the more reform-minded prime ministers. What was left was to put all bets on the old KGB and its modern-day reincarnation. This put the head of the FSB into a key position. He concentrated all the loose ends in his hands because he must have understood that in this situation the stakes were very high: win or lose, with very little in between. And there was no doubt that he wanted to win.

Win or lose

But Primakov, buoyed by his popularity at home, now began to give up his neutrality and put pressure on the oligarchs. This implied looking also at deals with which the 'family' was associated. Money-laundering and corruption were among the accusations hurled in the direction of powerful owners of powerful concerns. The General Prosecutor Skuratov was said to have in his safe a list of foreign bank accounts in the name of high-ranking Kremlin officials. Yeltsin, against a vote in the Duma, ordered him to stop his investigations. Was he a hero, or a gangster? How could people tell? What was going on was a struggle for control, and the stakes were as high as the spoils. In retrospect it looks like an unscripted fight for raw power. At the time, it was a cloak-and-dagger story defying description, let alone detailed analysis from outside.

One of the key figures was Berezovsky, and he might have been taken into custody had it not been for the protection extended by the FSB, more precisely by its chief. Berezovsky was close to Yeltsin, and if Berezovsky fell, Yeltsin would be badly hurt. Putin, however, stood by the oligarch and by the 'family'. This, in turn, earned him another promotion. In March 1999 he was appointed head of the National Security Council while continuing to be in charge of the FSB.

While the succession crisis was looming, East–West relations took a turn for the worse. Nato intervened against Serbia in order to prevent genocide or, in the modern version, 'ethnic cleansing' in Kosovo. The Albanian guerrillas fought Serbian troops, and vast numbers of Albanians fled north towards Austria, Switzerland and Germany. In Russia, age-old sympathies with Serbia threatened to boil over while the Kremlin recognized the mounting danger to the Russian federation if Kosovo set a precedent for other ethnic groups fighting for independence. Russians have not forgotten the separatist temptations affecting many of their minorities in the early Yeltsin years. Even where those concerns were seen as way beyond reality, the fact that Nato forces could attack while Russia's opposition in the UN was simply pushed aside was a shock, and has certainly contributed in no small way to the surge of Russian nationalism ever since. Kosovo was a traumatic experience, taking off the shine from Western democracy and encouraging strong-arm solutions to Russia's own problems, especially in the Northern Caucasus. But while Primakov tried to use outrage in Russia to consolidate his support in the population at large, the 'family' decided – and Putin obviously concurred – that given the sad state of the oil price and the looming succession crisis, discretion was the better part of valour. Kosovo and the future of Serbia's strong man Slobodan Milosevic were not the most pressing item on the agenda.

The power struggle under way reached crisis point, and high drama ensued. The Duma majority, dominated by Zyuganov's communists, went for the jugular and prepared impeachment charges against Yeltsin, citing five major reasons: high treason against the Soviet Union in 1991 and destruction of the army; coup d'état in dissolving parliament in 1993, which led to the bombardment of the 'White House' in the centre of Moscow; misuse of office in unleashing the Chechen war of 1994; failing the Russian people through misguided reform. If the Duma succeeded, Yeltsin, after having lost most of his political power, would also lose the legal right to run Russia. In constitutional terms, the legislature and the executive blocked each other. In real terms, the spectre of the erstwhile Soviet Union stood up from its shallow grave to threaten the new, post-Soviet Russia.

In the ensuing struggle, Yeltsin answered the opening move of parliament by firing Primakov, although his government had presided over a modest improvement of state finances, a reduction in runaway inflation, a slight economic recovery and had even secured new loans from the IMF. The Duma had the right to refuse three times Yeltsin's nominee for prime minister, but then the President could dissolve parliament; however, he could do so only if the impeachment process had not yet been set in motion. There was talk in Moscow about civil war.

These were trying times, especially for the man at the helm of the National Security Council and the FSB. Putin had gone too far to entertain second thoughts about where his loyalties lay, but he had his usual luck. The five-point impeachment vanished when the Duma, with the smallest of majorities, refused to open proceedings – whatever reasons lay behind the change of mind of a crucial number of deputies. The Kremlin administration had, by hook or by crook, won the day. Berezovsky, the Kremlin's éminence grise at the time, boasted to the communists: 'We shall never cede power to you.' The Kremlin had won back the initiative. The new prime minister was Sergei Stepashin, a former general in the police and, more recently, first deputy prime minister under Primakov and minister of the interior, in charge of the most powerful ministry.

Stepashin was more of a bureaucrat and by no means a mud-on-the-boots military type like Alexander Lebed who, with his considerable diplomatic skill and popular charisma, might have become a Russian Pinochet if given the chance. Stepashin was, for the time being, a compromise candidate, acceptable to the victors around the President, acceptable also to the vanquished in the Duma. His paramount task was, as Yeltsin's entourage put it, possibly with a sardonic smile, 'to safeguard the legal character of the elections'.

Once again, the choice was between returning to a Soviet-style regime or soldiering on, pursuing more or less the road to a post-Soviet sustainable system of government. 'God will be merciful,' a Soviet energy minister had said when on a visit to Bonn in 1998, referring to the lack of basic provisions. And God, or the archangel presiding over oil prices, was indeed merciful.

Siding with the oligarchs

In that summer of 1999 oil prices began to pick up, slowly but steadily, and the men running Russia could breathe more easily. But the cabinet imposed on Stepashin by the 'family' looked too much like an insiders' club of oligarchs and their princes. Berezovsky was suspected of picking his cronies, and together with young Roman Abramovich, using his Siberian oil wealth, he seemed to control all money matters of importance. They were powerful players, but none of them secured the trust of the 'family' to win the forthcoming elections. The prize would go to the man who could win the full trust of the Kremlin and ensure that, after the event, no painful questions would be asked, let alone criminal proceedings opened on the lines proposed, only a few months earlier, by the Duma.

Luzhkov of Moscow was a runner-up, enjoying much support on TV. Primakov could profit from his professional image and his posture as a kind of political patriarch, supported by the regions. On the liberal left Nemtsov, Kiriyenko, Gaidar, and Yavlinsky were preparing to run. The most dangerous candidate, in the eyes of the 'family', was Luzhkov. He formed a movement named 'Fatherland' to promote a leader much more than an ideology, gathering widespread support including that of Tatarstan's powerful president Mintimer Shaimiev, who brought not only the resources of his oil-rich republic but also the sympathies of a couple of million Muslims. The communists under Zyuganov campaigned against the President, renewing their wild accusations and promising re-nationalization of key industries. The 'family', meanwhile, drifted into a strange state of both nervousness and paralysis – a typical case of *fin de régime*. The only good news was coming from the oil markets: prices were rising, and tax receipts began picking up.

The Chechen rebels' attack on Daghestan brought developments to crisis point. It was open rebellion against Moscow. Rasayev, the rebel leader, promised an Islamist state and threatened to cut Russia off from the Caspian Sea; this of course would affect one of Russia's most important oil pipelines. The rebels were well armed with money and weaponry, some of it sophisticated. Where did the money and arms come from? And who were the fighters? Some obviously came from Pakistan, from Afghanistan, from Saudi Arabia, suggesting a concerted effort by radical Islamists planning to set up a bridgehead inside Russia. Moscow's rumour mill was in full swing, producing likely and unlikely scenarios, from an Islamist conspiracy to the hand of the Kremlin directing a spectre to frighten the people, justify strong-arm politics and secure the presidential elections. The Russian troops sent into the province, mostly raw recruits, were ignominiously repulsed. Some of their weapons, sold or captured, turned up on the other side.

Prime minister

This was not a time for the faint-hearted. The Kremlin fired Stepashin, whose half-hearted crisis management had allowed things to go from bad to worse. On 9 August 1999, Vladimir Putin was appointed prime minister. Was he just another intelligence chief running the government? Russia had seen five prime ministers within seventeen months – why should a widely unknown Kremlin insider make much of a difference?

The difference was furnished by Yeltsin, who pronounced Putin his heir apparent. People in the street wondered at the FSB running the government, but Berezovsky contributed an appropriate explanation: 'During the transition we need authoritarian measures to protect our way of capitalism. This is the only way to find the perspective of a democratic order of society.'

Some people rise because they overwhelm the world. Others rise by being underrated, and so it was with Putin. The Duma confirmed his appointment without any of the usual fuss. Yeltsin's umpteenth premier was seen as a stopgap and not taken seriously; everybody was looking to the day after tomorrow. But the smart money, most of it belonging to Berezovsky, was on Putin. Berezovsky, visiting the Deutsche Gesellschaft für Auswärtige Politik in Berlin, explained his view of the situation back home: 'There were two criteria. Our candidate had to be a reformer and to be able to push through his policies' – as quoted by Alexander Rahr, who hosted the meeting.

But there were only a few months left to turn the widely unknown Putin into a national leader prominent enough to beat Luzhkov and Primakov in the forthcoming elections. The war in the northern Caucasus was an unavoidable test, but very risky. Putin lost no time in throwing more and more troops into the raging battle. He wanted, once and for all, a military answer to a political challenge. Official media reported from what was called the campaign against terror but failed to impress the general public. Meanwhile, time was running out, there was no Kremlin party, and opinion polls saw Putin only among the 'also ran' at a modest 5 per cent. In addition, new rumours about corruption among the 'family' made the rounds, and high-ranking Kremlin officials were said to have channelled vast amounts of IMF money into their private accounts out of Russia.

At this critical juncture war seemed to knock at the gates of Moscow. Several bombs went off, one bringing down the apartments of officers' families in the northern Caucasus, another ripping apart an eight-storey building in a south-eastern suburb of Moscow, with 200 casualties. Four days later, the carnage was repeated, and 130 people died in a Moscow apartment block. The authorities accused Chechen terrorists of having instigated and coordinated the carnage, though proof was never provided. Instead, vigilante tenants in an apartment block in Ryasan apprehended a group of intelligence officers hiding sugarbags full of explosives in the basement. The excuse given by the embarrassed services was that they wanted to test the reaction of people.

Whatever the chain of responsibility, Russians were convinced that fighters from the Caucasus mountains were out to get them, and patriotic fever gripped the people. The miseries of daily life were conveniently forgotten. Questions of life and death dominated public discourse, and the security services moved to centre stage in their patriotic effort to save the Russian people. The name of Osama bin Laden was mentioned as the ominous financier in the background, sending a message to the outside world.

Putin put an ultimatum to the Chechen president Maskhadov to apprehend and extradite the terrorists – or else. When nothing happened, Putin had villages bombed and much of the Chechen capital Grozny flattened.

Saviour of the nation

Overnight, the war made the prime minister a hero, saviour of the Russian nation. When, on top of the political turmoil, Berezovsky mobilized the full furore of television and the provincial authorities followed advice from the Kremlin, the presidency seemed no longer out of sight. While war was unleashed on Chechnya, a new political party, Edinstvo (Unity), was called into being, with a bear – *medved* – as its emblem. The price of oil was rising, the state budget was recovering, and after the catastrophic breakdown of the past few years some modest growth was in the offing. The stage was set for Yeltsin's not-so-secret crown prince to take his place centre stage. The Duma elections put Edinstvo, the hastily produced child of oligarchs and the Kremlin, into the pole position and prepared the launchpad for Putin.

On 26 March 2000 Zyuganov collected 29.4 per cent of the popular vote, Grigori Yavlinski put up a brave fight but reached not much over 5 per cent, while 52.6 per cent of the overall vote, with more than 70 per cent of the voters caring to go to the polls, carried Putin to the presidency of Russia. What was his past? What would his future be? And what are the implications of his political philosophy?

In September 2004 he hosted a group of Russian experts, columnists and ex-diplomats from the US and Europe to provide his own answers as part of a long, free-flowing conversation. Organized through RIA Novosti, this experience has been repeated every September since, in Moscow and in Sochi. These meetings in 2004 were a rare opportunity to meet personally a man whose training had been secretive, whose passion is communication, whose patriotism is Russian and whose fascination is power.

3
Meeting Mr Putin

'I noticed, with an unvoluntary pity, that the Tsar cannot smile with his eyes and his mouth at the same time.'

Marquis de Custine, *Journey for Our Time*

In the middle of some well kept parklands to the west of Sochi the palatial residence of Bocharov Ruchei is hidden behind a winding road and a simple 'no entry' sign, its ochre walls reminiscent of tsarist days. The wide arches offer a view of the grey waves of the Black Sea rolling to the shores of what the ancient Greeks called the land of Colchis and the Roman poet Ovidius, living in exile under the Emperor Augustus, decried as brutal and barbarian lands.

It was here that under the auspices of the Valdai Club, presided over by Sergei Karaganov, a small group of Western academics, journalists and think tank specialists was invited to dine with Mr Putin and ask questions. First the dark dog trotted into the dining-room. The master followed suit, smartly dressed in a light grey Italian suit, shirt and tie matching almost too harmoniously. Vladimir Vladimirovich greeted each guest with a handshake and that discerning look straight into the eyes that he had obviously taken from his former incarnation as an intelligence officer. Putin's guarded manner, his head always a little bent and his eyes looking upwards, does not give away much of the man and his feelings. But he wants to know, at once, everything about the person he is talking to.

On the two-hour flight from Moscow's ultramodern Domodedovo airport I had recalled earlier encounters with the man who in the autumn of 2007 was, without any doubt, the commanding presence of modern Russia and who, despite all the dissonant advice from his entourage and the vast popularity he enjoyed, intended to abide by the constitution and part with the presidency after his second term. Meanwhile, how he would exit, and where to, was something he kept to himself. He reminded many people of a chess-player who looks many moves ahead and would find it unwise to commit himself to one particular combination sixteen moves away. There were many options, and Moscow was awash with rumour and speculation. But one option, to simply see a willing United Russia party change the constitution and extend his tenure, or open the chance for a consecutive third term, had been firmly excluded. He probably meant what he said, and sometimes repeated: 'I shall leave the Kremlin, but not Russia.' And, a little more precisely: 'I cannot imagine that the Russian people would easily want to do without my experience and authority.'

In those September days of 2007 the guessing had not yet come to an end – let alone to a firm conclusion. The top positions in Russian politics can be redefined, modifying, for instance, the presidential system in a way that resembles more the British or German model centring on the authority of the premier. Yes, no doubt, Putin plays with the idea of leading United Russia, the Kremlin party, while at the same time staying, as befits the Tsar, above party. He might for a while be a more powerful prime minister only to return to full presidential honours and powers. But can Russia live with two tsars at the same time, one, to borrow Sir Walter Bagehot's famous phrase about the English constitution, representing the 'dignified parts' of the constitution, the other the 'efficient parts'? One in the Kremlin, and one in Moscow's White House? And for how long would a stopgap tsar be content with nothing but the mantle of power, and not its hard core? Putin will keep his distance from partisan politics. In Russian mythology the Tsar cannot and will not take sides. He is above everything mundane, answering only to Mother Russia and to those heavenly forces represented by the gilt St Andrew crosses scraping the sky over the Kremlin – while piercing the defeated Islamic crescent underneath.

As I was flying in the direction of Sochi my thoughts went back to a memorable evening in 1992 in the Rheingau. Princess Tatiana Metternich, née Vassilchikov, had invited a number of industrialists and politicians to the Palace of Johannisberg, a former monastery secularized in 1803 which the Austrian Emperor had given to Prince Metternich, of Vienna Congress fame, together with the fabulous Riesling vineyards beneath the well-kept Abbot's residence. When it comes to German Riesling wines Johannisberg sets an absolute standard of both finesse and strength.

A Russian princess who fled revolutionary turmoil in 1917, first to Kiev and then on to Berlin, Tatiana Metternich had never given up the idea of the eternal Russia, very different from the bloody mess the Bolsheviks had created. In Berlin in the 1930s she had been a celebrated beauty, and some decades later she still radiated a distinctly *ancien régime* charm – while also being an eminently practical organizer of the Rheingau festival, a manager of the estate and a great hostess. Ever since the Soviet Union collapsed, she did everything she could to introduce the standard-bearers of a Western-oriented Russia to German industrial and political leaders.

This is how that memorable evening at Johannisberg had come about. Guest of honour was Professor Anatoli Sobchak, elected mayor of Leningrad, the very city that had just been renamed St Petersburg in a highly symbolic gesture – a gesture, however, for what? Certainly a rejection of Lenin and his brutal regime, but what was to come instead? The answer was open then and will remain open for a long time to come. Sobchak was a constitutional lawyer, arguing in St Petersburg and beyond for the creation of a parliamentary system instead of an ersatz tsar. Highly respected as being untainted by the past and above any suspicion of corruption, he was rumoured to be one of the future leaders of post-communist Russia. The princess had also invited Rolf Magener, then chairman of the overseeing board of BASF, the chemical giant of Ludwigshafen on the Rhine, whom I knew through the international council of the JP Morgan Bank, and Professor Hans Lutz Merkle, legendary former CEO of the House of Bosch, second successor only to the founder Robert Bosch. On the commanding heights of Germany Inc. Merkle was known as the Godfather, and a telephone call from him was enough to settle many a question. Among the numerous public offices he held, he was also president of the Stiftung Wissenschaft und Politik in Ebenhausen, where I had been director since 1988. And then there was a youngish-looking man of indeterminate age and light blue eyes, whom Sobchak introduced, in English, as a member of the administration of St Petersburg. His task, obviously, was to help with the translation. His German was remarkably good, and I remembered having met a few KGB officers whose English was flawless, Etonian. Meanwhile, the man in the grey suit contributed little to the conversation that ranged across Russia's past and possible future. His name, Vladimir Putin, did not ring any bells – noticed and forgotten.

Two years on there came an invitation from the Bergedorfer Gesprächskreis, a kind of movable think tank of great repute for plain speaking, especially between West Germans and Russians. A meeting took place in St Petersburg, in the snow-covered guesthouse of the city government, still presided over by Professor Sobchak. The subject was, naturally, the future of Russia after the Soviet Union's demise, debated by the German hosts and their American, British, French and Russian guests. It was remarkable how little attention was focused on the reasons for the decline and fall of the Soviet Union – not unimportant for any predictions about Russia's future. Instead, the agenda listed economic reform, industrial modernization, eastern enlargement of the European Community, the future of the North Atlantic Alliance, its role after the Cold War and its future borders. Around the table there were about thirty participants, among them, next to Professor Sobchak in the chair, the man in the grey flannel suit whom nobody knew. I remembered, however, Princess Metternich's invitation to Johannisberg Castle. The mysterious man, by now in charge of the foreign dossier in the St Petersburg city government, listened attentively without saying a word until the discussion touched what the Russians by that time called – in ominous vagueness – their 'Near Abroad'. What was meant were the lost provinces of the empire to the south and west. Clearly, the wisdom of the Western experts assembled around the table failed to impress Mr Putin. He must have found some of the opinions expressed about the saviour role of the European Community and stabilization through Nato rather provocative. When he took the microphone he made no bones about his dissenting views, saying that there were around 20 million Russians now living on the wrong side of the border. 'For us, their fate is a question of war and peace.' Such outspokenness was unusual among the mild-tempered people gathered around the table, and all the more memorable. Was this the authentic voice of the new Russia? And how much weight should be attributed to this kind of outburst? At any rate, most of those present made a note of the name: Vladimir Putin.

In 2001, having been promoted by Boris Yeltsin to chief of intelligence and prime minister, and by now president of Russia and master of the Kremlin, Putin came to Berlin. In the reconstructed Reichstag building the Bundestag held a plenary session, and Putin addressed the German parliament in his near-perfect German. It was the time of the Fischer–Schröder coalition government. He talked, as might have been expected, about Russia's relations with Western Europe in general and with Germany in particular – with little sympathy reserved for the US and their presence as a European power. The price of oil had been steadily rising for a long time, almost without interruption, and the price of gas followed suit. Nobody knew better than Putin, who in 1997 had presented his doctoral dissertation on the role of energy in the reconstruction of Russia's place in the world, that fortune had dealt him a glorious hand of cards, and that the oil bonanza could be translated into political power and influence.

When he came to geopolitics, Putin cited a sentence which I had written a few years before: 'Between Western Europe and Russia there are only a few dotted lines while between Europe and America there is an Ocean.' Although he was courteous enough to attribute it to me and it sounded innocent enough, the conclusion which Putin drew was very different from mine. He spoke of a natural affinity between Russia and Europe, Moscow and Berlin being the two centres of gravity. I had, on the contrary, concluded that, given the geographic distance across the Atlantic, it was especially important to invest a great deal of energy and imagination into the Atlantic relationship in order to prevent Nato nations from drifting apart. By the time Putin quoted me, I had forgotten the occasion which had prompted my original remarks. It was only years later, when I was sorting through old files, that I found the original source. It was a manuscript drafted for a Nato ambassadors' meeting in Brussels, and not meant for wider circulation. Putin's speech writer for that Reichstag address certainly had a dark sense of humour.

In September 2005 there was another meeting with Mr Putin, by now well into his second term, in the Oval Hall named after Catherine the Great in the Kremlin, a neo-classical masterpiece of perfect proportions. Catherine, the little princess from Zerbst who had become Tsarina after her lover Prince Orlov had killed her childish husband – 'Mother, oh mother, he has fallen onto my sword' – and rose to autocrat of all Russians, is perhaps the patron saint of the new Russia. In her own time she wanted to be celebrated as the Semiramis of the North. She sent lavish gifts to those Paris intellectuals of the Enlightenment who sang her praise. But she also suppressed without mercy the peasant uprising of Pugachev. In her tastes she remained wedded to the delicate charms of French and German neo-classicism. And while her latter-day successors buy Porsches and BMWs and Mercedes-Benz, she ordered governmental silver for all of Russia's provincial capitals from Paris and Augsburg, furniture from the Roentgen factory at Neuwied on the Rhine and pictures from Philipp Hackert's studio in Naples. Putin was late and the chief of protocol had to apologize. A Kremlin diplomat offered to show us other rooms, including the formal office of the President.

'*Le style c'est l'homme*' – if the old saying has any truth in it, Putin's office provided some insights. In the centre was a big fireplace, accompanied by a pair of French *dix-huitième* gilded armchairs that would do honour to the Elysée in Paris. In front stood an equally antique desk, carrying a heavy inkwell of malachite. This was old Russian style, the bigger the better. More impressive were the greater-than-life-size statues of former rulers of the Kremlin, placed in all four corners of the room and looking down on their late successors. Peter the Great was the modernizing autocrat, turning Russia's face to the west and south, ordering St Petersburg to be built and a Mediterranean escada created. Catherine II expanded the empire but was also famous for the flourishing villages that hardly existed but were a mirage invented by Prince Potemkin. Nicholas I was a tyrant who claimed a *droit de regard* over Germany and Europe and sent rebellious aristocrats, and especially the reform-minded Decembrist officers, into internal exile to Siberia. Alexander II was a reformer, cut short by assassination. What inspiration would incumbents gain from the brooding presence of those bronze figures overlooking his office? His answer might give a better clue as to Russia's future than a thousand statistics.

In those Kremlin halls in 2005, Stalin and Lenin were conspicuous by their absence. There was no trace of the two great tyrants whose memory still haunts Russia – Lenin displayed in bronze in many a Russian city's central square, while Stalin, except in his home town in the Caucasus, has become all but invisible. From their day only a portrait of Marshal Zhukov greeted the visitor, poorly painted from a photograph and impressive only in the double-breasted display of military decorations. All along the walls of the long corridors there were nineteenth-century gouaches and oil paintings much as in the manor house central to a Chekhov play. In the elegant waiting-room, richly endowed with insignificant Italian neo-Rococo white-painted furniture, a white-gloved butler served tea and biscuits to help the guests while away the time.

Then a brief walk to the Hall of Catherine. Name tags in English and Russian were prepared, within sight of the President. Suddenly he was among the guests, unannounced, greeting every one of them in his characteristic manner, head slightly bowed, his eyes like a laser beam examining everybody to determine whether friend or foe. He welcomed the guests and asked them to put questions to him or give their comments. Unlike the procedure in Soviet times, no question had to be submitted in writing. Every one of the twenty-five participants was free to ask whatever they pleased, most questions being rather on the tough side. But Putin seemed to like a sporting event. There was no one to slip him a note, no one daring to add to the President's remarks, let alone act as a kind of expert mentor. Putin seemed comfortable with this kind of discussion and the participants in their majority obliged him by not spoiling the event with awkward questions about, say, the past and future of Chechnya or the country's weak record in crime prevention. The man was obviously enjoying his role.

For just over three hours Putin explained Russia – Putin's Russia – to this circle of Western experts. His messages were unequivocal. Stability is the leitmotif in his thinking. He demands predictability, from himself as well as from others. He thinks in terms of Russian *raison d'état*, but he would not deny that what is good for Gazprom is good for Russia Inc., the emerging super-corporation. Does he believe in political friendship? He knows – maybe inspired by Lord Palmerston – that great states have no permanent alliances but only permanent interests. Friendship is a personal matter.

Putin fills the grandiose frame of the hall named after the German tsarina, a manager of *raison d'état* – this is how he wanted to be seen by everybody around the table. The man in the grey flannel suit displays an impressive amount of both nervous energy and self-assuredness. His outward appearance – inconspicuous tie, no decorations, let alone adornments of any kind – would in the City of London be described as casual elegance. This man clearly wishes to be seen as a no-nonsense type. If there is a whiff of vanity it is that of a man who does not need to cut a colourful figure. He cultivates the air of the CEO of a global corporation. He is popular, his ratings are at an enviable – and plausible – 60 per cent, not the 99 per cent of the Soviet past, but also not the dwindling numbers that Western leaders tend to achieve after six years in office. The political train is on track, the oil price high, and rising, almost too good to be cheered in Moscow. Russian shares at the nearby stock exchange are soaring towards an all-time high. All of this works in his favour. Russians admire his luck and want to have a little share of it.

Russia's strength stems from oil and gas, but it is also Russia's potential weakness. Putin remembers that the Soviet Union went down, together with the world market price for oil in the mid-1980s, and that post-Soviet Russia was near collapse in 1998–90 when the oil price – the price for gas is, in most cases, pegged to oil – went, once again, down to a catastrophic US $10 per barrel. The reason was not a secular reversal of the terms of trade but a slight recession in the Far East's roaring economies. The ensuing small reduction in demand translated into a major crisis of the oil market, a sharp decline in investment, and an economic disaster for most of Russia's city dwellers. But ever since the oil price knew only one direction: up and up. However, Putin is painfully aware of the fact that Russia's fortunes are inexorably dependent on stable prices, preferably well above $50 per barrel – but not too much, as consumer countries would then be forced to look for alternative energies, from nuclear to ethanol, from solar panels to maize. 1998–9 was the low point of Russia's post-Soviet curve, and Putin knows how dependent on the world economy Russia is and how brittle the newly found wealth could be. Oil, Putin knows, can only be a bridge to a much more broadly based economy.

Referring to energy relations with Western Europe in general, Germany in particular, he mused: 'We are happy with the situation. Even at the worst of times Russia has never allowed interruptions to take place.' He was hinting at the strange paradox of the early 1980s when the Soviet Union directed its ultramodern nuclear-tipped medium-range missiles codenamed SS20 at Western Europe while Germans and Soviets, much to the dismay of the Reagan administration, continued to negotiate, and conclude, the gas-pipeline deal:

the German government under Chancellor Helmut Kohl was not only interested in swapping pipelines and pumping stations for gas but also in sending a signal of business as usual – while the German electorate, driven by nuclear angst, expected the end of the world. It was a balancing act and a masterful manoeuvre.

Now, Russia's Gazprom reigns supreme, aiming to add a third pipeline on the bottom of the Baltic Sea to the two older and landbound ones carrying natural gas to the West, and Putin is the state monopoly's prophet: 'An additional pipeline in the direction of the EU is due in order to broaden the distribution system for Europe.' But why, the question is bound to follow, not via Eastern Europe this time but on the bottom of the Baltic Sea, from near St Petersburg to Pomerania in Germany and on to the Netherlands and England? 'The revolutionary movements in Ukraine,' Putin says with disarming openness – and with more than a little *schadenfreude*. Poland failed to come up with the money. 'And this thing should stay outside of politics, anyway,' he says with a wry smile, as if oil and gas could ever exist in a politics-free zone. 'We want to exclude nobody,' he says, and tries to calm rising concern. Then he turns to detail and shows his mastery of the small print: 'We have concluded contracts for more than sixty billion cubic metres.' Moreover, Russia is slowly ridding itself of surface pipelines: 'The first tanker carrying liquefied natural gas [LNG] is on its way to the US.' As if to warn the Europeans that Russia can find customers all over the world, he adds that soon a pipeline will bring natural gas to Turkey via the Black Sea (by late 2007 around 60 per cent of Turkey's needs were met in this way). More pipelines are being built in the direction of the Far East. To northern China's industries or to Japan? 'Relations with the People's Republic of China are good. When, fifteen years ago, the Soviet Union collapsed, there were security problems. By now we have reliable treaties concerning borders.' Did he hint at fears, back in 1991, that China might take advantage of Russia's time of troubles? Or did he allude to the Russian concern about vast numbers of Chinese looking at the empty spaces of Siberia? Or about filling the power vacuum left by the demise of the Soviet Union in Central Asia? Putin, instead of addressing hidden fears, assured his audience that economic relations with mainland China were good, especially when it comes to military-industrial cooperation. That tends to help the Russian arms industry – but it also leaves Russian generals worrying about the future. In the past, Russia would sell at best second-rate goods to China. By 2005, only the best would be accepted by Chinese buyers paying US dollars.

What role for Japan in the Far Eastern puzzle? 'For us, Japan is a strategic partner. In the Asia Pacific region we see a balance of power at work.'

Of course, Putin is aware that this complex balance could be seriously upset by North Korea acquiring the bomb. Here, once more, he cites common interests with China and the US, mentioning Great Britain and France in passing. The Nuclear Club has its own set of rules, and its own exclusive interests, and preserving the Non-Proliferation Treaty is essential not only for reasons of security, but also for status and prestige.

The conversation, at this point, was bound to drift towards Iran. In Busheer on the northern shore of the Persian Gulf the Russians are building, after Siemens gave up the site in 1979 due to the second coming of Ayatollah Khomeini, a nuclear power plant which the Americans resent and the rest of the world, especially the Israelis and the Arabs, view with a watchful eye.

Putin: 'Is it meaningful to summon the Iranians to the UN Security Council? We have talked to our Iranian friends and advised them to keep their unilateral promises. Everything they have done so far is within the rules of the NPT. But we have warned them that throughout the Greater Middle East an explosive situation is forming. We do not exclude referring the matter to the UN Security Council.' Unlike German Chancellor Schröder, Putin refrains from any criticism of the US in this matter. Controversy ends at the NPT's edge. 'Between the US and ourselves there is no problem if there is cooperation.' And, 'by the way', he added a reassuring note to often-heard concerns, 'Russian control over our own nuclear facilities is watertight.'

In the summer of 2005, Moscow was abuzz with talk about the 'orange revolution' in neighbouring Ukraine. Could something similar occur his side of the border? Putin sounded less than relaxed: 'I think we have no reason to expect destabilization' – codeword for democratic change. But he is obviously aware of the potential for trouble, especially through the vast gap between the super rich New Russians and the rest of the population. 'We have to continue the policies which we have conducted so far. Over the last few years real income of the broad population has grown by ten per cent. We have to strengthen the middle classes, the party system and independent mass media.' The last point in particular visibly raised some eyebrows and made everybody wonder what he meant. 'The main reasons for the Ukrainian revolution were poverty and unemployment, on top of endemic corruption.' We are not against change in the post-Soviet space. But we want to make sure that those changes do not end in chaos.'

Does he see Western intentions to meddle in Eastern Europe? His answer was clearly more diplomatic than realistic: 'We entertain, to be sure, nothing like a hostile attitude towards the EU. We want stability in the former Soviet space. We want to avoid a split between east and west in Ukraine. The Russians in Ukraine deserve a safe future. We cannot go back to the Russian Empire. Even if we wanted to – it would be impossible.'

Managed democracy or authoritarianism – is this the style he wants? 'Democracy exists, or it does not exist. A state of law, democratic elections are part of it. All politicians draw criticism. How would that materialize without free institutions? We try to optimize the fabric of society. We aspire to peace and prosperity for the people.' Sometimes Putin cannot help using Western jargon. 'Of course we have to grapple with the traditions of this country. We cannot live on imitation. I listen to criticism. And if it sounds justified, I act accordingly.'

How does he see his own future after the end of his second term as president in 2008? 'I shall leave the Kremlin, but not Russia,' he answered, avoiding anything more precise. But the question was thrown back to him. There were rumours that he would aim for a third term. What role would he play? 'I would like to see that my experience and my knowledge are being used by the Russian people.' But the question was tossed back a second time. Were there not indications that he might seek a third term? 'Is that a recommendation?' Putin quipped. And then, on a more serious note: 'I repeat, I shall not run for President in 2008. The most important thing is to secure stability. No, we shall not change the constitution. You will see.' As for the oil price: what will the President do when and if the price for a barrel reached $80, and windfall profits continued to accrue. Putin answered,

'Eight months ago I had a visitor who wanted to know my prognosis for the oil price. I quoted roughly eighty dollars. Without the shocks and upheavals of the last few months the price would have been between forty and fifty US dollars. This I see as healthy. What we are going to do with the money? Presently we have a budget surplus and a positive balance of trade. Our gold reserves are high. We recognize a high risk of inflation. Therefore a good part of the petrodollars will go into the stabilization fund, another into the repayment of foreign debt. A third into social improvements, education, science, reduction of taxes.' In fact, only a few days before, Putin had decided to improve the tough lot of Russia's underpaid public employees and announced a programme of financial improvements for doctors, nurses, teachers and the like. It was a sign not only that the losers of the reform deserved some belated help but also that Putin and his people had taken a page out of Western democracies' book on how to win elections. While the Porsches and Jaguars zigzagging across Moscow's vast highways and byways are the toys of the newly rich, those left behind in the new Russia must receive a consolation prize and a share of the vast petro-dollar fortune that Russia had amassed ever since Putin had come into office.

The shifts in the population and the future imbalances between the old and the young, but also the rising percentage of the non-Russian population are strategic concerns of the first magnitude for the Kremlin. Russia, in the nineteenth century a land of infinite population growth, is now a land of elderly women, mostly widows, as men tend to die in their mid-fifties 'of excessive drinking and work accidents resulting from booze' – as Putin put it, disapprovingly. Children are a rare sight in Moscow's busy centre but also in the suburbs. Except in Muslim areas like Tatarstan, Russia is the land of the one-child family, and of early death. What is to be done about it? Putin indicated a panoply of social improvements. 'The solution is obvious. We are lacking, above all, a comprehensive and efficient health-care system. That can be set up administratively, but no longer through the centre, which is too far away from the real needs of the people. The regions must be made to administer health care. Therefore, the regional gov-ernors will receive the necessary budget allocations. In addition, we have targeted programmes to help young families. Economic growth will also do its part. But we have no magic wand. And as far as those twenty-five million Russians beyond our borders are concerned, we want to harmonize legislation with the other CIS countries and make the respective health-care and pension systems mutually compatible. Moreover, we do hope to transform Russia so that people queue up to come home on their own account.'

In the end, Putin put in a note of warmth and sympathy for the Americans hit by Hurricane Katrina: 'I have talked to George [Bush] and offered all the help that we can give. What does this disaster mean? We are nothing in the eyes of nature and of God Almighty.'

Putin, inspired by his tsarist predecessors, posed as a social conservative, fearful of instability abroad and social disruption at home. In his youthful days he must have repeated, time and again, Karl Marx's famous exhortation that it is not enough to interpret the world, but to change it. In the Kremlin there was a man keen to present a picture of himself as a pillar of world order and of Russia as a status quo power, part of an emerging world balance, trying to recover from post-imperial blues.

One year on, in September 2006, another meeting with what by now was known as the Valdai Club took place with Mr Putin as host. This time the venue was a princely dacha just outside Moscow called Novo-Ogarevo. When we had exited from the eight-lane motorway, the well-kept winding road, with a policeman standing guard at every hundred metres, passed woodlands and extensive 1930s villas as well as more modern buildings, including the stylish mansion that Mr Khodorkovsky, when CEO of Yukos, had built for himself. The billboards crowning the road at regular intervals advertised Western luxury goods that most Russians probably had never heard of. After about ten kilometres, a narrow road branched off, allowing no entry except with special permits. It ended in front of a steel gate painted white and adorned with two imperial double-headed eagles. The remote-controlled gate opened and allowed access to a park, with a wooden church in the distance, a small lake and a yellow-painted mansion in the timeless heavy neoclassical style at home in Russia since the tsars, but most probably built in the 1930s. It would have been interesting to know whose ghosts inhabited the well-kept structure. Instead, the President's guests were ushered into an extensive dining room on the first floor. A lavish early dinner awaited them, announced on an eagle-

and-gold-embossed menu card and prepared by an Italian cook.

Putin came unannounced, greeted the guests one by one with a hand-shake and a softly spoken word of welcome. He had come back from an African tour only a few hours before but looked as fit and energetic as ever. He gave a brief introduction, referring to the recent G8 Summit in St Petersburg where he had been in the chair, relishing the global exposure. He immediately raised the issue of energy demand and supply, and made it clear that for the foreseeable future the combination of oil, natural gas and – 'of course', he said – nuclear energy would be the basis for growth. Oil prices, the Middle East, Iran, the future of the nuclear non-proliferation system – all of this would develop as a function of energy. 'We have much in common, there are overriding interests. But it takes a proactive effort.' Energy security is the key theme: his particular theme since the days as an adult Ph.D. student at the mining institute of St Petersburg.

But the age of oil will one day draw to a close. How is Russia preparing for the time after cheap oil or, indeed, after oil? Putin offers an optimistic perspective: 'We are working on hydrogen energy. In the medium term we will invest massively. Moreover, we shall continue to develop nuclear energy. Today sixteen per cent of our needs is covered by nuclear energy. In the next fifteen to twenty years this will rise to twenty and perhaps twenty-five per cent. Renewable energy sources like solar power are not particularly effective, not only because of our climate. A vast potential is still in hydroelectric power, although much less than China can tap. We believe in diversification.'

Is Russia aiming to be an energy superpower? And what is the meaning of energy security – the key item on the G8 agenda? Putin rejects the term superpower. It smacks of the Cold War era. But only recently his minister for energy espoused Russia's strategic objective to be a superpower in the energy field. Putin distances himself from unwise rhetoric: 'I have never said that Russia is or should be an energy superpower.' He leaves it to the audience to decide what is fact and what is politically correct modesty or, perhaps, *maskirovka*. He mentions Russia's vast resources in Siberia, oil for more than three decades, the most voluminous gas fields of the world. But he recognizes the risk that Russia remains caught in the role of the purveyor of raw materials.

He knows about what the West calls the oil curse: the rule that riches make you lazy. The energy wealth of Siberia, he insists, will have to be used not so much for happy consumption but for the creation of a future science-based economy.

Energy, he points out, is 'the national wealth. We have to use it in a responsible way.' What he means is responsibility towards future generations but also, he hastens to add, towards the world community. Coming back to energy security, he points out that it has two aspects: supply and demand. 'The West needs security of supply, Russia security of demand.' At the G8 Russian expectations, he says, were disappointed. But sooner or later there would be consensus. In the realm of high technology Russia feels excluded, especially by the United States. France wants to sell its nuclear energy. But: 'We want relations on the basis of equality.' Meanwhile, Russia's lines of development are pointing not only West but also East. The new technologies for liquefied natural gas make new markets accessible, independent of pipelines.

Where will Russia be in ten years' time? 'Economic power is shifting from the Atlantic to the Pacific. Growth in those parts of the world is impressive and will not soon come to an end. Russia, as a littoral state of the Pacific Ocean, enjoys natural advantages. We would like to settle each and every conflict still extant.' That sounds like an opening to Japan? Putin prides himself for having consolidated the old uncertainty about borders with China. Why should that not serve as a model for the territorial disputes with Japan, especially over the Kuril Islands? With China, Russia has reached a state of cooperation as never before. 'Even when in Soviet times we sang of eternal brotherly love there remained deep mistrust.' Today there are overriding concerns, from timber production to space technology. There is also military-industrial cooperation. But energy is at the centre. Today's 3 per cent of Russian exports go to China, Putin points out. This should rise within ten years to an ambitious – and strategic – 30 per cent. The West, in other words, will feel Chinese competition where so far the market has been almost exclusively oriented towards Western consumers. Hard times ahead, rising prices, more leverage for Russia. But it is not only natural gas that reshapes the Russo-Chinese relationship in the Far East. The first oil pipeline is under construction, bypassing Lake Baikal, soon to reach the Chinese border. The demands of the environment, he assured Western concerns, would be safeguarded. Explorations for a second, parallel pipeline had just begun in Eastern Siberia.

Is there, between Russia and China, something akin to a hidden agenda? The answer is no, he insists. 'In Asia there is a complex correlation of forces, and Russia is seeking a responsible role.' Would this include UN sanctions against Iran because of nuclear concerns? Is Russia against Iranian uranium enrichment, and would Putin, if necessary, support at least mild sanctions by the UN Security Council against Iran? Putin does not hesitate for a moment. 'It is very difficult to control from outside the point where permitted low-grade enrichment for civilian use transcends into weapons-grade enrichment for military use. Even the burnt-out nuclear rods are potentially weapons-capable.' Altogether Iran presented an exceptional problem. 'Yes, they have the right to modern technology. But in the constitution they have declared annihilation of another country the overriding objective. Moreover, in the Greater Middle East extreme caution and self-discipline are to be advised. As far as sanctions are concerned, we will, together with our five partners – US, UK, France, China, Germany – consider the question, talk to the Iranians and then, possibly, decide on mild sanctions. First and foremost you have to avoid confrontation ... In this context we demand from our Iranian partners to stop uranium enrichment.' He calls Iran a 'partner' while usually he likes to speak of 'friends'. Then he points at Russia's offer from last January, indeed sold as the Putin initiative, to take care of enrichment and processing of used nuclear fuel within Russia, on behalf of threshold countries like Iran but beyond their control.

What does he think about the European Union? In Soviet times, the Kremlin largely ignored European integration, believing that capitalist countries would sooner or later be at each others' throats. Shared sovereignty? This was certainly not for the Russians, trying to keep their vast land holdings together. As far as Europe's uneasy Union is concerned, Putin remains ambivalent. Can Russia cooperate with Brussels to master international conflict? It is not easy, Putin answers, 'to conduct political dialogue with the EU as long as it is structured as it is, weak and indeterminate'. Putin does not quote Henry Kissinger's famous quip asking for the European telephone number. But he is similarly critical. The presidency, changing every six months, is not a force for continuity and predictability. For Russia, he muses, 'this could also be of tactical advantage. But in fact we have never tried to play the game of divide and rule. A strong Europe would be to the advantage of world order.' Meanwhile, the Europeans should keep out of the conflicts within the post-Soviet space: Nagorno-Karabakh, South Ossetia, Transnistria: 'It would be a major mistake,' he warns, 'to disregard the resolutions of the UN Security Council.' But what about Kosovo, Serbia's uneasy province? Putin at that stage tried to avoid committing himself to more than general unease about what he called 'uncontrolled and uncontrollable developments', once independence from Serbia has been stated. For Serbia, too, any future settlement would have to be acceptable. If this was advice to the West then it meant that no unilateral solution would be acceptable. Russia had not forgotten that the 1999 Kosovo war had been conducted by Nato against the advice from Russia. That this was still seen as a humiliation calling for redress.

Will Russia use its veto in the Security Council? 'We shall use our veto according to our national interest.' In the middle of a lavish dinner the Russian bear had growled. And what about relations with Germany? Just one year before, everything seemed to be in the hands of Gerhard and Vladimir, but by now Chancellor Schröder and the Social Democrats had been replaced in government by Angela Merkel from the Christian Democrats – and things looked different indeed. Ms Merkel, he remarked philosophically, would have her own priorities in shaping the EU agenda while President of the European Council. As far as Russia was concerned, energy of course would continue to dominate the agenda. Russia wanted to have its full share of political and economic competition throughout Europe. Some partners – meaning France – disagreed. 'But Russia is no longer the Empire of Evil' – he joked, referring to Ronald Reagan's famous remark about the Soviet Union. The future North European gas pipeline would not, he insisted, defending the Schröder-Putin project, take anything away from others.

The pipelines via Ukraine and Poland would continue to be needed. The criticism of the additional pipeline, he hinted at Warsaw and the Baltic states, could only be 'politically motivated'. In a nod to Berlin, he added: 'Serious people do understand.' Moreover, after Kiev had severed the bond with Russia fifteen years ago, the Russians had subsidized Ukraine to no small extent, selling oil and gas well below world market prices. For years on end the Russians, not least under pressure from the World Trade Organisation to go for market prices, had tried to arrive at a negotiated settlement. Then the orange revolution occurred. 'This has a price,' Putin added with a wry smile. 'In spite of so much frustration we have stabilized the situation. In the old days we concluded agreements with Ukraine year after year, and they included transit fees. The West Europeans had no idea that their energy security was a cliffhanger. By now we have a five-year agreement for transit to the EU. This is an important step in the direction of European energy security.'

Again and again the Russian President comes back to energy. Everything develops, he says, as a function of energy and its price. What does this mean for the economic development of Russia, the state budget, rate of inflation, welfare, and demography? Putin seems to love facts and figures, and he gives his listeners an impressive lecture on Russia's present and future macroeconomics. Above all, he insists, the state budget should not grow faster than the real economy to prevent inflation. 'The Russian economy needs diversification, especially in the direction of high technology.' Putin, as a former KGB officer, must have been aware of the Soviet system's fatal weakness in information technology. This was systemic, no doubt. But it had been recognized as a mistake not to be repeated. Infrastructure in general, roads in particular, needed massive investment. The main burden of taxation would in the future fall on energy, and this would inevitably make for higher prices in domestic consumption. The present rate of inflation, he stated, was at an unacceptable 9 per cent. In a few years' time both the government and the Central Bank intended to bring it down to 4 or 5 per cent. 'This, however, will limit our chances to use our oil income for improving general welfare. The most serious aspect is demography.' The Russian population – he did not say 'the population of Russia – was greying and shrinking. The growing economy needed a growing workforce. Additional labour could come from the Central Asian republics, working in construction. 'While there are serious labour shortages almost everywhere, I am more concerned about the decline of population throughout Russia. I have made this the leitmotif of this year's annual state of the nation message in the

Duma. Special leave for young mothers, a bonus for parents who want to have more than one child, or who adopt children. After maternity leave mothers should be able to return to their jobs without being disadvantaged. We need many more crèches and kindergartens. General political support is wanting. The family is the core of society.'

And in this context, what is the role of religion? All over the world, a religious renaissance can be observed. In the Zagorsk monastery, the day before, newly-weds and young recruits in uniform had made the pilgrimage to the holy fountain, washed their faces and drank of the water. Is that the future? When he answered, it was the only time that Putin made a personal reference. 'Russia,' he said, 'has always been a very religious country. Since the seventeenth century my father's family has lived in a village not far from Moscow. Only recently the church registers yielded the information that my forebears had always attended church and visited the confessional.'

Is there future in the past? 'The Orthodox Church has always been a moral institution and an element of political order. Since 1917 the ideological context changed. But there was no other moral institution to fill the ensuing vacuum. The Orthodox Church has suffered great pain, much as Jews and Muslims. Those wounds have never been accounted for. The separation between the state and the church will continue. Religious freedom is fundamental.'

After three hours it was time to ask about his vision for the future and his legacy. Above all, Putin said, it would be necessary 'to strengthen the state in Russia, to reinforce moral standards and to encourage efficient institutions. Russia's industry needs to be modernized, indeed reinvented and modernized – Russia's currency reserves have risen from a meagre $19 billion to $270 billion. Hyperinflation has been stopped. We have full employment. At present the economy registers growth at 7.4 per cent p.a. Meanwhile, four out of ten Russians still live below the poverty line. A great deal needs to be done.'

What measures does he see as a priority? 'To fight the ubiquitous corruption, to stabilize a multiparty system. Power has to be better divided between the centre, the regions and the municipalities' – so says the man who is in love with 'the vertical of power'. A multiparty system? He is concerned that the vested interests of different classes and groups in society are too strong. A multiparty system would channel those divergent forces into a more manageable system.

Putin's philosophy combines his Russian experience and his German vision, the essence of both Dostoevsky, the Russian writer, and Hegel, the Prussian philosopher. The strong state is needed in order to protect society from the demons of anarchy. 'In Russia, the political system is underdeveloped.' So much so that it could become necessary for him to continue in office beyond his second term? 'The great majority wants stable government. But it is not for one man alone to create good governance.' The constitution, he adds without a discernible moment of regret, is very clear on this point. And if there is a temptation to bend the letter of the constitution, he does not want his interlocutors to sense it: 'There is no exception for me, because this would be destabilizing. We cannot make the destiny of an entire country dependent on the fate of one man – even if this man is me.'

That was in September 2006 near Moscow. A year on, in Sochi, the time to say goodbye had drawn nearer. But Putin in his remarks sounded as if he would be around for a long time to come: We will do this, we will do that ... Who is 'we'? The party United Russia that he had called into being? The intelligence services running the administration? The President of today? Or the President of tomorrow? Or would Putin part with the presidency and come back in another incarnation? Speculation was rife in those mid-September days of 2007, less than a week after Putin had unexpectedly fired the government of Prime Minister Fradkov. In his stead he had appointed an unknown tax official, Mr Subkov, whom he knew from St Petersburg days. Subkov had made a reputation as head of the financial police. He was so little known outside the political class that, when his name was aired in Moscow and the rest of the world, it was difficult even to find a photo of him, let alone a CV. Putin, once again, had surprised almost everybody and opened a new round of guessing what this manoeuvre implied for the presidency – and the future of Russia.

Sochi is what Russia has inherited from the former extensive holdings of the Soviet Union on the shores of the Black Sea. The small and – by Soviet standards – elegant town is just beginning to prepare for the 2014 winter Olympics: major road building, brush clearing, hotel building and refurbishing of sports arenas in Sochi and in the mountains above the city, plus a tremendous amount of upgrading, will have to be done. Putin, when he persuaded the International Olympic Committee in Guatemala in early summer of 2007, had displayed his Sunday-best English and French to convince the sports officials that Sochi, although blessed with a Mediterranean climate, was really made for the winter Olympics; that Russia, never mind global warming, could still guarantee enough snow on the mountains to the north of the city, and that money was no object.

The airport is on one side of the city – which is essentially a narrow settlement between the steep mountains with their dark forests and the misty clouds above and the seashore. The mansion of the President is on the far side of the city. Travellers without a presidential escort flashing blue and red lights will experience endless traffic jams. Nobody was indiscreet enough to ask Putin directly whether or not he would still be around to oversee the realization of his pet project.

Russia, Putin said, is 'a multireligious country'. Throughout the centuries the fate of the country depended on the ability to coexist and cooperate. When mistakes were made – did he mean the Bolsheviks? – the consequences were painful and long-lasting. The future he sees in strong government – he indicated that only a presidential system could deliver enough authority. However, strong parties were also needed, preferably in a multiparty system. At present, and for a long time to come, United Russia looks poised to supply the necessary societal foundation. But Putin left no doubt that the party was more dependent on the President than the President on the party. He also mentioned Just Russia which, for good measure, he had created to the left of the Kremlin party – an exercise in Russian social democracy. Together those two parties were well equipped to win the December elections and control the State Duma for the next four years.

But who, the question was on everybody's mind, will be President? And would not every successor, whoever he might be – a 'she' would have been the surprise of all surprises given Russia's macho society – be forever in the shadow of Mr Putin, and therefore rather weak? Putin: 'I am not interested in a weak president after me. Russia cannot exist without a strong president – or did he mean strong authority, in whatever constitutional guise? Whether he could imagine returning to the Kremlin after a while? Putin leaves the answer open. 'I hope I will be fit enough. That would be one factor.' Meanwhile, rumours from Moscow suggest that Putin might want to become chief of Gazprom in St Petersburg in order to make real money.

But in late summer of 2007 all of this remained mere speculation. Putin would not be the gifted tactician if he were to unveil his plans. Either everything was still open, or everything was already settled and, known only to a small circle inside the Kremlin.

For the time being the new government and what it means are the focus of attention. Why the new premier? Why just now, before the Duma elections in December and the presidential elections three months later? And why Mr Subkov? Putin responds angrily to the hint that the reshuffle was undemocratic. What about France? Or the US? Or Germany? Everything happened strictly within constitutional lines. It was a 'technical decision'. On the one hand the ministers had paid too much attention to their friends and their own personal future – did he hint at corruption in high places? – while a government ought to work 'like a Swiss clock'. On the other hand, he put much emphasis on 'continuity'. But why, of all people, Victor Subkov, arguably the most faceless of bureaucrats? Putin answered that the man from St Petersburg brought much experience to the job, first as an agricultural expert who had made the Kolkhoz under his thumb a model for many others, then as a financial expert and, during the last six years, as the head of the tax police where he had obtained no fewer than 421 convictions. Subkov, Putin concluded, was the right man to steer the country through the uncertainties of the forthcoming elections. But would Subkov also be the right man to modernize Russia's desolate infrastructure? To clean up Russia's cities? To reinvigorate the education system, even under the Soviets the pride of Russians and now in a state of decay? To reverse the destruction of the environment? Perhaps an experienced apparatchik type might be best equipped to channel the wild dynamics of Russia's economy and give them productive direction. But doubts linger on.

Therefore, once again, the inescapable question was who would be his candidate to succeed him as president. It cannot have been convenient that Subkov, in his first press conference, had hinted that he could conceive of himself running for president. Who else? 'There are five or six excellent candidates.' All of them enjoy the support of United Russia, the Kremlin's party. It is obvious that Putin plays his cards close to his chest, and does not want to have his hands tied. 'I am still around, and 2012 is far away.' Is there a roadmap? 'Much can change in the course of a few months,' he says, to end that particular subject.

With gusto he went on to answer the next question as to the economic future of the country mercilessly running through facts and figures: more than 7 per cent overall growth each year since 1999 – that was the year when the oil price, after its catastrophic fall to $10 per barrel, picked up. The rouble is now a hard currency. Russia, until 1999 a basket case, was able to repay its debt. Unemployment was down to 5 per cent, inflation reined in from a destructive 40 per cent to 8 per cent over the last twelve months: 'But you have to pay attention.' In fact his experts fear, if too high a proportion of the petrodollars were channelled into pensions and infrastructure, rampant inflation.

The question as to 'sovereign democracy' gives him the cue to express bitterness at the sight of the massive US presence throughout Eastern Europe: 'ministers have to be approved by the US ambassador'. At the same time, Russia claims its own path. He does not mention human rights. Instead he praises the role of democratic institutions, more specifically law and order, civil society, a multiparty system and freedom of the press. It sounds good when he adds: 'We cannot build the country on the will of one person or a single group.' Is what he says an attempt to please and reassure his interlocutors? Or is it a vision for the Russia of his dreams? It is with admiration that he speaks of the older, 'mature democracies' of the West, able to manage complex societies. Russia, he adds, was still on its way. 'But we do not have to invent our own wheel.'

Could not Russia, by selling less and earning more, increase oil revenues? Putin's answer comes like a conditioned reflex: 'On the contrary. We have to produce. We shall even expand production. Demand continues to rise. We have always acted responsibly. Our interests [he addresses the Westerners] should be in harmony. We are not part of OPEC. We are not interested in monopolies or excessive pricing. If we did, it would put a premium on substitution and ersatz. Everywhere the search is on for other sources of energy. This we have to take into account.' As far as distribution is concerned, he is looking for more outlets. Again he mentions construction of two major pipe-lines to the Far East and a giant oil pipeline in the same direction – 'bypassing Lake Baikal by a wide margin', he adds, referring to envir-onmentalists' criticism of the original route. And who knows what new opportunities for transport along the northern shores of Russia climate change will one day open?

The blessing of oil will end, sooner or later. Putin is thinking about the day after oil and talks of a science-based economy – a kind of Walter Rathenau vision that so captured Lenin's imagination for the future of the Soviet Union. In fact he is aware of what is being described as the 'oil curse' – the counterproductive addiction to oil coupled with neglect of a broad-based economy: 'What we need is economic modernization, a new middle class as the backbone of the economy, German style, secure property rights and affordable housing.' There is now, he adds, 'a well-oiled market for mortgages, including specialized banks, and the people make use of the new facilities. Investors need security' – does he mean physical or legal security, predictability of taxes or the weeding out of corruption? Clearly, this President's insights reach far beyond his power.

Putin does not trust stock exchanges abroad. Investment in equity, he warns, is not secure enough. He would rather convert petrodollars into securities. But, if that is the philosophy at the top, what is the meaning of a 5 per cent stake, required recently, of EADS-equity, the Franco-German high-tech giant? Putin is on his guard: 'We do not wish to infiltrate other countries. What matters is mutual integration of energy interests. If the West makes concessions downstream, we are willing to admit investment upstream.' Is this the outline of a deal?

After two hours the conversation turns to foreign and security policy. Would a complete withdrawal of US troops from Iraq be good for regional stability, or bad? His answer surprised everybody around the table because of its well-balanced perspective. 'The Americans are not in Iraq to keep the country forever occupied. We were against the invasion from the beginning. What the objectives are at present [he adds with an ironic smile] is beyond my understanding.' In this, Putin is certainly not alone. And what about democracy for Iraq and the Greater Middle East? 'In Chechnya we had occasion to learn that democracy cannot be created through war. Sooner or later the Ameri-cans have to withdraw their troops. But not before the Iraqis themselves are capable of guaranteeing domestic security. It might be useful to give a date so that Iraqis are under pressure to act responsibly themselves.'

And what would be the worst-case scenario? The answer is unequivocal: 'Partition into three statelets. This would not be the end of fighting but the starting point of even more vicious conflicts.' What about Afghanistan? 'We are very concerned, especially about what goes on throughout the border areas between Pakistan and Afghanistan. We do what we can to help our Western partners to succeed. But a good ending is far away.' There was not a hint of *schadenfreude* or I-told-you-so, but rather the concern that the conflict might be contagious and, once again, affect Russia.

On Kosovo, obviously Putin was reluctant to commit himself. 'Once the Kosovo Albanians declare independence towards the end of this year, everything depends on the West's reaction. Support in cultural and economic matters would be acceptable. Full political recognition would be another matter.' His advice to Western nations, especially the Europeans, is to go slow. But to what extent Russia will seek compensation elsewhere, and in what dimension, remains an open question. At the G8 meeting in Heiligendamm, two months before, Putin had hinted that the frozen conflicts in the post-Soviet space might be revisited. Maybe, he hints, the EU could make the Serbs an offer impossible to refuse? Putin makes it clear that the present state of uncertainty is better than a solution forced upon the Serbs and, by implication, upon Russia.

How to deal with the European Union? Putin remembers the European Council meeting of heads of state and of governments at Lahti, under the Finnish presidency, in late 2006. He was clearly nonplussed. He had been accused of not taking the EU seriously and of always choosing a bilateral approach. Russia (and he sounded bitter at this point) felt rebuffed. 'There are outdated stereotypes, a silly Atlantic solidarity. The position of many European countries is not reliable. Russia is a European nation – with several million Muslims. We have vast interests in Asia. With China we have thousands of miles of border. China is an attractive place for producing industrial goods. We shall not waste our chances with the EU.' Suddenly, there seemed to be another Putin in the room, no longer suave but angry and abrasive. And what about the

Baltic pipeline? 'The North Stream pipeline is good for Europe. Do we tread on anybody's rights? We have to diversify. But we meet with obstruction.'

Once back to oil, Putin continues, anticipating unfriendly questions: 'We have subsidized Ukraine for fifteen years. If the West wants an orange revolution, please pay for it. Do you think we are fools?'

Yes, things are improving. But there is no guarantee: 'The trend is not irreversible. We in Russia, you in Europe and in North America – we should be more patient with each other and stay away from lecturing each other.'

Then, as an afterthought, he mentions that teenagers from both countries are working together to look after the graves of German and Soviet soldiers from World War II. 'We must overcome the distorted values of the past.'

And what are the guiding ideas, the last question is put to him, for the future of Russia? Panslavism, Putin says, is a thing of the past. And so is world revolution. Under the tsars as much as under the commissars, an expansive foreign policy had to complement and support the domestic order, and vice versa. Lenin's Russia was built on the idea of world revolution, and caught by it: 'People were cheated of their land, the fruit of their labour and a humane way of life. Russia refuses to repeat those mistakes. We do not pretend that we are a world power. We pursue no missionary ideas. We seek self-respect and fairness among nations.'

Talking with the Russian President is an experience like none other. He is self-assured. There is no notetaker, let alone an advisor who might from time to time intervene. Putin is proud not only of his sporting achievements but also of the facts and figures he has at his fingertips. He is the man for the big picture, but also for anecdotal evidence, putting every little detail into the wider context, especially when it comes to oil and gas and pipelines. This is where he earned his doctorate at the celebrated mining institute of his home town. But he is also a shrewd operator. 'Communication' is how he once described his profession. It was one of those rare occasions when he talked about his earlier incarnation. Communication is indeed what became second nature to the man who joined Soviet intelligence at the tender age of twenty-two. The means employed in the service of communication are variable indeed, and sometimes Putin is both Mr

Nice Guy and Mr Tough Guy. His roles range from factual analysis in business style to the grand design for Russia's future, from open flattery to confessions of friendship. But for good measure there is also, from time to time, a hint of threat or cynicism, well hidden behind a wry smile. Anybody in the West or, for that matter, in Russia underestimating Mr Putin would do so at his own peril.

4
Putin's people

'The Russians' Byzantine policy, working in the shadows, carefully conceals from us all that is thought, done and feared throughout the country.'

Marquis de Custine, *Journey for Our Time*

It was in the foggy winter days before the recent Duma election. On 30 November 2007 *Kommersant*, the reliable Moscow-based business paper, carried a substantial interview that was, by any standards, unusual. Somebody, until that day largely unknown, had dropped a brick on the polished floors of the Kremlin administration. It is reasonable to assume that this came as an unpleasant surprise to some of the *siloviki*, Russian slang for those in power, including members of the armed forces, the FSB and other security services.

Normally the red-brick walls of the Kremlin are impregnable, especially when it comes to intimacies between big government and big business, more than in Wall Street or the City of London. Not so in this case. What *Kommersant* offered its readers was a rare X-ray picture of the workings of power in today's Russia, a juicy story with an ominous outcome.

Siloviki and vacuum cleaners

The man to spill the beans was Oleg Shvartsman, and the fact that he gave the interview and survived its shocking frankness – at least so far – meant either that he was not taken seriously, the whole thing regarded as a hoax, or a fantasy perhaps, or, much more likely, that he had high-placed backers who wanted to expose practices that are compromising to the people in power. Shvartsman immediately retracted, mumbling the usual 'taken out of context', but knowledgeable people around Moscow like Anatoly Chubais stated, on the record, that everything Shvartsman had said was true. Everyone was left wondering what the real story was.

What happened was a bombshell fired in the middle of pre-election uncertainty. Shvartsman, head of a holding in the venture capital business Finansgroup, was talking in the interview about 're-privatization' – i.e. undoing the privatizations of the 1990s – and the way that high-placed Kremlin personalities would profit from the process. 'Investments are channelled through a special project called Venture Ru. That is our own. We are providing the biggest pipeline to channel capital into the regions. ... Moreover, we have acquired a foothold in the Ministry for Science – unofficially of course. This concerns approximately 4000 projects. Whatever moves in the market or does not move we try to integrate in Venture Ru. There is a real chance to attract foreign investors; our complete website is available in English.'

Shvartsman was unequivocally proud of what he was doing. 'I am president of Finansgroup. We have USD 3.2 billion under admin-istration. I am not involved in operational management. What I do is strategic planning, policies for society as a whole.' So far so good. What followed was more contentious: 'We are closely connected to the structures of political power, including some political characters, and we administer their assets. We are also linked to the presidential administration, with its security structures. We own large assets in oil resources. I am president of a company called Russian Oil Group. There are more of the same calibre, like Russian Diamond Economics and Russian Machine Tool Technologies. The holding Russian Busi-ness Group is a very serious structure. As far as private participation is concerned, a lot is offshore, via Cyprus etc. ... The holders of power are not involved, but their family members, members of the administration. They are FSB people, people from internal intel-ligence.'

Kommersant asked for more details about the political involvement, and Shvartsman obliged by naming names – a dangerous and most unusual thing to do: 'There is an organization by the name of Union for Social Justice in Russia. I personally had a hand in setting it up, in administration and finance. It was created in 2004 when Putin advised that not only the state but also big business should carry some respons-ibility. After that, our colleagues from the FSB decided to use this organization for going after all the Khodorkovskys. Patrons are all the power ministries: Defence, Home Affairs, Emergencies etc. It turned out, however, that it did not work properly. Each and every oligarch had his special relationship with this or that power structure. So we tried another path. The new concept means that a partnership is being set up with companies under scrutiny. We planned various cooperations. That is how Russian Oil Group came into being – the result of an alliance between Lukoil, TNK and Rosneft. We bought parts of the smaller subsidiaries of those companies. They ceded part of their income to us.'

Kommersant wanted to know more about the future, and Shvartsman's answer was even more revealing: 'At the moment we are developing a structure to be called Social Investment. It will soon be a state corporation. The concept was drawn up by us, the Russian Civil Service Academy and the Russian Economic Academy. The concept could be called "velvet reprivatization". That we do in the interest of Rosobornexport.' Everybody in Moscow, of course, knows the name of the Russian holding for weapons exports. Shvartsman went on to explain: 'This is a market-compatible form of taking over strategic assets throughout the regions. The goal is to stop the faulty mechanisms of tax evasion. Pensions for civil servants throughout the regions should be paid out on time.'

But the journalists from *Kommersant* asked: how does it all work in practice? The answer made it round the world and became known as the vacuum-cleaner method: 'It works like a vacuum cleaner that sucks up the assets of companies into a structure which soon turns into a state corporation. Those assets are then passed on to the professional leaders. The measures applied are both voluntary and mandatory. People understand which institutions we come from. This is no expropriation, as in the Yukos case. Our senior comrades put things right whenever conflict occurs, but people are compensated, generously, even if it is at the low end of the market price. This is today's guideline – consolidation of assets in the hands of the state. In all of this, the state helps us. Our employees are former operatives from the intelligence services, 600,000 all over the country. It is through those relationships that we can drive out the power of disloyal entrepreneurs. There is another preventative structure looking into the problem of debts that are not being serviced. This one is about to become one of the most powerful state structures.' And who, the journalists wanted to know, had given

Shvartsman those instructions? The answer was short and simple: 'The party. Today it is being led by the *siloviki*, represented by Igor Sechin. There is a real problem: 600,000 people doing nothing and being corrupt. Our measures give them something to do.'

Sechin? For the outside world something of a dark horse. On the Kremlin website he was listed as the man over whose desk all the laws of the Federation and all the president's decrees had to pass. Moreover, he was also responsible for all intelligence briefs; this was certainly not a man to short-change.

Shvartsman's activities, *Kommersant* suggested, were much broader than normal, far beyond a classic venture-capital fund. He obliged by saying that: 'Venture capital for us is petty change, not to be taken too seriously. Behind this there is a bigger issue lurking. The state has the duty to develop new sectors and turn Russia from an exporter of resources into a progressive and innovative big power.' And would he report directly to Sechin? 'There are others, such as Varennikov, member of the state Duma, chairman of the union of heroes of Russia. For us, he is a link to Sechin. He fully supports our idea of reprivatization.'

Muscovites were not alone in wondering, after Shvartsman had opened a small window on to the inner workings of the Kremlin administration, what it all meant. Was Shvartsman trying to commit suicide? Or was he doing somebody else's bidding? The answer came three weeks later when, suddenly, Sechin went on holiday, and rumour had it that he had fallen into disgrace. However, after a while, he resumed his responsibilities. One of the most powerful movers and shakers and a long time adviser to Putin from St Petersburg KGB days, Sechin showed an unusual ability to survive the power play of FSB factions. In 2008 he joined Putin in Moscow's White House. The comment by Anna Politkovskaya, murdered on 7 October 2006, sums up what happened: 'In Russia a great deal is being played out behind the scenes; many people wander around with a bad conscience.'

Corruption

It is rare in the West for newspapers to be invited to the inner sanctum of money and power, and even rarer in Russia. But it is not unknown. A little after Shvartsman went public, Putin shared his concerns about the domestic power structure in Russia with – of all journals – *Time* magazine. The presidential administration soon afterwards put the full text on the internet. Putin was asked how he controlled corruption, and his answer was, by any standards, a blunt one: 'Unsuccessfully. We are addressing the issue without success. ... In a transitional economy and during the restructuring of an entire political system dealing with such issues is more difficult because unfortunately there is no response from civil society to us. ... We must speak frankly and openly admit that we have not worked out a system that encourages social control of the activities of public institutions.'

Civil society in Russia? The master of the Kremlin seemed to be well aware of the disease but unable to administer any medicine, let alone a lasting antidote. Yes, the country had abundant resources and vast amounts of money were in the hands of some individuals and some companies. But the President could not offer much reassurance except by sending highly placed officials on secondment to the top echelons of big companies. There they would represent government control and also be able to put something aside for a rainy day: 'Incomes in the public sector for government officials still do not correspond to the nature of the decisions they have to make. That is: the payment for their work on the one hand and the importance of the decisions they have to take on the other hand are incompatible. ... The activities of officials on whose decisions billions (of USD) depend should be awarded appropriately so that there is no temptation. All of this, including increasing opportunities for the media to expose corruption, all of this taken together is certainly one of the tasks that we have to deal with.' He suggested what his American interviewers wanted to hear: 'strengthening the political system, civil society, improving market mechanisms'. But he also seemed to warn that the Kremlin would continue 'making governmental and administrative decisions about economic management', and have the Kremlin representatives compensated by more than the official salary which, in the eyes of well-off businessmen looks like a pittance. Keeping Kremlin staff loyal is not only a matter of power and promotion to be granted, but also of money to be dispensed. This is also a method designed to make everybody dependent and vulnerable the very moment when disloyalty is suspected.

All the President's men

Who are the people with real political power in Moscow and St Petersburg? It has been said about Putin that he trusts nobody. This is unlikely as the running of a large country requires reliable lines of command, division of labour, and the creation of both official and unofficial networks. Moreover, he would hardly have insisted on leaving the Kremlin after eight years in office if catastrophe or revenge beckoned – or indeed a settling of accounts. Over the last eight years Putin has surrounded himself with people he could control and trust. Much of this was planned and executed with a long-term perspective in mind. It is interesting to remember that, four weeks after Putin's re-election in 2004, it was Dmitri Medvedev, in 2007 the tsar designate, who stood side by side with Putin and the newly appointed prime minister Fradkov, formerly of the KGB, on the Easter night at the entrance of the Christ Redeemer Cathedral in Moscow, after the Kremlin Russia's most hallowed place.

On close inspection, there are two groups sharing power uneasily, the old and new St Petersburg clans, most of whose members had served with Putin either in the KGB or in the St Petersburg city administration, or both. At one time, the old St Petersburg clan was represented by people like Anatoli Chubais, head of the Russian Joint Energy Systems; by Alexei Kudrin, deputy prime minister; and by Sergei Ignatiev, chief of the Central Bank. Until the end of 2007 German Gref, with his belief in liberal economics, played an important role as minister for economic development; other pals from old St Petersburg days were Alexander Pochinok and Deputy Finance Minister Alexei Ulyukaev. Some of Putin's more recent protégés were also close to the clan, among them two deputy directors of the presidential administration, Dmitri Kozak and Dmitri Medvedev; the latter shadowed Putin almost from day one in St Petersburg and was proclaimed heir apparent towards the end of Putin's second term. He is unlikely to show anything but gratitude towards his mentor over so many years. When proclaimed crown prince, Medvedev even went so far as to say that, if elected, he would need continuous tutoring by Putin. But, as they say, *l'appétit vient en mangeant*.

And then there is the new St Petersburg group, called 'special agents' in a reference to the KGB background that has launched most of them on their post-Soviet career. It includes many former colleagues of Putin's in the St Petersburg KGB establishment, including Sergei Ivanov, a former lieutenant-general in the KGB, with experience abroad, soft-spoken and tough-minded, until mid-2007 minister of defence and, since then, deputy prime minister for high-tech development. He was a runner-up in the race for the presidency, but Putin probably saw him as too much of a rival. On the day after Medvedev was nominated Ivanov could hardly conceal his disappointment. There is also the human resources manager of the presidential administration, Victor Ivanov (no relation, just a common name) and FSB director Nikolai Patrushev, a KGB agent who rose through the ranks, helped by his closeness to Putin. The same is true for his deputy Yury Zaostrovtsev and foreign intelligence chief Sergei Lebedev. The group also includes some former colleagues of Putin's from the Sobtschak administration in St Petersburg, notable among them presidential affairs director Vladimir Kozhin and the head of the presidential administration Igor Sechin – one time *éminence grise* in the corridors of power who became the chief target of the Shvartsman revelations in *Kommersant*. Important also are Alexei Miller, powerful CEO of Gazprom, and other business leaders like Sergei Pugatshev (Mezhprombank) and Vagit Aleperov (Lukoil).

In retrospect, the Soviet days in Leningrad and the post-Soviet days in St Petersburg look like a long march to the top. Just before he became President, according to the London *Economist*,* Putin told his colleagues that a group of FSB operatives were 'dispatched under cover to work in the government of the Russian Federation'. Maybe it was just a joke, or maybe it was the truth. At any rate, the mentality, the culture and the world view now prevalent in the Kremlin bear the hallmarks of the old KGB. Much of the security forces, the government and the economy is now, directly or indirectly, under the control of the intelligence services. Three out of four senior Russian officials today were once affiliated with the KGB or related organizations. The fact that Dmitri Medvedev, when named heir apparent, did not seem to have a KGB background could mean that either Putin wants to reduce the influence of the old KGB on Russian politics and society or, on the contrary, that a president not affiliated to the KGB but renowned in

* *Economist*, 25 August 2007

the West for his unorthodox views and his belief in democracy and the market would provide a cover for the real power play going on inside the Kremlin walls. The outside world will have to wait and see.

Meanwhile, the *siloviki* are firmly entrenched in the seats of power. The patriotism on display is a mix of Soviet nostalgia, revenge for the failed coup of 1991, the desire to translate oil wealth into political punch – and the self-serving instinct of an elite corps convinced that the spoils of power are legitimate compensation. Vast sums are quoted when it comes to discussing what top officials, including the President, are putting to one side. Some Kremlin insiders have hugely enriched themselves over the last few years, and their chief desire must be to secure ill-gotten gains abroad or at home.

Lubyanka

Does it matter that the people who run Russia are more or less linked to what Russians still call, with fear and uneasiness, the Lubyanka, meaning not only the stately building on Novaya Ploshad (New Place) but also the institution, the tradition and the clandestine violence associated with the secret service? The formative phase of the Kremlin's incumbents today has a direct impact on domestic affairs as much as Russia's foreign policy. The post-Soviet Russian elites, with the exception of the majority of business leaders, still define power in terms of distrust and control, awe and anxiety.

When spies take over the political process, it is in a way their field of competence, but in the economy they can do a lot of damage. Russia's economy is still today almost one-dimensional. Everything depends on the continuing flow of oil and gas at high prices. Russia is conspicuously weak in manufacturing, except in the weapons sector and high-tech industries. Spooks can be relied upon to understand power, but do they understand real-world business? What do they know about modernizing companies, developing markets, cooperating with partners abroad, managing ever scarcer human resources? Both the brutality of the early years, when enemies were jailed and assets seized, and the more subtle 'vacuum-cleaner' method exposed by Shvartsman are not conducive to running efficient businesses that have to compete in the world market. Compared with China, Russia has attracted little direct foreign investment except in the natural resource sector. What the 'vacuum-cleaner' recipe amounts to is a practice where accusations can be fabricated and assets acquired at artificially depressed prices and redistributed to cronies irrespective of their management genius.

A bullying foreign policy combined with intimidation at home, however, is a deterrent for those investors from the West who are badly needed to upgrade, or in most cases reinvent, Russian industries for both consumer goods and capital assets. On both counts Russia is not yet part of the modern world, and the key problem is that the ex-KGB echelons do not think in market terms. Russia does indeed present, from time to time, some high-tech marvel at air shows abroad or sells to China cutting-edge information technology for sophisticated military and intelligence use, or boasts the biggest vacuum bomb the world has ever seen. But this is not representative of Russian industry at large, not even in the civilian aircraft industry which badly needs Western input. When a 100-seat passenger aircraft was rolled out in summer 2007, needed in large quantities to replace an ageing fleet of converted bombers, it was clear that both avionics and electronics had come from Western suppliers. Meanwhile, the expectation around the Kremlin that a flourishing weapons industry could be the fountain of rejuvenation for Russia's economy fails to take into account that defence industries work in specialist markets, are not particularly sensitive to competition, are politically driven and are not renowned for their efficiency.

The *siloviki* republic

Perhaps the most serious area of insecurity is the political nature of the *siloviki* republic. The men around the Kremlin have shown that they know how to quash opposition, intimidate people, lean on television channels and sow fear in many people's hearts. What they have failed to do is inspire long-term trust in the future, in the stability of institutions, in the continuity of political management. This is precisely what intelligence services are not good at. They are nervous about the future, and the mysteries surrounding the succession to Mr Putin are a worrying symptom of uncertainty that affects not only Russians but also the world beyond the Russian confines.

Putin and his people have built a new sort of corporate state through a combination of money and power without precedent in Russian history. About one quarter of Russia's senior bureaucrats are *siloviki*, and the proportion rises to three quarters if one includes people who are affiliated in one way or another. This top echelon is linked through upbringing, outlook and material interest – a new ruling class. In the old Soviet Union what the communist leaders always feared was 'bonapartism', meaning the rise of a successful general, Napoleon-style, to prominence and power. The old KGB, comprising about half a million operatives working as secret police, intelligence organization and security agency, was never more than a combat division under the watchful eye of the Central Committee of the CPSU. It was a state within a state, subservient to the party bosses. Its leaders, however, were invariably among the better informed players in Moscow, sensing the slow decline of the Soviet system during the early 1980s, opting for reform from above and seeing, with ill-disguised horror, how everything was spinning out of control. Their low point came when the coup of 19–21 August 1991 failed, the head of the KGB who had helped to orchestrate the action against Mikhail Gorbachev was arrested and a jubilant crowd celebrated in front of Lubyanka – the headquarters of the old Cheka just as of Stalin's NKVD. The anger of the people concentrated, instead of storming the building and seizing the files, on the statue of Felix Dzerzhinsky standing in front. 'Iron Felix' was duly dismantled by a huge crane. Neither Gorbachev nor Yeltsin seized the moment to dismantle the intelligence establishment and bring a reformed system under their control, thus implanting a self-destructing device into every attempt to create a more democratic system of control. Meanwhile, the intelligence experts sensed the danger and, humbled by the inept performance of their own superiors and by the conspicuous show of disdain by the Moscow crowd, vowed that this should never happen again. In due course, 'Iron Felix' returned, his bronze statue installed at Petrovka 38 – the headquarters of the internal criminal police: it is still open to debate whether the godfather of all Tscheckists will be reinstalled in front of the Lubyanka.

Now Russia is experiencing, instead of military bonapartism, feared by Soviet rulers, the rise of a former KGB colonel to the top, while it is not clear whether Putin is the product or rather the creator of today's power-sharing system. Most likely he was a product in the early years, and the creator the longer he served in office. Nobody can say no to the FSB people at the top, as long as they run a tight ship and do not quarrel among themselves. The FSB has become the state itself. The government and the Duma are not in any way able or willing to challenge the Kremlin's authority. The government executes the will of the presidential administration, and parliament rubber-stamps legislation coming from elsewhere. Of all the Soviet institutions, the intelligence services survived best, together with their mentality, their methodology, their omnipresent suspicion, and their methods of enforcing their will. Authority seems to be firmly in the hands of the *siloviki*.

The limits of power

Russia comes from a Hobbesian world and needs to make the transition to the social contract devised by John Locke to protect life, liberty and estate. As Russians get richer, whether at the top of the oligarch pyramid or closer to the bottom, they want security above all else. This not only includes physical security against murder and theft but also security of investment, guarantees of real-estate holdings and the protection of property in general. What the *siloviki*, through their upbringing, are unable to appreciate is the reassuring force of transparency, open debate, even political criticism – in short the wider attributes of the rule of law and liberal democracy. Dmitri Medvedev, judging from his 2007 Davos speech, seems to be the exception among Kremlin incumbents when he praises the purifying forces of the market and the need for democratic control. But whether this is lip-service to impress gullible Western audiences, or a deeper conviction of what Russia needs, only time will tell.

Kremlin leaders instinctively surround their regime with the fog of authoritarianism. They should not be surprised if one day complaints about cronyism, corruption and mismanagement undermine the throne. Today it drives Russian money out of the country and allows this foreign money into the country only where, in the natural resources sector, the rewards are tangible and reasonably safe.

By posing as the biggest bully on the block, Russia, instead of developing the CIS into a meaningful Commonwealth united by common concerns, division of labour and complementary interests, or building a stable, energy-based relationship with Europe, falls victim to a self-fulfilling prophecy. It was at the 2007 Munich Security

Conference, when the US Secretary of Defense gave a reply to Putin's outburst, that Robert Gates remarked, jokingly: 'From one ex-spook to another ex-spook, I have gone through re-education.' The trouble is that most Russian ex-spooks still have to graduate in the real world.

5
Russian breakdown

'What is Russia? Russia is the country where one can do the greatest things for the most insignificant results.'

Marquis de Custine, *Journey for Our Time*

Sometimes the remains of empires past can be awe-inspiring and an inspiration to later generations. This is certainly true of the Romans from the Jordan river to the pillars of Hercules and from the wastelands of northern Africa to Hadrian's wall on the British Isles. The British Empire left not only the sombre architecture of its military cemeteries all over Europe, Africa and Asia but also had a lasting imprint on institutions and the layout of capital cities from Toronto to New Delhi. Even the Russian Empire left its military citadels, monasteries and Orthodox churches across the wide stretches of Eurasia, from the white snows of the north to the shores of the Black Sea. The Soviet Empire, by contrast, will not be remembered for the beauty of its buildings or the fascination of its institutions. The promise of the workers' and peasants' paradise, mobilizing a dead-tired population at the end of the First World War and subsequently fascinating its intellectual fellow travellers and artistic admirers all around the globe, ended, inevitably, in misery and poverty, frustration and bitterness. Even today's rulers of Russia draw little inspiration from a failed empire once believed – and feared – to inherit the earth.

Vestiges of empire

What Muscovites call the Northern River Port is a case in point. A wide-berthed canal links the capital with the Volga river to the north. The many hundreds of miles of waterway were dug under Stalin in the years from 1933 to 1937. No fewer than half a million human beings, men and women alike, are said to have been worked to death, and the earth walls on both sides of the canal are haunted cemeteries – unless a capitalist suburbia for Russia's nouveaux riches takes possession, bringing with it clubs, marinas and golf courses. In recent times, just opposite the landing bridges, a nuclear submarine, black and menacing, is rusting away at some time in the future it is supposed to house a museum for Soviet naval ambitions during the Cold War. On the side of the Leningradskoye Chaussee white luxury liners of generous proportions are moored. The passengers seem to be elderly American Rotary members, husbands and wives, who have booked a package tour to see not only what is left of the evil empire of the past but also to get a taste of post-Soviet capitalism's rough and tumble. Perhaps, as in my case, they are also participants in a conference which helps today's Russia to present itself to the outside world in a way compatible with the self-respect of an imperial power that has lost its empire and is searching for new meaning, direction and equilibrium.

The long landing quay is separated from the adjacent parklands by a building with huge arches that could have been transplanted from the Crimean peninsula to these northern shores were it not for the brutal foundation walls of a huge spire which still carries the conquering Soviet star adorned with hammer and sickle. More than 130 metres into the sky, under Stalin and his successors it celebrated the glory and the threat of Soviet power. Today it is a shabby reminder of a past which Russia's modern rulers have by and large chosen to relegate to the archives. No one can tell for how long the hands of the big clock, halfway up the spire, have remained frozen at twenty past five. The building is by now, no doubt, a hazard to everybody walking through it or shopping at some of the stores selling tickets or guidebooks to the city. Everywhere decay is conspicuous, but without the charm of Rome and the Roman Campagna so attractive to northern visitors in the seventeenth and eighteenth centuries. Here no grand tour is on offer but only the melancholy of a suffering past and endeavour wasted. The people who go about their business, young couples flirting or busy mothers pushing prams seem to be completely unaware of the deeper meaning of those ruins. Or they find it useless to ask for sense and direction in a past that they refuse to own. Moreover, almost two decades after the fall of the Soviet Union, they have grown used to the less horrific expressions of Stalin's horrors; Stalin is no closer to them than Ivan the Terrible or Peter the Great. If they find anything meaningful in the remains of the revolution and its bloody aftermath it is a recognition that life can be, as Thomas Hobbes once put it, solitary, poor, nasty, brutish and short, and that you had better enjoy the good post-Soviet days while they last. Who can tell for how long? Today, it is the order of Putin, of the oligarchs and the FSB – heir to the KGB and the Cheka and the Tsar's Okhrana – reigning over the 13 million inhabitants of Moscow and throughout the far-flung Russian domains.

The charms of the Leviathan

The new order justifies itself by being, after a century of turmoil and upheaval, a sort of order. This legitimacy will hold as long as it can deliver the goods. Over the best part of a decade and probably well into the future, rising oil and gas prices are buoying the government of President Putin and his successor. Moreover, the government has successfully suggested to the people that it is not the world market, globalization and the demand from the industrial world outside that drives Russian growth but the wisdom of the people running the Kremlin, Gazprom and internal intelligence. Muscovites, except in the poorer neighbourhoods beyond the inner city, look better fed and better clad than ever in living memory. They no longer look like the characters populating Mikhail Bulgakov's novel *The Master and Margarita* or Boris Pasternak's *Doctor Zhivago*, haunted, hungry and nervous.

The long queues in front of the shabby shops of the past, selling standard staples, are no more. Instead, middle-class cars crowd the streets twenty-four hours a day, causing gridlock and aggression, with many a Porsche and black BMW, not to mention the huge Mercedes limousines preferred by high government officials or, in the even more expensive armoured version, by oligarchs, caught in the middle of never-ending traffic jams. Kremlin cars, invariably black limousines driving in convoy, force their way, blue and red lights flashing, through the lanes respectfully opened by motorists who are not normally lacking in punch and aggressiveness.

The rouble is now an internationally traded hard currency, accepted everywhere on equal terms with dollars or euros. It is not only those in power but also the man and woman in the street who show a modest prosperity, while young, long-legged blonde beauties display the marvels they have bought at Chanel or Dior boutiques round the corner from the Kremlin. The new Russia is immodest, impatient, and eager to live life to its fullest. The past is an ever-present reminder that things can be much worse than they are now.

Meanwhile, at the Northern River Port, a very different Russia can still be seen. The ceiling of the main building is still adorned with the insignia of former Soviet republics. Vast quantities of sickles, hammers, rising suns and bushels of corn are displayed. When he opened the canal, Stalin must have liked what he saw: totalitarian classicism, and God help those who dared to differ. Everything is written in Cyrillic letters, except for three of the republics. They are the three Baltic states of Lithuania, Latvia and Estonia who escaped Russia's rule after 1917 and were added and annexed again according to the secret provisions of the Hitler–Stalin Pact of 23 September 1939. The ignominious complicity of Europe's great tyrants in carving up Eastern Europe along the Curzon line – still today Poland's eastern border – allowed Hitler to attack Poland from the west and Stalin to come in from the east – thus opening the gates of hell for the whole of Europe. Here history has stopped, like the clock halfway up the tower over-looking the entire edifice. No one cares to get it moving again, nor even start a modest clean-up operation. If ever in a distant future archaeologists excavate the remains of the Soviet Empire, what they find will be sad or threatening, without much meaning and mostly worthless, a Kafkaesque universe.

The reasons for final failure

The decline and fall of empires, long before Gibbon published his magisterial three volumes on the *Decline and Fall of the Roman Empire* in 1776, has always captivated the minds of rulers and generals, philo-sophers and historians. The decline and fall of the Soviet Empire is no exception. But the reasons for final failure are much clearer than in the case of, for example, Rome. The implosion of the Soviet state and, indeed, the Soviet bid for world power, throughout the 1980s, were part of the imperial overstretch of Russia, while today Russia's resurgence is owed not only to the shedding of the imperial burden and the retreat from global ambition but above all to the control of oil and gas for decades to come. The old industrial economies of the West need more energy than ever before, while India and China join the race for power and prosperity. This is bound to create growing and almost unlimited demand, driving prices to spiralling heights and indeed opening a worldwide scramble for resources as never before.

At the time of the Cold War it was not fashionable, nor politically wise, throughout the West to point at the inherent weakness of what the Pentagon in its annual review of Soviet power habitually called the 'Soviet threat'. But it should be noted that as early as 1947 George Kennan, who coined the phrase, and the concept, of 'containment',* diagnosed the Soviet system as suffering from 'deficiencies which will eventually weaken its total potential'. This would, Kennan continued, 'warrant the United States entering with reasonable confidence upon a policy of firm containment, designed to confront the Russians with unalterable counterforce at every point where they show signs of encroaching upon the interest of a peaceful and stable world.' If the United States were to live up to its own promise, 'the aims of Russian Communism must appear sterile and quixotic, the hopes and enthusiasm of Moscow's supporters must wane, and added strain must be imposed on the Kremlin's foreign policies'. Kennan's policy advice was: 'The United States has it in its power to increase enormously the strains under which Soviet policy must operate, to force upon the Kremlin a far greater degree of moderation and circumspection than it has had to observe in recent years, and in this way to promote tendencies which must eventually find their outlet in either the break-up or the mellowing of Soviet power.'

Rarely in the history of diplomacy has an analysis been more poignant, a prognosis more coherent, a policy more appropriate than the one suggested by the then head of the State Department's planning staff.

There were limits, though. Kennan, who never wanted the United States to be locked into a global confrontation with the Soviets and even doubted the ability of the US system of government to run a global defence alliance, was, tragically, of two minds. He saw that at the end of the Second World War both the Soviets and the US wanted the Germany of their choice, but that this implied two mutually exclusive maps of Europe and, indeed, the world. While he succeeded in designing 'containment' as a long-term strategic confrontation over central Europe in general, and Germany in particular, he failed to keep

---

* *Foreign Affairs*, July 1947, 'The Sources of Soviet Conduct'

10 February 2007, keynote speakers at the 43rd
Munich Security Converence: US Defence Secretary
Robert Gates preparing his notes after Putin had
attacked the sole surviving superpower as aiming for
the domination of the world. 'I have my re-education
behind me.' (Associated Press)

Left: The man who dared to challenge Kremlin power. Mikhail Khodorkovsky, one-time CEO of energy giant Yukos, was accused in 2003 of tax fraud and other crimes and sent to Siberia for eight years. Yukos was dismantled, other oligarchs learnt their lesson. (Associated Press)

Above: Day of remembrance. The head of state and the head of the Orthodox Church pay their respects to Stalin's victims. The date is 30 October 2007. The place is Butovo near Moscow, where in 1937–8 NKVD officers routinely conducted mass executions. (Associated Press)

The centre of Russia: the Kremlin and Red Square on the evening of the duma elections of 2 December 2007. Nasi youth are celebrating an unsurprising victory in a stage-managed procession reminiscent of Soviet-era mass demonstrations. (Associated Press)

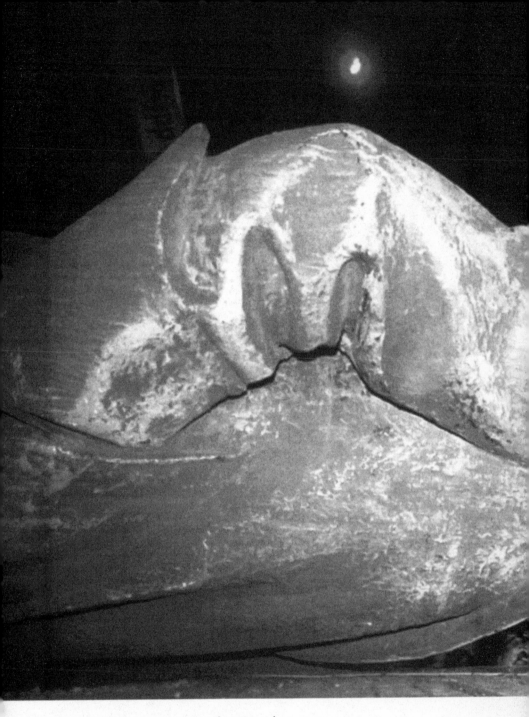

'Iron Felix' falling, August 1991; the KGB cadres
pledged revenge. (Associated Press)

Top: In front of the FSB headquarters at Lubyanka the Solovietsky stone, a memorial to the many millions who perished during Stalin's regime of terror. 'Memorial', a group of people who refused to forgive and forget, brought the stone from the Solovki island, the first establishment of the Gulag archipelago. Today political protest movements gather around the giant boulder. (Anastasia Dergacheva)

Above: Gazprom tower in Moscow, thirty-four floors for administration, business and power. On top is the control room, showing pipelines in existence, pipelines in the planning stage and pipelines that Gazprom would like to control. (Yelena Firsova)

the US military out of the confrontation. His plan B for German neutrality, unfortunately proved to be incompatible with his plan A for containment of Soviet expanionism. The bid of two opposing world powers for 'the whole of Germany', as defined already at the Potsdam Conference in the summer of 1945, had become the unintended consequence of the Second World War. Both sides had an idea of Europe and of the world: but those ideas were mutually exclusive. As Berlin was the key to Germany, and Germany the key to the domination of the European continent, neither side could cede precedence. The result was what Walter Lippman, in his critical response to Kennan, called the 'Cold War'.

Containment

While the Soviet Empire under Stalin reached its apogee, those 'present at the creation' – to quote the memoirs of Dean Acheson, Secretary of State at the time the North Atlantic Pact was signed on 4 April 1949 – believed not only in containment but also in the eventual weakening and, as a consequence, 'mellowing', as Kennan had put it, of Soviet power. Containment itself was a two-pronged strategy, economic-financial and military-political. The economic element began even before the end of the war with the Bretton Woods system for the post-war reconstruction of an American-sponsored world economy, based on a strong dollar and free trade. What was needed was an economic blood transfusion to Europe and, above all, West Germany. This strategy was administered by the Marshall Plan, more precisely called the European Recovery Program (ERP).

But sound economics was not enough to stop the Red Army. The military framework was constructed around the Brussels Pact – the 1948 West European Defence Union directed against the Soviet present and the German past – when the US invited Canada and the Brussels Pact allies to join the North Atlantic Pact in early 1949. The Truman administration was convinced that for the time being Soviet appetites had been satisfied. This was due, among other factors, to the nuclear bomb which the Americans had and the Soviets had not but were desperately trying to manufacture through their own research, espionage and the kidnapping of German scientists the US was enabled to translate its initial nuclear monopoly into what came to be called 'extended deterrence', extended from the American heartland to the faraway shores of Europe. Washington, true to its fundamental philosophy of open sea lanes and free trade relations, saw it as a vital US interest to strengthen liberal economies on the other side of the Atlantic Ocean. The 'wise men' of Washington – as they were referred to in an excellent book about Kennan, John McCloy, Chip Bohlen and General Lucius D. Clay – set out to build a dam against more communist takeovers and eventual Soviet control of the whole of Europe. Germany, by virtue of its geopolitical position between the Eurasian landmass and the sea-bathed islands and peninsulas of Western Europe, was the centre of gravity, nowhere more so than with the precarious allied position in the divided city of Berlin. Without the territory between the Rhine and the Elbe, Truman wrote in his memoirs, the defence of Western Europe would have been 'nothing but a rearguard action on the shores of the Atlantic Ocean'.

In essence, the US offered the Europeans double containment – against the Soviets as well as against the Germans – while President Truman made it clear that part of the bargain was that the Europeans would put their economies together and coopt Germany into the club. This, one could say, was not only the origin of Nato but also, after the American-inspired OECD (Organisation for European Cooperation and Development), of the European Economic Community that was to become today's European Union. Measured against the rise and fall of Soviet power in the second half of the twentieth century, US strategy was immensely successful in combining economic and military means, soft power and hard power, in order to contain and frustrate Soviet ambitions for world domination. In all of this, divided Germany, whether the Germans liked it or not, had a key role to play, both the catalyst of competition and its chief prize.

Containment, however, went through hard times. With Suez in 1956 London and Paris discovered that American nuclear guarantees did not cover post-imperial excursions beyond agreed Nato territory; it was only much later that the Americans recognized the vital strategic importance of the eastern Mediterranean, of the Suez Canal, of oil and nearby bases. Once Russian scientists, with the help of espionage and German experts, had tested nuclear weapons in 1949 and the hydrogen bomb in 1953 and sent intercontinental missiles into space, the correlation of forces changed in favour of the Soviets.

But how far? The answer to this question was to dominate much of the 1960s, starting with the Berlin crisis of 1958–61 and leaving behind uncertainty over whether the building of the infamous Berlin Wall was the end of the confrontation or just a pause in an unforgiving contest. Or was not the Cuban missile crisis just one year later an attempt to translate, once again, nuclear potential into geographic and political gain? Was Cuba an attempt to leverage the Soviet position in central Europe?

Soviet power goes global

Soviet outreach was long in coming. It did not start in Egypt and Syria, when Gamal Abdel Nasser, Egypt's strong man, invited the Russians to build the Aswan Dam and allowed them to station troops in what had, for the best part of a century, been a British protectorate. Ethiopia, Angola and Mozambique were turned into military colonies, mostly by proxies from Cuba. Afghanistan in 1979 was not only the last of those interventions which pretended to foster the cause of liberation, but it turned out to be the most disastrous one when casualties mounted and Russian mothers began to organize protests against the senseless sacrifice of their sons.

The Soviet Union had been extending throughout this period in a combination of ideological doctrine and military occupation. The Hungarian revolution of October 1956 demonstrated to the West the naked brutality of Soviet rule and sowed the seeds of doubt among communist sympathizers in the West. Inside the Soviet Union it provoked dissident movements among people who refused to believe any longer in the capacity of the Soviet system to adapt and to reform itself. Just over a decade later, the Prague Spring of 1968, once again crushed by Soviet tanks with a little fraternal help from the Warsaw Pact countries, was an open admission that Soviet power was about nothing but raw power. Even among some of the power elites throughout Eastern Europe doubts were growing.

Throughout the 1970s dissidents were persecuted, irrespective of the lofty aspirations signed by heads of government at Helsinki in 1975. But from then on, Helsinki Committees sprouted among the intelligentsia. In the Soviet Union samizdat and tamizdat made the rounds, shrouded in secrecy. Among all the satellite states only the leadership of the German Democratic Republic remained unques-tioningly loyal to the cause. Faced with the freedom and prosperity of the western three quarters of Germany, and scrutinized by West German TV day and night, Ulbricht and Honecker had nowhere to go but to Moscow. When the winds of change began to be felt in the mid-1980s, they were left alone, no longer trusting their Soviet protectors, waiting for the end game: another Tiananmen Square in the summer of 1989, or the fall of the wall in November.

The long nuclear peace

All of this happened under the grim shadow of nuclear weapons, but these also imposed the sternest of discipline upon Soviet leaders. Moreover, they inspired a kind of Metternichian conservatism on all political leaders irrespective of which side they were on. They joined an informal and silent cartel of war avoidance. Raymond Aron, the French *maître a penser*, described the situation as '*à guerre improbable; paix impossible*'.

There was good reason to handle world affairs with care. Berlin and Cuba offered the two superpowers ample opportunity to imagine what nuclear war between them would mean: the end of the world. All of a sudden they found they had more in common than anticipated. As a consequence, they started formalizing their relationship through the so-called red telephone or hot line, linking centres in Moscow and Washington to avoid accidental war, and continuing with the Test Ban Treaty: no more nuclear tests in the Earth's atmosphere. Moreover, they found that they had to avoid at almost any price another direct military confrontation.

The superpowers also learnt that nuclear weapons, whatever the generals told the politicians, were not for fighting wars, and once small powers got hold of them, were brutal equalizers among states. From this followed the two-tier system of the Nuclear Non-Proliferation Treaty (NPT), limiting the number of nuclear 'haves' to the five permanent members of the UN Security Council, who by the end of the 1960s were established nuclear powers anyway. More than one hundred nations signed up to a treaty that was clearly iniquitous – five 'haves' and the rest 'have-nots' – with Israel, Pakistan and India remaining outside. The strength of the treaty lay in its supervision by the International Atomic Energy Agency. Its obvious weakness was the absence of sanctions and corrective action should a signatory to the treaty one day decide to break out. South Africa, Brazil and Libya tried and gave up. North Korea is still in the bidding. In today's world Iran seems to be the most conspicuous offender, supported half-heartedly by Russia, and opposed wholeheartedly by the US.

Philosophically, by the end of the 1960s both the superpowers had resigned themselves to the global status quo, the US not bent – except in rhetoric – on making the world safe for democracy and creating the 'new world order' promised on day one of the USA; the Soviets no longer engaged in a worldwide do-or-die campaign under the Leninist motif of 'peace to the huts, war to the palaces'. Instead of policies short of war that had characterized East–West confrontation from the Korean War (1950–54) to Indochina, to Suez and to Berlin and Cuba, the nuclear world powers went through an agonizing learning process that resulted in a kind of long nuclear peace.

Of course, the ensuing arms control negotiations, both nuclear and conventional, gave both sides ample opportunity to use strategic bargaining as a means to lock in the other side, to gain strategic information, and to use arms control as the continuation of warfare by other means. But still, the SALT (Strategic Arms Limitation Treaty) agreements of the early 1970s were not useless, and the ABM (Anti-Ballistic Missile) treaty of 1973 helped to give both sides a better understanding of strategy and politics and later on helped to create, develop and practise confidence and security-building measures of all kinds. Basically the two sides were united, as Raymond Aron was the first to observe, in a cartel of war avoidance, both conventional and nuclear. Moreover, both sides believed in progress and that their system would inherit the earth, though in a mutually exclusive version.

The arms control edifice, with its concomitant confidence- and security-building measures, became the strange and unexpected condition of strategic co-existence. But the correlation of forces was never stable. Both sides tried to put new officers on the global chessboard, using various technologies to gain advantage, the Soviets through MIRVing their missiles (Multiple Independent Re-Entry Vehicles). The Americans put the neutron bomb on the chessboard, only to retract it when it became clear that it would upset every future arms control equation.

The oil curse

In fact the Soviets gained strategic advantage when the price of oil shot up as a result of the Arab oil boycott, producing less and earning higher prices in 1974. But what looked like a blessing, the abundance of Siberian oil and gas, turned out, after more than a decade, to contain the seeds of a curse. For well over ten years the petrodollars allowed the Kremlin leaders not only to fill the gaping holes in their domestic economy with imported goods, including high-tech expertise from Germany such as high seas fishing equipment, or even the Sheremetyevo airport in Moscow, a straight copy of Düsseldorf airport. However, the billions of dollars in the Kremlin's accounts also encouraged Soviet leaders to engage in foreign expansion, Syria (where Russia still today keeps and expands bases) to Egypt and Ethiopia, Angola and Mozambique, where Cuban troops, well trained and Soviet-equipped, conducted low-level warfare against South Africa. But what to the outside world looked like war for ideological reasons was also meant to secure for the Soviet Union the rich mineral resources and port facilities of host countries.

The first oil crisis of 1973–4 and the windfall profits it brought had already seduced the Soviet leadership into an expansionist foreign policy. The second oil price hike in 1978, immediately following the return of Ayatollah Khomeini to his native Iran and the subsequent Mullah revolution, seemed to herald an age of ever-rising oil revenues. In fact this prospect must have encouraged the Kremlin leaders to give up their usual geriatric restraint and get themselves ever deeper into engagements beyond their control. The invasion of Afghanistan in 1979, at first successful in conquering the cities and establishing a communist regime, soon turned into a quagmire, costing blood and financial resources, shaking the Soviet consensus at home and revealing the weaknesses of the army. Technically, the Russian generals received a severe warning when the resistance, via Pakistan's inter-services intelligence, was equipped by the CIA with Stinger missiles of the 'fire and forget' type. That gave the mujaheddin – among them a certain Saudi Arabian citizen by the name of Osama bin Laden – the capacity to deny the Russians control of the skies, the valleys and, finally, the entire rugged country.

If Afghanistan had offered a strategic warning, the 1982 Middle

East war over Lebanon became a watershed. What happened was an unmitigated disaster, in fact a moment of truth for both the military leadership and the Moscow intelligence community. One summer morning no fewer than seventy Syrian-piloted MIGs were shot out of a sunny sky by the Israelis in their F-16Is – the I standing for the Israeli version, equipped with US-procured Sidewinder air-to-air missiles. This news must have been a tremendous shock to the defence ministry in Moscow. It appeared even worse because the Russian analysts assumed, in a mirror image, that the Americans, like the Russians with their satellite armies, would never give their allies first-rate equipment, but only second- or third-rate. Little did the Russian analysts understand that the Pentagon gave the Israelis cutting-edge technology to prevent them from thinking nuclear in time of crisis. This had been the lesson from the Yom Kippur war, when the Israelis, closely watched by US satellite intelligence, had displayed a willingness to go nuclear.

Strategic defeat

What had happened over the Bekaa Valley in that summer of 1982 was more than a tactical defeat. The terrible truth was that the Soviet Union lagged behind in the martial arts of the present and future, information technology and, more especially, miniaturized data processors. This was not just something the Soviets could easily obtain in the international marketplace or through well-established channels of espionage. What was needed was control over very complex production processes. There was no way to re-engineer the components, let alone entire C 4 I systems ('command, control, communication and information'). From articles in top-secret Soviet military journals Western intelligence learnt that Russian leaders, including the KGB and the top brass of the military, notably the then chief of staff of the Warsaw Pact Marshal Ogarkov, were aware that nothing short of a revolution from above was needed if the Soviet system was to survive into the twenty-first century. This was when Secretary General of the CPSU Yuri Andropov hinted to Chancellor Kohl, in Moscow for the funeral of Leonid Brezhnev, that the man of the future, recently coopted by the Politburo, was a youngish party leader by the name of Mikhail Gorbachev.

The Soviet system was in crisis. It had to cross the threshold to the information age, and this could only be done if the secretive and suspicious system of control was opened up. But the information crisis was not the only ill that befell the Soviets in the 1980s. Shortly after the Red Army had marched into Afghanistan and into its defeat, the Iraqi dictator Saddam Hussein sent his troops into war against Iran, believing that after the mass cleansing of the Shah's officer's corps Iran and especially the oil terminals at the northern tip of the Persian Gulf would be easy prey. What followed was butchery on a large scale, but also missile warfare against Iranian cities, especially Tehran. Unexpectedly, the Iranian Pasdaran, the elite corps of the revolution, put up fierce resistance, and the old Persian army remained loyal against the Arab invasion. To break the deadlock, the Tehran regime sent battalions of youngsters into Iraqi minefields, promising the young believers instant martyrdom and eternal pleasures in the other world. How could all of this seal the Soviet Union's fate?

By 1985 it looked as if the Iraqis, in spite of being backed by the Saudis and the West, especially the US, were about to lose the war. But suddenly, against all reasonable expectation, oil prices began to drop; in fact they sank to a meagre $10 per barrel. What had happened? The Saudis, following strategic – and not unselfish – advice from America, had opened the taps and worked the refineries to full capacity. The result was that the Iranians lost their main source of hard currency and had to come to terms with their threatening neighbour. The contest in the Gulf, however, and the decline of oil prices were only the precursors of revolutionary changes all around the world but nowhere more so than throughout the Soviet Union. While keeping up with the West's IT revolution could perhaps be done within a mildly reformed Soviet system, with Gorbachev's glasnost and perestroika still compatible with traditional Soviet concepts, the sudden collapse of oil prices turned out to be cataclysmic, in fact the beginning of the end, and a lasting trauma for Kremlin leaders today and into the future. From now on, the reformers in the Kremlin were driven by events beyond their control, the reactor burnout in Chernobyl in May 1986 creating a terrible symbolism for the uncontrollable state of the ailing empire.

The global correlation of forces was changing rapidly. What was bad for the Soviet Union was good for Western nations. Suddenly, after the agonies of the first and the second oil price crises and the vast transformations they had effected throughout the West – governments falling, new parties emerging, attitudes changing – now it was the time for the likes of Margaret Thatcher, Helmut Kohl and Ronald Reagan to turn the tide. Angst was out, hope was in. A tectonic shift in world affairs was beginning to make itself felt that would not only put an end to seven decades of Soviet rule but also bring about a new world order – or, as it turned out, a new world disorder.

A revolution from above – derailed

The story of the decline and fall of the Soviet Union, first the Outer Empire and then the Inner one, has been told many times and will be retold again and again, as it contains mysteries and miracles as much as outright failure and incompetence. Not the least complication is that it took most people by surprise, and many, especially in the West, reacted with outright fear at what would happen if the nuclear edifice, so carefully constructed over many decades, suddenly collapsed.

The 1980s were characterized by changes from below and also from above. A controlled revolution was what Andropov had in mind and what Gorbachev was groomed for. Leaders in the commanding heights of the KGB and the army began to understand that the technological race was no longer about vast amounts of steel and coal but about command control and communication, and the electronic means to steer complex processes; they also understood that the system they had inherited was doomed unless agonizing change redefined the worlds of learning, of industry and the military. Top military leaders even went so far as to argue – in secret journals for Russian eyes only – that the Soviet system, in order to accommodate modern information technology, had to undergo thorough change, embracing openness and transparency.

This is what Gorbachev meant when he famously demanded glasnost and perestroika and wanted to 'revitalize' socialism, only to discover that it was by now a corpse. If ever there was a masterplan in the mid-1980s, it did not extend much beyond accelerating arms control in both the strategic and the conventional dimension. The rest was soon derailed. The chief reasons were the drop in oil prices and the nuclear burnout in the Chernobyl power plant at about the same time, the latter showing catastrophic weaknesses in the Soviet leadership structure. A rapid deterioration of living conditions did not help. Meanwhile, at the highest levels, in the Politburo Yeltsin wanted to cut Russia free from the oppressive state of the Soviets while Gorbachev wanted to preserve both the fundamentals of socialism and the Soviet empire. Everything came to a showdown when civil protest movements in the Baltic Republics demanded independence (the publication in Estonia in 1989 of the secret annexe to the Molotov-Ribbentrop treaty had utterly delegitimized Soviet rule) and military hardliners refused to withdraw the crack OMON troops of the Interior Ministry. The Baltic states declared independence from the Soviet Union, stating that the annexation of 1939 was a flagrant violation of international law. In December 1991 Ukraine, White Russia and Russia came together at Belovezhskaya Pushcha to put an end to more than seventy years of the Soviet system.

Rising from the ashes

Today, one or two revolutions later, you shake the Russian kaleidoscope and an altogether different picture presents itself. The Leningradskaya Chaussee, ringed by supermarkets full of Western consumer goods at top prices and fenced in by billboards advertising the fanciful expressions of wealth, luxury and comfort, brings every visitor back to real life in a city full of nervous energy, bristling with business deals, some shady, some spectacular and many in between. This is a city, also, where journalists live a dangerous life once they dare to venture into that big money or big government does not want to be explored. Some have paid with their lives, like Paval Khlebnikov, the editor of the Russian edition of *Forbes* magazine, who was shot when leaving his home, or Anna Politkovskaya, who was on the trail of some business crooks with links to high places – or, perhaps, some Chechen gangster, as the authorities maintain – when she, too, was gunned down.

If democracy means casting a vote from time to time for one out of several party candidates, Russia would qualify. If, however, democracy is seen, and practised, as a system of governance limited by due process of law, a predictable set of rules, a reliable constitution and a system of checks and balances – then Russia has a long way to go. Putin's idea that 'the vertical of power' should reign supreme, that a government should work like a Swiss clock, and that everybody and everything should live under the 'dictatorship of the law' is nothing but a rough sketch. Everything depends on who will fill in the detail. Meanwhile, the big question remains not only for Russia but for all of its neighbours whether the vast Eurasian country will finally follow the technocratic-democratic welfare mix on offer from the West, or the combination of centralized one-party-control, state planning and free-for-all economics that China has to offer. The answer will not only be decided in the upper echelons of power and money, somewhere between the Kremlin and the Gazprom Headquarters, but will depend to a large extent on the cultural foundations of Russia, the hidden fears of its denizens and their unspoken assumptions about prosperity, power and personal life.

6

An army humbled

'... progress of the Empress Catherine to the Crimea, the façades of villages set up at spaced intervals along the way. The façades made of wood and painted canvas were placed a quarter of a league from the route to make the triumphant sovereign believe that the desert had been peopled under her reign. Russian minds are still presented by similar preoccupations. Everyone hides the bad and presents the good to the eyes of the master.'

Marquis de Custine, *Journey for Our Time*

The date was 12 August 2000. At 11.28 Central European Time seismographs at Western monitoring posts registered a major explosion in the Barents Sea, off the Murmansk coast, and a mere 135 seconds later another one, ten times stronger. It took the Russian naval staff more than two days to admit that the *Kursk*, Russia's most modern submarine – Oscar II class in Nato code, put into service in 1994 and armed with twenty-two nuclear-tipped cruise missiles, the entire structure surrounded by a titanium-plus-rubber skin – had been lost at sea, together with all 118 of her crew.

It took days and weeks to uncover the true story of what had happened. Clumsiness, secretive habits and outright lies surrounded the catastrophe. First the admirals wanted to hide the terrible truth from the Kremlin, then from the families and general public, and finally from the world at large. The reasons given for the *Kursk* disaster varied, from running upon a Second World War German mine to collision with a Nato spy submarine thus turning it into a public relations breakdown and a serious test for the President. None of this contained any truth, but even a moderate and well-informed Duma member like Alexei Arbatov from Yabloko, member of the defence committee, thundered that Russia had to expect 'growing tensions with the West'.

President Putin at first refused any help from other countries to lift the wreckage, which was of course full of sensitive military information but also implied human tragedy and political mismanagement. After a few days of humiliating ineffectiveness and failure, including official lies about the sailors still being alive and Russian rescue teams working their way close to them, a Norwegian offer was finally accepted and a salvage company from Norway brought in, but the divers were not allowed to go anywhere near where the Russian naval command knew the sensitive information was hidden. Putin did not at first find it necessary to interrupt his holiday at the Black Sea. After six days of handling the crisis from a distance, however, he realized that this indifference would not be forgiven by the man in the street, the sailors' widows and the men in uniform, so he took action to avoid the impression that the political authorities were heartless and out of touch, that the naval command was only interested in saving its skin, and that, Soviet system or no, human lives did not count. It is to Putin's credit that he finally decided to invite the Norwegians in, regardless of the admirals' interest in letting the *Kursk* – and the truth – rest on the bottom of the sea. Of course, Putin also wanted Russian naval engineers to find out what had really sent the pride of the Russian navy to its early grave. Finally, he took the decision to allot substantial payments to the families of the dead men to help them rebuild their lives. It was late in the day when he preserved at least the appearance of competence and caring.

Beyond the world of conspiracy theories the *Kursk* prompted speculation that an ultra-modern torpedo with liquid fuel had been mishandled on loading, that the captain realized danger was looming and did not deem the submarine seaworthy, and that the few sailors who had survived the initial blast never had a chance to escape from the grave 120 metres below the stormy surface of the Barents Sea.

The loss of the monster submarine, twenty metres high, had many implications. It revealed not only the crew's poor training, inadequate for handling such high-tech wizardry as the *Kursk* and its dangerous cargo. It also revealed dramatic failure on the part of the Kremlin to handle the sense of frustration, doubt and open unrest set in motion by the disaster. Above all, it forced the General Staff as well as the Ministry of Defence into some serious rethinking as to the future of nuclear deterrence. Any effective modernization of the navy, which would also involve refurbishing the satellite systems guiding the nuclear-tipped missiles, would by far exceed the modest USD 16 billion defence budget of the time. So the *Kursk* disaster not only tested the government, the admirals and the President, it put a question mark over Russia's future nuclear strategy.

Moreover, ever since Peter the Great naval ambition had been Russia's attempt to overcome the limitations of a landlocked power and develop a naval capability second to none. The *Kursk* would have been one of the vessels accompanying the aircraft carrier that Putin had intended to send into the Mediterranean in order to demonstrate a naval presence approaching that of the mighty US Sixth Fleet. It was the navy that seemed to promise the Russians a chance to keep up with Nato forces and the very ambitious naval programme of the Chinese. That dream had disappeared off the coast of Murmansk for a long time to come. The refusal to admit defeat in the high-tech race for naval supremacy was the reason for both the initial clumsiness of the response to the crisis and the long-term inability to come up with a coherent strategy for the future of the navy and, by implication, the fine-tuning of the nuclear balance.

The strategic implications of the disaster were far-ranging. The political shockwaves could be felt even behind the red-brick walls of the Kremlin, and crisis management was visibly inadequate and poor. The *Kursk* catastrophe left Russians as well as the rest of the world asking, once again: who is Putin? It took the shine off the carefully crafted appearance of strong and decisive leadership. A naval officer in Murmansk complained openly: 'I thought I had a president. Now it turns out he is merely another state official.' Meanwhile, by the time Putin was up for re-election in 2004, the miserable death of the 118 sailors had been all but forgotten.

A claim to world power

Russia's claim to world power rests on three assumptions: its permanent seat on the UN Security Council, with the power of veto in matters big and small; the wealth of mineral resources; and the strength of its armed forces, especially the nuclear arsenal. The UN veto, however, has not been effective in stopping Nato from conducting the Kosovo war in 1999 or the US attacking Iraq in 2003, nor has it prevented the government in Pristina from declaring Kosovo's independence in 2008, followed by immediate recognition by the US and most Western countries – despite, in this case, very valid doubts on the part of Russia. Russia's participation in the Lebanon UNIFIL peacekeeping effort amounted to a meagre 400-man engineers battalion – as compared with 3000 Italians, 2000 from France, 1200 naval personnel from Germany, 1200 from Spain, 500 from Poland and 400 from Belgium. Is this the role of a country claiming to be a world power? Instead of displaying great power status, wielding the UN card can invite public humiliation and domestic frustration, while the nuclear arsenal looks rather inadequate and out of proportion in most of today's and tomorrow's regional and asymmetric conflicts: big toys for big boys, not good for export promotion and utterly useless in the nasty little wars Russia is facing.

After the end of the Cold War the thinking of the Russian General Staff and the Ministry of Defence in Moscow has gone through changes that amount to a revolution. In the Soviet past, the basic philosophy was that more is always better, until in the nuclear race the obvious question was raised: when is enough enough? The answer was obvious, that production and deployment of nuclear weapons had far exceeded any military rationale and had become a self-propelling process devouring ever scarcer resources. This sober assessment, when it dawned on both sides in the nuclear arms race, was fundamental in promoting and shaping the arms control processes throughout the 1970s and '80s and helped both sides to continue and in fact accelerate the reduction after the end of the Cold War.

No more military overreach

Modern Russian military policy is a component of national security policy, based on two lengthy documents, the National Security Concept and the Foreign Policy Concept of Russia. The Security Council, presided over by the President, adopted the official new version (after the first revision in 1993) of the National Security Concept in January 2000 – not long after Nato had reformulated its own Strategic Guidelines for the first time since 1991. Soon after, Russia's Security Council approved the military doctrine. Everything, however, continued to be dictated by the shortage of human, material and organizational resources. In short, military readiness was not a high priority.

It was at a Russian-Finnish military seminar in 2004 in Helsinki that the rationale behind Russian strategic thinking and military doctrine was partially revealed. High-ranking General Staff officers from Moscow brought a sombre analysis to the conference table, saying that contrary to much wishful thinking the significance of military power in the post-bipolar world had not diminished. On the contrary, they said, they observed more and more states, released from the grim discipline of the nuclear stand-off between the superpowers, asserting their economic and political interests through military power, while the overarching political institutions were clearly in decline. The US was not mentioned, but it was clearly implicated. The Russians expressed the need to fundamentally revise their thinking about international security and it sounded like an invitation to the West to help in the process and not stir up new conflicts.

The Russian military view expressed at that Helsinki seminar reflected not a parochial but a global approach. 'The end of the Cold War has given a new pulse to the thesis that a big war has no perspective. However, war as a phenomenon is hardly dead. At the present stage of human development it has simply changed appearance. During almost three centuries it had been considered the defining norm for nation states. There is nothing surprising in the fact that the appearance of non-state actors on the national and international scene has brought rapid growth of quasi-private armies and wild-card military formations who consider armed conflict as legitimate business. All of this means that new threats appeared over the horizon acquiring a military dimension.'*

In spite of the grim picture of poverty and overstretched resources painted by the military experts, the Kremlin, whenever there is a suitable occasion, tends to put on an appearance of power and glory, mostly for home consumption. At great receptions in the Kremlin young cadets in elegant tsarist uniforms line the corridors and stand at attention. Putin himself, although never a military man, likes to put on a uniform, flying into Chechnya or sporting naval attire. But Russia looks stronger than it really is, and the army is no exception. In fact the *Kursk* catastrophe was a sad reminder that Russia's ambition to be a naval power second to none has hit disaster several times, from the Crimean War of the nineteenth century to the sinking of Russia's

* Sergei Yermakov

99

battleships by the Japanese near the island of Tsushima in the early twentieth century to the involuntary retreat of the Mediterranean 'escada' at the end of the Cold War.

The army as a whole was hit hard by the years of Soviet decline, by underfunding, poor leadership and the loss of a sense of purpose. Today, the state of the armed forces seems to be much worse than officialdom dares to admit. Russia, according to most observers, cannot base its claim to world power on its military capabilities, notwithstanding some spectacular new weapons systems proudly paraded for both the benefit of potential buyers abroad and the prestige of the Kremlin at home.

After the Cold War, the transition was slow and hindered by lack of money, initiative and imagination. Even the housing provided and paid for by the German government to accommodate the officers left stranded after their return from East Germany, was mostly handed over to non-military users better connected. Transformation was inevitable, and it was guided by more or less the same strategic analysis as throughout the West.

Transformation

In 2006–7 the armed forces of Russia, according to figures provided by the London-based International Institute for Strategic Studies, comprised altogether 1,027,000 men and women (army 395,000, navy 142,000, air force 160,000, strategic deterrent force 80,000, command and support 250,000), plus paramilitary forces of 480,000. In theory, there is a reserve of twenty million, of whom only one out of ten has served during the last five years. Reserve status is mandatory until the age of fifty. The defence budget is minute compared with that of the US, and even taking into account real purchasing power it is small. Counted as a percentage of GDP, however, the two countries allow themselves about the same outlay for the military. Sergei Ivanov, while still defence minister under Putin, stated at a meeting with visitors from abroad that Russia would not repeat the fatal mistake of the Soviet Union: to arm itself to death.

In the army, ethnic Russians prevail by far. Only the Tatars at 4 per cent and Ukrainians at 3 per cent make a noticeable contribution; all other nationalities, like Bashkirs, Belarusians, and Moldovans, count for 1 per cent or less.

The deterrent forces, known to the West not only through strategic spying but even more so through various arms control agreements and a remarkable amount of cooperation in securing nuclear warheads against accidental use, are the one element of the military establishment that still allows Russia a claim to world power. There are, after the *Kursk*, fifteen nuclear-powered and nuclear-armed strategic submarines, some of them probably more dangerous to their own crew than to any enemy, and not seaworthy. Six of the Delta III class are stationed along the Pacific coast, five Delta IV are attached to the Northern Fleet. The land-based systems comprise three rocket armies operating silo and mobile missile-launchers. There are 506 intercontinental ballistic missiles and the long range aviation command called the 37th Air Army. Some aircraft, Nato code Blackjack and Bear, were put back into active service by Putin in the summer of 2007 to patrol the open seas and fly the flag. It was a gesture to remind the world that Russia still has a claim to world power, at least in military symbolism. There are about twenty-two anti-ballistic-missile radars, placed for 360-degree control of airspace and covering approaches from the west and south-west, north-east and south-east, and partially from the south. The space forces number altogether 40,000 personnel in various formations and units withdrawn from strategic missile and air defence forces to detect missile attacks on Russia and its allies, to implement ballistic missile defence and to conduct military and dual-use spacecraft launch and control.

The navy's overall serviceability is generally seen as low. There are four major forces: the Northern fleet with air arm and naval infantry, the Pacific Fleet, the Black Sea Fleet and the Baltic Fleet plus the Caspian Sea Flotilla.

Deployment abroad is very limited. What is controversial for the West is the 3000 soldiers in Georgia's disputed areas South Ossetia and Abkhazia, and the so-called 14th Army with 1400 men (365 accepted as peacekeepers) in Moldova. Those troops are the ones Russia wants to keep where they are while the West is demanding their withdrawal. This has recently translated into Russia suspending the CFE (Conventional Forces in Europe) Treaty, which offered confidence and security-building measures to both sides. There are still 3500 Russian soldiers in Armenia, some anti-air units in Belarus, a small naval detachment in Syria, 500 soldiers in Kyrgyzstan, some more in Tajikistan. In Ukraine, where the Russian Fleet has leased berthing and port facilities on the Black Sea in Sebastopol, the Russians have deployed one regiment of marines and a small flotilla, a naval headquarters. The rest are small units under the blue helmets of the UN or, as in Lebanon, one batallion of engineers, placed there by bilateral agreement, parallel to the UNIFIL mission.

Except in the nuclear dimension, Russia is no longer the military giant of 5 million men at arms that the Soviet Union was even in the days when it had passed its apogee. On 10 May 2006 Putin, in his annual address to the Federal Assembly, spoke about the state of the military. He maintained that in spite of many economic weaknesses, the army would still be able to fulfil its mission and guarantee the defence and security of the country. Looking back at 1999–2000 – the time of Nato's Kosovo war and Russia's Chechen war – he said that the country had not been able to field a minimum of 65,000 well-trained and combat-ready soldiers and send them to fight the rebels in Chechnya. At that time, according to the President, Russia had altogether no more than 55,000 soldiers ready to go, and they were dispersed all over Russia. Putin sounded like Nato's Secretary General at the time, Lord George Robertson, when he complained that out of 1.4 million Russian men and women in uniform no more than a few were ready for active combat.

Back in business

In 2006, in his state-of–the-army speech Putin went on to present a much improved picture. Modernized and high-tech weaponry had been introduced into the forces, but chiefly in the strategic dimension and patently useless for deployment against Chechen rebels hiding in the northern slopes of the Caucasus. Putin praised the introduction of two intercontinental missile complexes, Topol-M and Bulawa-30, and the building of two new nuclear submarines – the first since 1990. As far as conventional arms were concerned, Putin had little to offer. He praised improved training, a better fighting spirit among soldiers and officers, and the high morale of the troops. But not much hardware would be coming their way though Putin asked for high-class performance: 'We must have forces capable of taking up the fight in global, regional and, if necessary, several local conflicts, and at the same time.' In this, Putin echoed the Pentagon in the mid-1990s, which had boasted that two and a half wars could be fought simultaneously, and be won. Time and again, the US is the mirror image that sets the standards for the Russians.

In particular, Putin singled out six objectives for the next decade, some hard, some soft, some strictly military, some much broader – and altogether probably overambitious:

- The Russian forces should study and understand the planning and development of competing forces abroad and find superior responses. One wonders to what extent the Chinese armed forces on their way to Asian dominance are silently included in this threat assessment.
- Two-thirds of the armed forces should be transformed into an all-volunteer army, and military conscription reduced to twelve months – revealing a strategy based much more on high-tech weaponry than on the traditional Russian mass army.
- Adressing a problem unsolved since the withdrawal of the Red Army from much of Central Europe and Central Asia, housing for officers and soldiers should be of a much higher standard.
- Half of military expenditure should be invested in better training, more effective weaponry and technical development.
- Discipline among the troops should be enhanced, but no recipe was offered for how to transform the disciplinary code and rough customs throughout the army into behaviour consonant with a modern high-tech establishment.
- The prestige of those serving in the army should be restored. Somebody defending the motherland, Putin put it, should have a high social and financial status. But how to achieve this lofty goal, except by fiat, the soldiers were not told. One wonders what the reaction may have been among the rank and file, most probably the traditional Russian philosophy of 'The God is high, and the tsar is far away'.

The Kremlin is acutely aware of the shortcomings, and Putin's announcements in 2006 could also be read as an overall, and not too favourable, evaluation of what the five-year plan announced in the year 2000 had achieved – or failed to achieve. That plan, originally handed over to Defence Minister Sergei Ivanov, formerly of the KGB and not a military man, had been a roadmap for reform. But where did the road lead? First of all, and inevitably, into serious confrontation with the generals as no fewer than 300 general officers' posts would be scrapped, traditional arms programmes discontinued and the giant military establishment of the Cold War cut down.

In due course, Ivanov's first step had been to reduce the overall size of the army to its present numbers of just over 1.1 million personnel. He then proceeded to change budget allocations and, by implication, the composition of the army. Before, 70 per cent of the budget had gone towards manpower and maintenance, and only 30 per cent into research and development. Official figures for 2006 indicate a much improved ratio of 60:40. This should continue until in 2010 a 50:50 ratio will be achieved.

In addition, between 2010 and 2015 the armed forces will no longer be administered through military districts but organized according to territorial integration on land, at sea and in the air. The Far Eastern Command will include the Far East, Siberia, the Volga-Urals district and the Pacific Fleet; the Central Asian Command will comprise the Northern Caucasus and the Black Sea Fleet; and the West European Command will include the military districts of St Petersburg and Moscow as well as the Northern Fleet and the Baltic Fleet.

A military-industrial complex

Taking a leaf from the American book, Putin created a high-level arms-industrial commission, a powerful steering committee superimposed on the military-industrial complex which throughout the 1990s had drifted out of the Kremlin's control and, by selling hardware to sinister clients like Iran and Syria, had created some strategic embarrassment. The new institution, with a combined general staff, arms agency and defence ministry on top of the older institutions, would also oversee all government ministries involved, controlling both the budget and the armed forces. Therefore, in early summer 2007, Sergei Ivanov was promoted from defence minister to deputy prime minister at the head of this commission – all powerful, at least in name. Henceforth, all government activities are to be organized and controlled by the commission, as well as production, procurement and foreign sales.

Most military establishments are given to waste and inefficiency but in the big league the Russian armed forces are probably the winners. In 2006 military expenditure, according to Russian statistics and corroborated by Western estimates, amounted to 2.74 per cent of GDP (equivalent to 667 billion roubles or USD 24 billion), up from 550 billion roubles and a mere USD 20 billion the year before). Procurement in 2006 amounted to 236 billion roubles. For 2007 the Russian government planned an investment increase of 300 billion roubles. Sergei Ivanov announced a huge armaments programme – huge by Russian standards, small by comparison with American efforts. But, relatively speaking, the Russians, given the vast difference in purchasing power, probably get more for their money.

At the time of the Soviet Union Russia used arms exports to buy influence, loyalty and dependence on a large scale. Therefore, much was handed over to foreign governments on long-term credit and never paid for. Today, while exports continue to flourish – in fact, after gas and oil, arms are Russia's third largest export commodity – the military-industrial complex is very keen not only to bolster its meagre income at home and make production more efficient through economics of scale, but also to be paid on time. What has also changed is the quality of weaponry sold. While under Soviet rule what was for sale was only second best, factories can sell cutting-edge technology – except, of course, nuclear and missile technology.

In the past mainland China, long seen as the great and ever-growing rival for hegemony in the Far East and, on top of the strategic threat, also capable of high-class re-engineering, had to be content with second- and third-rate military hardware. For some time, and within the framework of the Shanghai Cooperation Organization, the Chinese have been allowed to buy top-end technology for naval battle management and any number and quality of fighter jets. It is most probable that Russian general staff officers baulk at seeing this technology transfer going in the direction of their most dangerous rival, but the arms industry wants to survive and even recover its former key position. So exporting for ready cash whatever is on the shopping list of potential buyers, no matter what they may have in mind, is the lifeline for an industry that experienced breakdown not so long ago. While in 2000 exports brought in just over USD 2.7 billion, in 2004 it was already USD 4.7 billion, and the curve continues to rise. For 2007, according to Sergei Ivanov, an export volume of USD 7 billion was being planned. Another USD 22 billion worth of military goods, according to proud announcements by Ivanov, is already under contract from abroad.

Handle with care

In Russia Prince Potemkin, in or out of uniform, is still alive and well. Driving through Moscow along the Moskva river one sees with delight the beautiful mellowed façades of palaces of the past, especially those within view of the Kremlin. At close inspection, however, it turns out that giant canvases hide buildings in poor state of repair. Could it be that official pronouncements about the state of the armed forces are merely a shining canvas in front of a much more modest reality? The air force has only about half of its aircraft in active service. Most of the hardware is much older than five years, and often the aircraft are older than the pilots at the controls. The Russian air force is supposed to have no more than twenty aircraft less than five years old. The need to replace ageing and outdated jets after 2009 exceeds 3200 aircraft and 1500 helicopters. Over the last ten years modern replacements were bought only piece by piece. It will take a long time, and huge cost, to bring Russian forces up to date, and what is true for the air force is probably true for other parts of the services as well.

Even the state of the strategic forces – Russia's remaining claim to world power – is far behind the official assurances of strength and aptitude. Key projects are chronically underfinanced. The West has to worry not so much about fancy new weapons of the future but about the state of the missile and nuclear forces of the past. Sergei Ivanov assures the outside world that Russia's strategic systems are perfectly well guarded and fully under the control of the Ministry of Home Affairs and its special forces. But even during the time of the Soviet Union Western arms control negotiators like former ambassador Richard Burt were not always sure that the Russians had full control over all their nuclear hardware. Today, twenty years later, most Western experts look at the state of Russia's strategic forces with concern. Eighty per cent of Russia's mobile ICBMs are beyond their use-by-date. To keep up with the US, Russia would have to produce on average between twenty and thirty mobile ICBMs instead of the present seven per year. The Strategic Offensive Reductions Treaty of 2002 states that by 31 December 2012 both Russia and the US should be down to between 1700 and 2200 nuclear warheads respectively. Russian experts say that by that time Russia will not be able to field more than a thousand nuclear warheads. This may look, to an outside observer, fairly irrelevant, but given the psychology of the Russian population and especially the military, still steeped in Cold War thinking, the strategic balance with the US has high priority.

The outcry about those anti-missile systems that the Pentagon, prematurely, wants to deploy against a future Iranian threat in both the Czech Republic (a radar site) and in Poland (ten missiles) can only be explained in terms of prestige and anxiety, not in terms of military necessity. Those systems cannot threaten Russia – and Putin, while railing against them, has all but admitted their low-level importance by offering a radar site in Azerbaijan to help the US with policing the skies against Iranian missiles and learn something about state-of-the-art anti-missile defence – but they inspire the traumas and fears that are the stuff of politics. At a time of elections, even if in 2007 these were far from 'free and fair', those messages from the past were powerful. In the real world, Russia's military, its wings clipped and its funds reduced to a bare minimum, is in the middle of a thorough transformation, moving even further away from the mighty Red Army of the past. The military doctrine guiding this transformation process was slow to emerge and hamstrung, for a long time, by a dramatic lack of funds. Military policy is traditionally the dependent variable of military doctrine. It comprises the country's military priorities and directs the military process in general and the development of the armed forces in particular. It also defines the conditions, the potential, the needs, but also the limits of military force. And it is supposed to offer the military's political masters forms and methods for applying military force.

Cold War no more

For Russia as much as for everybody else the confrontation typical of the Cold War has disappeared from the defence layout. Russian military policy for the early decades of the twenty-first century is, according to the general staff, 'characterized by a balanced, constructive approach to the most complicated challenges and contradictions and by its focus on positive outcomes through political cooperation with other countries.'*

If this is the sanitized version for polite society – leaving aside the military mess, the brutality and the frustration of having to fight Muslim rebels in the northern Caucasus – the real emphasis is on deterrence: 'Strategic deterrence is among the priorities of Russian military policy to prevent both nuclear and conventional war as well as to provide for Russia's commitments towards its allies. Provision of military security for Russia by all means and resources available is of fundamental significance. Therefore Russia has to possess the nuclear capacity sufficient to reliably inflict a certain amount of damage upon any aggressor (be it an individual country or a coalition) under any circumstances.'

Russian military leaders, although they know that the Cold War posture has lost most of its meaning, like to dwell on nuclear doctrine. Control over nuclear weapons is what makes them equal to their American counterparts and allows them to punch above their weight. But they also know that to go nuclear means to get, as the Americans say, 'more bang for the buck'. That is why in today's Russian nuclear doctrine 'tactical' use of nuclear weapons figures much more prominently than in the days of the Cold War. It is a matter of necessity rather than of choice.

Official doctrine has it that 'Russia reserves the right to use nuclear weapons in response to the use of nuclear weapons and other weapons of mass destruction against Russia or her allies'. Of special significance is the doctrinal provision that nuclear first use can also materialize 'in response to a large-scale aggression with conventional arms in situations critical for the national security of Russia and her allies'.

Of course, all the above hinges on the preservation of the Non-Proliferation Treaty and the concomitant control regime in the hands of the Vienna-based International Atomic Energy Agency (IAEA). Russia, together with the US, the PRC, the UK and France, called the NPT into being after the nuclear stand-off over Berlin in 1961 and over Cuba

---

* Major General Valeri Leonidovits Manko in EU DG RELEX briefing at the House of Lords, 22 November 2007

in 1962. It was meant to exclude countries with nuclear ambitions, of whom there were a number, and provide a base for bipolar arms control negotiations and major accords first on limitations, like the two SALT (Strategic Arms Limitation Talks) agreements, and later also on reductions – START (Strategic Arms Reduction Treaty). The most important agreement among the two superpowers was what came to be called the ABM (Anti-Ballistic Missile) Treaty, which in fact stipulated that both sides should give up deployment of anti-missile defence and keep only one system operational. At the time, in 1973, this meant acknowledging that both the Russians and Americans had far from an effective system. In the meantime, both sides have worked assiduously but the Americans, due to President Ronald Reagan's Strategic Defence Initiative (SDI), forged ahead and President George W. Bush did indeed cancel the ABM system – much to the dismay and open anger of the Russians.

All of this makes the preservation of the NPT system even more important. The Russian general staff wants the effectiveness of the treaty system to be increased by way of bans, monitoring and any perceivable kind of technical applications. The Russians also want nuclear tests to stop – mature nuclear powers can by now do the testing through computer simulation – and a Comprehensive Nuclear Test Ban Treaty (CNTBT) to be introduced. This has become an important point of difference with the US, where the Senate has raised objections and blocked the process.

In view of their rapidly deteriorating nuclear arsenal the Russians are also willing to further reduce the number and calibre of nuclear weapons on a bilateral (with the US) or multilateral (with the other legitimate nuclear powers) basis 'to reach minimum levels required by the need for strategic stability'.

In a troubled world, overall strategic stability continues, much as during the later, more enlightened years of the Cold War, to be the linchpin of Russian military thinking. This is an element Russians want to retain from the old bipolar system, and to impress also on the Americans who otherwise would invest more and more in high-tech wizardry and leave the Russians behind. Strategic stability for the Russians is a mantra, meaning equilibrium. This has been, as high-ranking members of the general staff pointed out at various meetings, 'over three decades inseparable from the dialogue between Nato represented by the US and the USSR/Russia, and from the tangible results of this dialogue'. Russian officers also attach great importance to controlling the means of delivery, especially missile technology; in this, of course, they find themselves in conflict not with the Americans, who tend to think in parallel, but with the powerful Russian military-industrial complex ailing from many years of underfunding and loss of foreign markets. It is wishful thinking when the general staff lets it be known that 'Russia does everything possible to prevent weapons of mass destruction and their means of delivery from going out of control and is seeking innovative ways to curb proliferation.'

While in the past Russian military exports were mostly, if not always, of second-rate quality, so that the Russians would always have an edge over any users, be they Soviet satellites or Third World customers, in recent years Russian factories have taken to selling cutting-edge technology to, amongst others, India – which accounted for 40 per cent of Russian arms exports – and China. To what extent anti-air systems recently sold to Syria and Iran, much to the irritation of the US, Israel and all other Middle East countries, are of the more advanced category is, for most outsiders, a matter of speculation.

The spectre haunting Russia

The monster that the Russians perceive, however, is not conventional attack or even nuclear aggression – it is terrorism in all its varieties. They feel haunted by the spectre of asymmetric warfare which they experienced in the traumatic Afghan war, also in the Northern Caucasus. Moreover, Russian general staff officers understand, much as their Western counterparts, that the complex nature of modern societies invites terrorist attack against critical infrastructure and technological nerve centres. Referring to 9/11, Russian military leaders find themselves on the same side as the Americans and the rest of the modern world. Terror, they say loud and clear, 'has challenged the entire global community', and Russia can no longer cut itself off from the rest of the world. 'Terrorism has recently exceeded the limits of a national security threat and grown into a threat to international security. This challenge therefore takes a prominent place in Russian military policy – and even more so as Russia has for many years been engaged in combating the henchmen of international terrorism in the Northern Caucasus.'

It is interesting to note that the men in grey-green uniform, more than their political masters in pinstripe suits, are painfully aware of the limits of military action, and do not want to see the army sent into battles that soldiers on their own have no chance of winning. 'It is obvious that terrorism cannot be eradicated by means of force alone. Non-military means to control its feeding grounds should be explored' – advice, no doubt, to politicians in Moscow. 'Such ground is provided by social and economic cataclysm, poverty, large-scale unemployment, armed conflict, international organized crime, drug-trafficking, an illegal and uncontrolled arms trade. The evil of terrorism can only be fought by comprehensive means and in a joint effort.' If this is a caveat for the politicians in Moscow, it implies also an offer to collaborate with Western countries, and possibly worldwide. It would be foolish not to take up the chance.

The Russian general staff officers at that Helsinki seminar came back to the subject of terrorism again and again, taking pains to make this a common effort: 'No nation on its own can secure the homeland or counter the threat of modern transnational terrorism. Only by merging our capabilities can we protect our people, defend our societies, and preserve our ideas and principles for future generations. That is why Russia and European and transatlantic security institutions such as Nato and the European Union must work together to confront this dangerous post-Cold War phenomenon.' The Russians understand full well that this kind of anti-terrorist effort is a new model of cooperation, transcending traditional notions of national sovereignty. What they mean is 'direct involvement in the military operations against terrorists and also blanket overflight rights, access to ports and bases, refuelling assistance and stepped-up intelligence efforts and, last but by no means least, public diplomatic support'.

It is ironic to remember in this context that, when President Reagan met Secretary General Gorbachev in Reykjavik in 1986 for arms control negotiations, both men, in a more philosophical moment, posed the question as to when the East–West conflict would ever end. They came up with the answer: when planet Earth is invaded by Martians. By now, the Martians, this time mostly from the Greater Middle East, are at the gates, and some are already inside the walls. New enemies produce new alliances.

Nato: strained relations

Within the Russian military establishment the bitterness about Nato enlargement is not to be underestimated, and it grew throughout the 1990s. Relations between the Russian Federation and Nato were, for the Russians at least, a key issue in foreign and security affairs. There are overarching concerns, like the proliferation of weapons of mass destruction and terrorism. The Russians seem to have hoped for a reliable framework to consolidate the effort. The Nato–Russia Cooperation Council for them was a disappointment, especially after Nato's Kosovo air campaign, waged against Russian opposition in the UN.

But the military top brass wants results and is very concerned about deficiencies in the common anti-terror struggle. There is open self-criticism of the Russian attempt to split the Western Atlantic alliance. 'Any attempt to stop Nato enlargement or to create an anti-Nato block failed.' The reference of course is to the run-up to the Iraq war. 'Russia overestimated transatlantic contradictions in the security field.' The concept of treating the US and Nato as enemies and Europe and the EU as friends of Russia and aiming for a split was entirely misplaced. 'The present state of transatlantic relations is geared more towards common cause than towards separation.' This recognition in turn caused Russian policy-makers to be more realistic and pragmatic. Time and again Russian general staff officers come back to the refrain: 'Russian policy towards Nato must be based on a full understanding of contemporary threats to the country's security, such as international terrorism, not in the stereotypes of the Cold War era, still prevalent in Russia–Nato relations.' What they mean but dare not say is that the long-term strategic competitors are China in the east and Islam, in its many variations, to the south. The Russian military elite has, ever since the end of the Cold War, cultivated military-to-military relations and has made full use of the Nato–Russia Founding Act, the Nato–Russia Cooperation Council and the many variations on Russia–Nato cooperation, at Harvard, at Stiftung Wissenschaft und Politik in Ebenhausen, or on the strategic level.

The working groups active between Russia and Nato are comparing notes on air-space control, logistics and material-technical supplies, and – most importantly – on ballistic missile defence. The latter is by and large a code for defending the motherland against incoming missiles from the south. Over many years, Russian and US teams have explored avenues of cooperation, especially for theatre missile defence (TMD), notwithstanding the US cancellation of the ABM Treaty or, more recently, Russian protestations about the proposed US radar site in the Czech Republic and the ten anti-missile missiles to be put into Poland as a defence against potential Iranian nuclear-tipped missiles en route to the US or Europe.

When Putin raised the issue at the 2007 Munich Security Conference Russian anger seemed to be implacable. In the meantime the Russian military offered a disused radar site in Azerbaijan for cooperation with US anti-missile forces. Scoring political points among anti-American crowds in the West was one thing; gaining access to American anti-missile technology quite another.

Meanwhile, there was even talk of joint exercises and action as part of multinational contingency forces. After 9/11 those activities were enhanced. At the Munich Security Conference of 2002 the then Russian Defence Minister Sergei Ivanov mentioned work on the Status of Forces Agreement, allowing for joint training and exercises, both through command post exercises and field exercises. There is a framework Agreement – in response to the *Kursk* disaster off the Murmansk coast – about Submarine Emergency Crew Escape and Rescue: 'It may seem to be purely technical, but in reality it has brought Nato–Russia interaction up to quite a practical new level.'*

First and foremost non-proliferation

Among all these common concerns, keeping the lid on the proliferation of weapons of mass destruction is paramount, and the Russians as much as the Americans know that they have to do it together – or give up. This explains the close cooperation in dissuading North Korea from continuing on the nuclear path. It also helps in understanding the complex Russian–Iranian relationship: helping to construct the nuclear power plant at Busheer while keeping the nuclear fuel out of Iranian hands. The philosophy of non-proliferation dates back to the days of the Cold War when both Americans and Russians were united in preserving the nuclear monopoly, regardless of UK, French and

* Sergei Ivanov at the 40th Security Conference

Chinese aspirations, and restraining the ambitions of Third World countries. This has undergone no fundamental change and is not likely to change. Not only the Russians but also every US administration since Richard Nixon have always understood the paramount national interest in keeping the nuclear genie in the bottle.

Today not only Russia's security but also Russia's international standing depend on preserving the nuclear cartel with the US and, to a lesser extent, China, the UK and France. When Russian politicians talk about terror being their foremost concern they mean, of course, Chechen rebels and Islamist fighters in nearby territories. But the nightmare of all nightmares for Russia is terrorism with nuclear weapons. In this, the Russians are not alone. Nato leaders, instead of turning fear of Russia into a self-fulfilling prophecy, could and should overcome the shadows of the past and concentrate on the real dangers in the offing. Neither the state of the Russian army nor the layout of Russian grand strategy warrants a return to Cold War conditioned reflexes and policies. Never mind occasional militant rhetoric and boasting from Moscow loudspeakers when new weapons are put on display for potential customers, military spending in Russia has remained, for many years, well under budget. And those budgets were, to judge by complaints from the military, already modest by any standard. Russia is an exhausted empire, and it is not through the currencies of the past, tanks and Marxist ideology, that it seeks new power, but through oil, gas, pipelines and petrodollars. Welcome to the modern world.

7
Crescent rising over Kazan

'One has to come to Russia to see the result of this terrible combination
of the intelligence and the silence of Europe with the genius of Asia.'
Marquis de Custine, *Journey for Our Time*

When night falls over Kazan, the ancient capital of the Tatars where
the Kazanka river flows into the mighty Volga, the Kremlin of Ivan the
Terrible rises like a ghost from olden times over the city and its modern
high riser. Walls, crenellations and towers are bathed in an aggressive
white light. The ancient fortress is a monument to Russia's expansion
from Moscow into both Europe and Asia and to the centuries of
imperial glory and pity that were to follow.

The most recent addition to the architecture, however, tells a different story. A brand-new, white-marble mosque, built by a Turkish
company, towers over the old Russian buildings and tells the story of
the politico-religious upheavals of the early 1990s, of Saudi money,
and of an uneasy peace between Islam and Russian Orthodoxy, the
past and the present, the many children of the Muslim women and the
few children of the Russian women. The huge cupola of the mosque,
rising high into the ink-blue sky, is framed by four giant minarets
which at nightfall are bathed in blue and green light. The symbolism
of Islam triumphing over Russian conquest cannot be overlooked, and
it carries all the way to Moscow eight hundred kilometres to the west
a strong message not about who the troubled past belongs to but about
who will own the future.

Defeating Ivan the Terrible

Four centuries ago Ivan the Terrible came from Moscow leading a
force of 60,000 fierce and battle-ready soldiers to break what Russians
to this day, with a feeling of horror, self-doubt and awe, call the yoke
of the Tatars, meaning 300 years of domination by the people of the
Eurasian steppe. The Tsar, once the city had been duly raped and

plundered, had the fortifications strengthened, and in this shape they survived difficult times: forever a powerful bulwark against Asian invasions and, even during Soviet times, a strong reminder of the self-ascribed Russian mission to conquer, to civilize and to stay. The golden crescent, however, now rising from the bell tower of the tsar and pointing in the direction of Mecca in the far south, is hardly what the grim conqueror could have imagined, let alone welcomed. In Kazan, from time immemorial the point of entry for Asian hordes into Europe, a Muslim reconquest is being announced to the Russians – but also, if they care to listen, to the peoples further west. This reversal of history is counted not in years but in generations, and it has only just started. The wild martial dances, performed by horsemen for the benefit of foreign travellers in the evening, are certainly more of Tatar than of Russian origin. And the message they carry may be more serious than mere folklore.

A notably successful survivor from Soviet decades, proud of his wide popularity and his indisputable democratic credentials, is Mintimer Shaimiev, president of the republic of Tatarstan. His almond-shaped black eyes reveal his Tatar lineage. In the past, he must have been a dutiful Soviet agricultural apparatchik as, at the tender age of twenty-nine, he had already been appointed head of what the Soviets called an agro-industrial complex. When he went into politics, middle-aged, accumulating decorations, offices and influence, he managed the turn-around after the fall of the Soviet Union, kept things around Kazan mostly peaceful and was reelected three or four times. He makes no bones over the fact that he feels embarrassed by the recent confirmation in his leadership by order of the Kremlin. People, he insists, should be allowed to elect their leaders themselves. This reservation, however, does not detract from his conspicuous friendship with Vladimir Putin, displayed in brochures and on billboards of no small size along the short stretch of motorway leading out of the city, where a southern Kremlin chief shakes hands with a northern one. Shaimiev is also one of the leaders of United Russia. His popularity is such that his black Mercedes S-class is not the armoured version. Nor does he need a convoy of similar cars to mislead and frustrate would-be assassins. He is the boss, and he means business.

Shaimiev presents himself, credibly, as the father of the Tatar father-land, an enlightened ruler. In Moscow he is credited with having prevented major bloodshed at the time of the first post-Soviet Chechen uprising, possibly even the secession of the oil-rich republic. He did this with a combination of financial appeasement, remarkable powers of persuasion and a firm hand. Therefore, he will be irreplaceable for a long time to come. It does help that Tatarstan produces a neat 18 per cent of Russian oil. The reserves untapped so far are estimated to last for at least another thirty years or so. It hurts local pride and egotism, of course, that the Moscow overlord demands close to 90 per cent of the revenue.

The Caucasus and the Chechen capital Grozny – named after Ivan Grozny, also known as Ivan the Terrible – are far away to the south, almost a thousand kilometres, even further away than Moscow to the west. But ideas travel fast. The old Orthodox archbishop and the young Mufti, the latter educated in Medina, assured their visitors at a joint meeting in the mosque that everything was all right, that people were listening to each other, that there was no risk of Islamist contagion and that everybody was happy. The Americans, however, much to the chagrin of the local dignitaries, had captured some young Tatars in Afghanistan who reemerged at Guantánamo Bay, America's notorious prison where Islamist fighters are kept in legal limbo. Caution was advised.

The number of mosques throughout Tatarstan, in Soviet times fewer than a dozen, has grown to many hundreds. The Tatar language, closely related to Turkish, has come out of hiding and is now the second official language.

More mosques

The green night-sleeper train from Kazan to Moscow's Kazan station takes eight hours, slowly rumbling over creaking tracks, while matrons in green uniforms serve tea and vodka in ample quantities. From Moscow the east and south are seen with ill-concealed concern. Even in its reduced post-Soviet form Russia, with about 20 million Muslims, still has a much higher percentage of Muslim population than Germany with three million Turks, but comes close to France with an estimated number of seven million, mostly of Arab origin.

In Chechnya there is a sort of peace, uneasy and unpredictable. The local president Ramzan Kadyrov, an opaque character if ever there was one, for the time being collaborates with the Russians, their special forces and administrators, but has also seen to it that women wear the veil, that a mosque of enormous proportions is being built, and that Moscow does not interfere too much. Nobody can tell what his designs may be on the day after tomorrow. Muscovites do not like to imagine what Russia's Muslim population is dreaming about for its destiny in the years and decades to come. The Muslim future will be decided less under the crosses and eagles of Moscow and more through what happens in the lands under the rising crescent. Meanwhile, everything is quiet in and around Kazan.

Putin has never made a secret of his belief that the decline and fall of the late Soviet Union was an unmitigated disaster of the twentieth century, and four out of five Russians seem to be of the same opinion. But, on reflection, the demise of the vast Soviet Union can also be seen as a kind of liberation for Russia and the Russians. Much as France, in restrospect, has to thank General de Gaulle for cutting the umbilical cord to Algeria in 1962, the Russians got rid, without major revolts and uprisings, of many millions of Muslims living in the southern republics of Azerbaijan, Kazakhstan, Turkmenistan, Tajikistan and Uzbekistan. When those republics left the sinking ship in 1991, they took with them vast amounts of mineral resources, imperial glories and military installations like the Baikonur Cosmodrome in Kazakhstan – but they also put an end to the Soviet illusion of a peaceful multi-racial and multi-religious empire, happy and at peace with itself. The wars of succession within or between those newly invented states were cruel, notably between Azerbaijan and Armenia. The surgical separation of South Ossetia and Abkhazia from the Georgian republic – not without a little help from neighbouring Russia – was mercifully brief. It became a frozen conflict on the dividing line between Russia and Georgia – only to unfreeze in the brief brutal war of August 2008.

Shedding what Rudyard Kipling in the heyday of British imperialism had called the 'white man's burden' was a blessing in disguise for the overextended motherland. The Soviet Union took its leave from history, quite unexpectedly, not with a bang but with a whimper. The wars over Chechnya and along the Northern Caucasus could have been the rule, but have been the exception – so far. There may be disasters waiting to happen, in neighbouring Ingushetia or multi-national Daghestan, for example. But so far they have failed to materialize.

Things could indeed have gone very wrong, certainly at a time of Islamic reawakening all over Asia, and especially along the southern borders of Russia, defined only haphazardly by tsarist generals and, following the reconquest by the Red Army's commissars after 1920, by the new Soviet rulers. What they imposed upon the vanquished was a mental map designed by communist ideology and Russian expansionism.

'My home is not the house and the street, my home is the Soviet Union' – a favourite song of the Sixties that still remains popular. Soviet man could not replace ordinary people, and Soviet ideology could not wipe out the longing for nationhood, the tribe, the clan. Indeed, throughout the Central Asian republics as much as in Ukraine it was never forgotten, until the end of the Soviet Union, that they had been the first nations to be victimized. The brutality of the civil war continued in the *korenizacija*, i.e. suppressing traditional elites and creating new ones from local red commissars. As a matter of course, the traditions of nomad people had to be broken. This civilizing 'mission' put an end to centuries or indeed millennia of ethnic tradition.

The Soviet inheritance

While under the tsars the people of the steppe had been largely left out of central control, the Caucasus mountains were too important to be left to themselves or the designs of local tribes. Protest was born together with Russian rule, and the Soviets inherited a legacy of bitterness and rebellion. The Chechen people never forgot the endless wars they had been subjected to through three centuries. When the German Wehrmacht approached in 1942 they finally hoped to be redeemed from Soviet rule, and in 1944 they paid a horrendous price, being shipped in open wagons into the Kazak steppe, the survivors to be brought back only under Khrushchev in the 1950s. Georgians in many ways shared their fate. Not even the existence of a Georgian socialist party could bridge the gulf; the socialists of Georgia happened to be firebrand nationalists, or like Stalin and Beria; the bolsheviks from Georgia, the worst executioners.

The seventy years of Soviet rule, however, at least kept ethnic tensions under an iron lid. Even before the Soviet Union finally dissolved, the nations around the Caucasus, sensing the impending end, did not wait for the exodus but started their own wars of the Soviet succession. What happened throughout most of Yugoslavia after 1989 had its close parallel when Soviet rule collapsed in the south. While vast areas were redistributed, 'ethnic cleansing' accentuated the horror and the butchery. To the present day most of the conflicts have not found a lasting answer. The natives of Georgia, Azerbaijan, Armenia, Abkhazia, Ossetia and many others recall their founding myths and claim all the land that they remember. At worst, mass murder was the answer, at best frozen conflicts.

The Russians, from Stalin to Gorbachev, had combined a policy of brutal repression of traditional elites, of Islam and its teachers, with long-term attempts at coopting new leaders. With what success? 'We were here in the seventh century, and I can assure you that there will be more of us on the day after tomorrow,' said Sheikh Abdullah, deputy chair of the government-sponsored Council of Central Asian Republics and Kazakhstan, in January 1989.*

This awakening was, after the Russian catastrophe in Afghanistan, not merely the result of tradition and remembrance. When a thousand years of Russian Orthodoxy celebrated in 1987, of 1100 years of Islam on the Volga, with Kazan as its capital, and 200 years of the Muslim Spiritual Council of Orenburg coincided, a religious renaissance was in the making. The rehabilitation of the Orthodox Church under Gorbachev and, even more so, under Boris Yeltsin, had strong reverberations not only among traditional Russians and closet Christians, but also among the Muslim population throughout the Soviet Union. All of a sudden, the Muslims within the Soviet Empire discovered their history, their identity and their potential strength. In those years Shafaq Stanizai, a member of the Writers' Union of Free Afghanistan, who had lived in Central Asia for many years, cited the 70 million Muslims throughout the Soviet dominions, with no more than two institutions to educate and train future imams, both administered by the Muslim Council of the Central Asian republics and Kazakhstan. Both were on a short ideological leash, and the curriculum followed more or less the dogmas of Soviet ideology, including no small amount of anti-capitalist and anti-religious routine. Altogether, no more than eighty students were enlisted. The graduates were employed not to look after their

* Erffa, Wolfgang von, *Das Vermachtuis Des Eisernen Emirs*, 1989.

religious flock but to cultivate relations between the Soviet Union and emerging Islamic countries as much as for Soviet peace propaganda in international bodies.

Under Stalin Islam had been seen, not unlike the Christian churches, as outright reactionary and anti-Soviet, 'opium for the masses' in true Marxist fashion. In the 1960s, as a response to the Algerian uprising against the French and various other anti-Western liberation movements throughout Islamic countries, and as an offer to the non-aligned movement, a Soviet-impregnated Islam was seen by Moscow as a useful tool. In the 1970s Soviet rulers were slowly recognizing Islam as an element of social improvement. Stanizai estimated that between 95 and 99 per cent of ethnic Uzbeks, Turkmens, Kazakhs, Tajiks and Kyrgyz kept Islamic ritual in their family and communal life, entertaining little sympathy for Soviet domination. Their xenophobia was directed mostly against their Russian masters. The Afghan war thoughout the 1980s accentuated the bitterness. The Soviet high command had committed the strategic blunder of sending mostly soldiers from Islamic republics as cannon fodder into Afghanistan. Their bitterness, frustration and contempt for their Russian masters became an important force in the splitting apart of the Soviet Union.

Six of the fifteen republics of the Soviet Union counted a majority of Muslims. The most important centres were Tashkent, Kazan, Boynaks, the centre of Bashkiria, the city of Boynyaks, Baku on the Caspian Sea, and Daghestan – the latter bordering on Chechnya. The Islamic revolution effected in Iran after the return of Ayatollah Khomeini in 1978 had enormous international implications, nowhere more so than throughout the southern republics of the Soviet Union. It was in response to the dramatic reversal of the Shah's fortunes and the humiliation of the USA that an Islamic reawakening began, with no separation between religious and political motives. For the Muslim population in the Caucasus area the Islamic revolution was a fascinating experience, inviting imitation. Those little cassettes carrying the spiteful sermons of Khomeini throughout Iran and the neighbouring countries were smuggled across Iran's northern border into the Islamic republics under Soviet rule. Meanwhile, the Iranian communists, emerging from the underground, offered their collaboration to the mullah regime but were rejected and persecuted. North of the border, many young Muslims asked for permission to emigrate to Iran. Baku, oil rich and strategically situated on the banks of the Caspian Sea, is only 300 kilometres away from the other Azerbaijan – the one behind the Iranian border. During Soviet times half of the population (1.5 million) was Muslim, mostly Shia.

From 1928 on a kind of Iron Curtain had been put up by the Soviet occupiers along the southern border and maintained for the next four decades. It ended only when in the 1960s Moscow saw the chance of world revolution through the Third World, imagined future allies and wanted to demonstrate its socialist achievements. But this was a kind of KGB-produced mirage, and proved to be short-lived. The Iranian revolution, the defeat of Soviet military might in Afghanistan by Islamic resistance fighters (with some electronic high-tech help from their US sponsors), and the revival of Russian orthodoxy had powerful and long-lasting implications. Long before the end of the Soviet Union the Moscow-controlled media tended to refer to 'the Islamic problem', meaning those tectonic shifts happening on both sides of the southern border. All of a sudden, but not out of the blue, religion, held in official contempt and persecuted throughout Soviet times, became a force to reckon with, while Soviet ideology was, to all intents and purposes, a spent force without spiritual promise, economic success or deterrent military potential. In addition, throughout the Islamic republics of the Soviet Empire, communist ideology never overcame the opprobrium of being the veneer of foreign, white, northern oppression. But Soviet defeat in Afghanistan held the promise that the power of Moscow over the lands of Islam was not permanent. During the last years of Soviet rule the authorities noted that the main organizations of Afghan resistance had even managed to have their propaganda translated into Russian and were able to circulate the texts throughout the southern republics, notably Kyrgyzstan, but also in Samarkand, Tashkent and Bukhara.

The Soviet authorities, in their turn, started their own anti-Islamic campaign in the early 1980s, reminding the locals in no uncertain terms that in the past the Tsar's armies had conquered the Caucasus and that, in the twentieth century, the Red Army had smashed the Basmachi – the southern rebels or 'bandits' who had put up their own short-lived statelets at the time of the civil war between the Whites and the Reds. Foreign diplomats saw this as an undisguised warning for those Muslims dreaming of independence.

Today, throughout the lands from the Caspian Sea to the borders of China mosques are being refurbished or built anew. Before the revolution the number of mosques in those parts of Russia was estimated to be close to 25,000, plus another 100 in the Emirate of Bukhara and in the Khanate of Khiva. In 1942, the total number had gone down to 2000, and in 1966 only 400 mosques were – in Soviet speak – 'working'. Obviously, the KGB took what was the result of severe repression as a sign of voluntary conversion to the Soviet religion. In May 1976 comrade F. Furov, chairman of the Council for Religious Affairs with the Ministerial Council of the USSR, listed 300 'registered' mosques as well as 700 'non-registered' ones. At the same time, an official in Tashkent was quoted by diplomats who cited 143 mosques as 'working' for all of Soviet Central Asia. There was, on average, one mosque for a quarter of a million Muslims. In the last years of the Soviet Union Igor Beliaev, reputed to be the number one authority on Islam, wrote in *Literaturnaya Gazeta* about '365 mosques, filled with worshippers'. Today, throughout the Central Asian republics but also across the Muslim provinces of Russia – or, for that matter, the Muslim parts of ex-Yugoslavia – mosques are being built in great numbers with both local money and generous support from petrol-states like Saudi Arabia.

How to live with Islam?

The Russians are ambiguous, Putin included. He may mourn the loss of those Central Asian treasure houses, but he must also be aware of the fact that, given the chronic demographic implosion among Russians and the demographic explosion among Muslims, the end of empire has rid Russia of a major problem, insoluble in the long term. Those 70 million at the end of the Soviet Union would, in the meantime, have come close to 100 million, on average much younger, more agile and more aggressive than the Russians of Russia. If demography is destiny, Russia after the Soviet Empire is, more than before, the master of its own – demographic – fate.

But the end of empire also meant that many millions of Russians left the wastelands of Siberia to look for softer living conditions in the western part of the country, while forced labour has gone out of fashion since Brezhnev and would not in any case be helpful in running oil wells, or building and maintaining pipelines through hostile territory.

Throughout its history Russia had an abundance of people, and those in power treated the masses just as masses, to be dispensed in war or peace without much regard for human life or human dignity. Nobody knows just how many people perished in the Gulag or were sent into bloody battle. This has changed, not through a conversion to a different philosophy but through the unwillingness of many well-educated young people to stay in Russia or, if they stay, to produce children and raise them. Today's Russia is rich in resources except the most important one: people and their pursuit of happiness.

In 2007 a report was published, endorsed by President Putin, on Russia's demographic predicament and the proposed policy to stem the tide. RIA Novosty reported the findings: every 21 seconds on average a baby is born into the Russian federation, and every 15 seconds a person dies. Every hour the Russian population is reduced by about 100 people, every year overall numbers shrink by between 800,000 and 900,000. The UN's relative optimism gives a forecast of 113 million overall for the mid-twenty-first century; pessimists in Moscow put the number, if the tide does not turn, at 96 million. If this is the case, the consequences are grim not only in overall numbers, but also in terms of the balance between Russians and non-Russians, especially Muslims. Within fifty years, at current rates, Islam might be the predominant religion throughout Russian lands. Venyamin Popov, the President's special envoy to the Organization of the Islamic Conference, at a press conference in October 2007 opened a window into the future. Few Russians liked what they saw: 'Almost 20 million Muslims live in today's Russia. In twenty years' time they will exceed one third of the population and by mid-century Muslims will outnumber all other groups of believers.' The explanation is clear: Muslims tend to have more children than Russians. Asked about the outlook for the rest of Europe, Popov was equally clear. The decline of indigenous population throughout Europe was 'inevitable'; 'in two to three generations Europeans will become a minority in Europe.' Russians like a good nightmare. So it came as no surprise when Popov predicted that the next five or ten years will witness acute confrontation between the Muslim world and the West in international politics. Note that all of a sudden Russia is counted as the 'West'. The conflicts throughout the Middle East, in Somalia, or even the war in Iraq are the harbingers of more crises and conflicts to come.

To frustrate these forecasts and to keep ahead in the competition for numbers is what the Kremlin calls the 'number one national project'. Putin time and again comes back to the bleak prospect of a dying Russia. When the Soviet Union fell apart, the trickle of Jewish emigration to Israel increased to a mass flight of over one million people who headed for the Holy Land or used it as a way station en route to the United States. By now, the ex-Russians have a conspicuous presence in Israel, flourishing in business, in the army, in politics and in other professions.

A similar exodus has taken place in the direction of Germany. Almost two million ethnic Germans took the Western exit, and close to 100,000 Jews also decided to go the same way and seek their fortune in Germany and beyond. Russians, too, have left the motherland in great numbers, notably in the direction of Berlin and London. Thus, Russia has lost many more school teachers, university professors and doctors than the country can afford. The Russians speak of a 'brain drain', deploring the loss of most or all of their technical elites. The most obvious consequence is that there is not enough manpower to run basic industries, let alone to modernize them along Western standards.

Decline

At the same time, the decline of population throughout Russia, except in the Muslim populated areas, was also fed by a serious decline in living standards as well as mounting housing problems. In addition, Russians were influenced by the same complex forces of cultural standards, attitudes and identity at work throughout Western countries. By now, the demographic crisis is the most serious hindrance to economic growth, technology and progress in research and development. In a recent interview Alexander Goncharuk, CEO of AFK Sistema, a Russian telecom giant, was asked about the shortage of highly qualified manpower. His answer can stand for many companies short of experts and expert training: 'This year [2007] we open, near Moscow, a super-clean room on a par with best practice throughout Europe. All the specialists that we need we have to train abroad. Whoever has something in his head, or a high IQ, is being sent abroad for further education. Our people come to understand and practise not only a certain knowhow but also a holistic technological culture.'

As to long-term emigration, Goncharuk was sanguine: 'Those who have left will come back. Here they find what Americans call a challenge. What concerns me, however, is the fact that the middle management has broken away and that there are too few technicians. We produce accountants, lawyers, experts in marketing and public relations. But where are the engineers?'

Goncharuk warned that lack of experts could be a serious brake on the development of Russia: 'You can have a market. But without experts long-term growth will collapse.' Foreign managers in top positions? Putin had publicly voiced his misgivings, but Goncharuk qualified the message: 'Putin meant something else. How long can Russia still rely on Western human resources? If we make Sistema off limits for foreigners, this would hit hundreds of high achievers.'

Putin sees the government duty bound to start a high-tech offensive. But can Russia catch up with the top-performing companies all around the globe? The industrial managers view the state directives with mixed feelings: 'We feel more and more the state's support, be it as investor or consumer, whether civil or military. What needs to be maintained is the balance between state corporations and private enterprise. For private companies the question is ultimately of how profitable a project is.'*

Jobs on offer

Meanwhile, what is true for the high end of the labour market is also true for the middle ranks and even the lower end. Russia's booming economy is luring more and more people not only from the West but in much higher numbers from Central Asia. Many are ethnic Russians, coming back to the motherland from inhospitable and poor lands, but even more are natives of the Central Asian countries, seeking a modest living mostly in jobs where Russians are no longer willing to work,

* Full interview in *Die Welt*, 30 October 2007

Russia's per capita income being six times that of, for instance, Uzbekistan.

While the economic boom is powering ahead, driven by rising prices for oil and natural gas and most other resources which Russia has in abundance, the shrinking of the work force complicates the situation. Not only Moscow and St Petersburg need office space, hotels, apartments and shopping malls – along with people to build them. There is a deficit of labour, growing ever more serious. At the end of 2007 the number of migrant workers, published by Moscow's Russian Economics Institute, was put at 4.9 million, washing dishes, digging ditches and doing other menial jobs. The real number could well be double that figure, most of them coming from the former Soviet republics to the south. There are even those who left Russia ten years ago and are now applying to come back.

The vast influx of foreign labourers, most of them easily recognizable by their darker skin and Asian facial features, helps to solve an economic problem, but it creates others. These 'blacks' as they are called, sometimes with even less flattering names, are a visible presence in most major cities. Some, the majority, work hard while some turn to petty crime. Many corner the market in fresh fruit and vegetables, working against the clock to get fresh produce early to market. But it is a thankless task. Although Russia is a multi-ethnic society, with more than one hundred non-Slavic nationalities, the Russians resent the presence of those busy foreigners.

In the summer of 2006 in the Northern Kola Peninsula, in the city of Kondopoga riots broke out against the people who were visibly different, and from the south. The locals felt exploited and cheated by the immigrants who had most of the local business in their hands, and seemed to flourish modestly. Karelia, otherwise known as a tolerant part of Russia, suddenly opened a Pandora's box of racial hatred, envy and violence. Putin's express conviction that the Russians were, by and large, used, in Soviet times, to living with other nationalities seems to be wishful thinking. A law of April 2007 forbidding foreigners to work as vendors in Russian markets addresses deep-seated disdain among the Russians for their unwelcome but indispensable neighbours. Samuel Huntington's 'clash of civilizations' is not an alien idea throughout Russia; you don't have to travel all the way to Chechnya or Daghestan to meet it as a daily experience.

SOVA is the name of a courageous and pretty lonely Moscow-based group tracking hate crimes. In 2005 they reported 435 victims of race-based assaults in Russia. In 2006 the number had gone up steeply – whether as a result of better reporting or an increase in hostility is not clear. In early 2007 the number was still increasing.

Russia has registered an average economic growth of between 7 and 8 per cent per annum since 1999. Meanwhile, Russia's population fell from 148.7 million in 1999 to 143.8 million in 2006 and continues to slide. There are, as throughout the rest of Europe, fewer babies, and so far government programmes to encourage young women to have more children have met with an unwilling response – easily to be explained by the scarcity of good housing, the fragility of families, the need to have two breadwinners in the family, and the slow disappearance of the eternal and omnipresent Russian grandmother, the babushka.

The balance between Russians and non-Russians is continuously shifting in favour of the latter. The overall decline is particularly dramatic in the work force which, according to the Ministry for Health and Social Development, will drop from 74.5 million in 2007 to a pitiful 65.5 million by 2010. The high number of vodka-related deaths among men – Putin's interpretation of these figures is that 'they drink too much and then they cause accidents' – and low fertility rates among women are the fundamental drivers of this development. Even today, four out of ten farm or construction workers are already foreigners, many of them Muslim. Life expectancy for Russian men is by now somewhere between fifty-seven and fifty-nine years – compared to well over seventy in Western Europe.

Today's Russia welcomes – if that is not too idyllic a term – the second largest number of immigrants after the United States. When the Soviet Union collapsed, many ethnic Russians came back from the inhospitable colonies, followed by many millions of undocumented Tajiks, Uzbeks, Kazakhs, Ukrainians, Moldovans and uncounted others. Getting into Russia is not difficult, at least for the first three months. After that, immigrants need a work permit. Until recently, in fact early 2007, most immigrants were living in the grey zones of the economy. Exploited by their employers, paid miserable wages and vulnerable to harassment by the Russian police, they were, though badly needed, at the very bottom of society. Not unlike the US Congress giving legal status to immigrants from Mexico, the Russian state Duma passed a law in January 2007 setting quotas by nationality and by region. In 2007, according to figures from the World Bank, the quota was altogether 6.1 million foreign workers allowed to work, with more than one tenth, 700,000, in Moscow alone.

This does not mean that the process of immigration is quick and easy. It can take weeks for immigrants to work their way through waiting lists at the Federal Migration Service – while they remain in legal limbo. In fact, without a *propusk*, a special permit costing money, they cannot work legally or be housed. Bribing officials is the obvious way around such obstacles, but it can backfire. The fine for illegally employing a foreign worker can go up to 800,000 roubles. The law is rough and unfriendly, notwithstanding the fact that without labour from abroad the Russian economy faces a demographic implosion. Russia is slowly heading towards crisis point, and all the petroleum money of Khanty-Mansiysk in Western Siberia, of Tatarstan and other places will not help.

Demography is destiny

Demography is destiny, for Russia as much as for Western Europe and the rest of the world. There is no way to escape the fact that, much as the workers' paradise of the past wasted human endeavour and did not respect the individual, labour is now the one resource, high end or low end, that will limit the rise and rise of Russia.

In strategic terms, Russians cannot but feel apprehension when looking south or east. In terms of high-performance weaponry Russia is still far ahead of any conventional threat. But in terms of both population and asymmetric warfare Russians have every right to feel threatened – and in their heart of hearts they admit that, while oil and dollars continue to lift the economy and the political system, the masses of China and of the Muslim world represent a potential nightmare.

What to do? The Russian authorities were slow to recognize the problem and even slower to do something about it. It is thanks to Putin, with his all-encompassing strategic view of Russia, that as of 2007 the state is investing in massive programmes to stem the decline. The reconstruction of Russian power in the world at large would remain an empty gesture without the reconstruction of the home base, and nothing is more important than having a well-balanced population; yet today's Russia is far away from any balance or stability. But behind the broader agenda for population growth there is a silent, less visible agenda in order to keep the balance between Russians and non-Russians. Whatever the detail, religious and regional conflicts will increase.

In October 2007 Putin used an address to the Council of the Russian Public Chamber – not a legislative body but a deliberating assembly – to present the new policy. He spoke of three stages. The objective for the first three or four years is to reduce death rates tangibly; by 2015 to stabilize the population total at 140 million (at the end of 2007 the number was 142 million), then to lift overall numbers to 145 million. There are two aims: one is to encourage young families to produce more children, the other to create living standards that give people a healthier life and increase average life expectancy (for men and women) from the current sixty-six to at least seventy years.

The project includes programmes already under way like the Health Priority National Project and the Federal Programme 'Children of Russia'. Post-Soviet Russia is far behind in health care in general and pre-natal care in particular. No fewer than twenty-three special clinics are to be set up, working more or less on the same lines as the British National Health Service.

It has always been said that it is the women who keep Russia afloat, and Putin would subscribe to this time-honoured view. So it is small wonder that in May 2006 he took the initiative and promised young mothers the equivalent of USD 9,500 for the birth of their second child. In addition, new subsidies were introduced for mothers looking after their babies. The Duma has increased, pressured by the President, the monthly maternity allowance to 23,400 roubles (equivalent to around USD 1000). What Putin wants to push through the jungle of bureaucracy is an all-embracing concept for a new welfare state, focused on turning around long-established trends.

Putin and his people know that a vast country like Russia cannot, as the Americans say, turn on a dime. The four great 'national projects' will take time, money and enormous effort to push through, but they are integral to the strategy to turn decline into growth. Those programmes are popular, and the more money comes in from oil and gas the less they look like pie in the sky. Administrative control of these programmes destined to reverse the long-term ebb of the Russian population was in the hands of Dmitri Medvedev, in fact his core responsibility in the Kremlin. After he was named by Putin as future president, within less than a month his popularity rose to a staggering 80 per cent. In retrospect it looks as if he was groomed by his mentor from St Petersburg days to be the man who brings the good news to Russians and, as president, will be able to deliver.

Four avenues are proposed by the Kremlin to lead the Russian people to the promised land of higher living standards and a better and healthier life: fair-priced living, modern health care, professional training, effective agriculture.

So far, this land of milk and honey is still in the future, and doubts have not been dispelled as to whether it will ever turn into reality. An initial budget of 180 billion roubles (USD 7.2 billion) has been increased to 430 billion roubles (USD 17.2 billion) at the end of 2007. But costs have risen too, and organization is inefficient.

The national projects

To start with the housing market. The idea was that the state would subsidize mortgages and give money directly to families. This resulted in a rapid rise in prices while nothing was done to liberalize the market for land to build on or to control the corrupt practices of municipalities assigning apartments to tenants. The result was an increase in housing prices in the major cities, especially Moscow and St Petersburg, of between 85 and 100 per cent. When this national project started in 2005, it took 4.3 years of the savings of an average family to afford the down payment for a flat of, on average, 54 square metres. Meanwhile, the time of waiting and saving has increased to more than five years. The legal system has been strengthened to provide for mortgage banks, but building societies are slow in coming to Russia. There is not sufficient trust in the legal and judicial system.

By the end of 2006 failure threatened the project. To bring more apartments to the housing market, pilot projects were developed in eleven regions of Russia. Again, unexpected consequences followed. Building material was in short supply, and the price of cement rose by 140 per cent. Meanwhile, inflation had driven the price of mortgages to a staggering 12.5 per cent (instead of the 11 per cent planned). The principle was a discomforting learning-by-doing.

The reform of the national health system was bedevilled by incompetence and waste. Corruption was endemic both in the procurement of medical equipment and in the administration, where pharmaceutical companies were asked for 'compensation' in return for major orders. In 2006 a major health insurance company was taken to court because of kickbacks. Education, even under Soviet rule a strong component of Russian culture, suffered from underfinancing and the mass exodus of capable teachers throughout the 1990s and is recovering only slowly. Everywhere computers are being introduced to schools. The problem, though, lies in the software. There is not enough money to purchase licensed systems. So pirated ones are installed, more often than not unworkable.

There is little state money going into the agricultural national project. While the big holdings are booming, cooperating with commercial banks, for the small-scale suppliers market access remains the big problem. All this goes back to the inefficiency of Russian infrastructure, the absence of market-oriented distribution, and the endless entanglements of bureaucratic red tape.

The demographic nightmare haunting Kremlin leaders as much as ordinary Russians will not soon go away. In fact it is here to stay and get worse. In the Kremlin today, strategic theory is far ahead of administrative practice. It all comes back to strengthening the home base, to giving ordinary Russians a better deal, to encouraging and sustaining more trust in the future, to reversing the decline of population and to save ethnic Russians from being outnumbered, in the not too distant future, by the Muslim population.

Putin and his people know one thing. All the oil money in the world, if it does not ultimately translate into a better life for the millions of ordinary Russians, will not benefit the future of Russia. They know about the 'oil curse' – the corrupting influence of too much money in too few hands – and they understand, in theory if not in practice, the dangers looming if the national projects fail, if the majority of Russians lose faith in Putin and his regime, and if cynicism defines the future.

8

Gazprom: the new currencies of power

'So much gold, so many diamonds ... and so much dust.'
Marquis de Custine, *Journey for Our Time*

What is good for Gazprom is good for Russia – the words that used to be said about General Motors and the United States of America are not entirely out of place for a most unusual company. Gazprom is a state within a state, the owner of most of Russia's gas fields and all the gas pipelines from Siberia to European Russia and on to Western Europe. Gazprom, which is also acquiring and controlling pipelines from Central Asia, is reconstructing the more efficient aspects of the lost empire. By using the new LNG (Liquefied Natural Gas) technologies Gazprom also sees the potential of going global.

Gazprom strategy is Russian strategy. Or is it the other way round? Only two days after the G8 meeting in St Petersburg in July 2006, where all the heads of state and of government signed a document calling for more honesty, transparency and competition, President Putin enshrined into law Gazprom's monopoly position as the sole exporter of gas from Russia. By the end of 2007, Gazprom's market capitalization was well over USD 230 billion – second to none in the world of energy or, for that matter, any other world. Analysts advised a 'strong buy' and pointed to the fact that Gazprom shares in the recent past had usually outperformed forecasts. Only a severe recession in the US or China could stand in the way of further growth, driving the price of oil downwards. The fact that Gazprom has underinvested throughout the last decade did not deter market optimism, especially after Putin had named Dmitri Medvedev, the Kremlin's man at the helm of Gazprom, to be his successor.

Local touch, global reach

Gazprom's basis is control over three natural gas fields: Nadym-Pur and Yamal Peninsula in Western Siberia and, technology permitting, the Shtokman field off the northern coast of Western Siberia. While all those fields are situated in the most forbidding environment, Shtokman, because it is offshore and any drilling platform will be threatened by icebergs and the harshest of climates, is a challenge that the Russians can only master with outside help, especially from Norway.

Natural gas is clean by comparison with any other fuel except nuclear power, friendly to the environment, and, once the pipelines are in place and well looked after – a very big 'if' indeed – easy to handle. But gas is also unrivalled as an instrument of power. Europe is dependent on natural gas, and well over a third of EU gas consumption comes from Russia. In the years to come, when North Sea gas runs out, it will be even more. But Russia too is dependent on the unimpeded flow of gas to the West. This is where vast amounts of petrodollars and petro-euros have been earned in the past and, everybody hopes, in the future. This is how Russian companies, under the thumb of the Kremlin, gain a foothold in the West.

Apart from controlling pipelines, Gazprom has been buying up assorted pieces of gas infrastructure throughout most of Europe. Wingas (a subsidiary of Wintershall, itself part of BASF) is 35.5 per cent Gazprom owned. Ten per cent of the interconnector pipeline between Belgium and Britain is owned by Gazprom, which also wants a similar share of the Netherlands-United Kingdom interconnector pipeline. Moreover, Gazprom is eyeing investment in oil, electricity and LNG- technology and transport. The deputy head of Gazprom, Alexander Medvedev (no relation of the president) has claimed without undue modesty that Gazprom is out to retain the position of leading gas supplier in Europe, continue to increase market capitalization and become 'the biggest energy company in the world'. Note: not just gas, but 'energy'. Alexei Miller, the giant company's CEO, recently remarked that Gazprom has risen from national champion to worldwide leader.

Alexander Medvedev, in a briefing in London on 22 November 2005, announced that investments in new markets (UK, USA and Asia-Pacific) are on the to-do list. The product portfolio is set to include crude oil, oil products, liquefied natural gas and power, and market presence in gas sales should extend to individual consumers at the end of the value chain. Gazprom will also work to increase gas production and develop the mineral resource base. For the foreseeable future, however, Europe is the main target export market. In 2004 gas sales to Europe accounted for 60 per cent of Gazprom's revenues, while 10 per cent of income was generated in the CIS and 30 per cent inside Russia. Meanwhile, the ex-satellite states have been pressured to pay up. Gazprom is no longer in the business of subsidizing countries like Ukraine, who show little political gratitude. Gazprom is in the business of recreating an empire based on energy.

Russia's main market is – and will remain for many years to come – Western Europe. In Europe, two German companies are the preferred partners, E.ON of Essen and BASF of Ludwigshafen. In early 2005 Gazprom and BASF signed a memorandum of understanding with regard to BASF participation in developing the Yuzhno-Russkoye oil and gas field (it became operational by the end of 2007), preceded by another memorandum of understanding with E.ON concerning gas production and power generation in Russia. For Gazprom, this is a showcase of, as Medvedev put it, 'cooperation with Western majors in Europe and worldwide'. The strategy is simple, and ambitious: 'Pooling of partners' resources enables cheaper financing . . . both Gazprom and its German partners attain a presence in all segments of the value chain. Full collaboration of the partners – from the well to the end consumers – allows for chain optimization ... guaranteeing higher reliability and security of supplies.'

Gazprom's leaders understand that the key to future success is mastering LNG technology, which they cannot do on their own. Therefore, on 7 July 2005 a memorandum of understanding was signed with Royal Dutch Shell to exchange shares in their Russian gas assets. Gazprom would have 25 per cent plus one share in Sakhalin II (this has since been expanded to 75 per cent, not without massive political pressure from the Kremlin), while Shell would acquire a 50 per cent interest in the Zapolyarnoye-Neocomian field. The overriding concern on the part of Gazprom is to acquire first-hand experience in LNG technology all the way down the supply chain. Shtokman is earmarked for LNG technology at a plant near Murmansk, with production due to start in 2010. Another gas liquefaction plant is planned in the Leningrad region on the Baltic Sea. This is not in competition with the Baltic North Stream pipeline but aims for markets further afield, especially North America.

Downstream v. upstream in Europe

While LNG remains expensive and technically very demanding, the Europeans for the time being have not much in the way of alternative supply channels, except from Norway – where there is a good deal of offshore gas – and from Denmark, the Netherlands and Scotland, where there are only a limited amount left. As long as Gazprom plays by the rules, there is little that Western countries and the EU can and will do to tame the giant. On the contrary, once Gazprom has a major stake in Western assets, so the rationale goes, Russia will be careful not to compromise its own investment. The Saudi example from the 1970s is cited, but there is a significant difference, not only with regard to size but also in principle. Between the EU and Russia a struggle is taking place: the EU wants to impose its liberal rules, while the Kremlin wants to control an ever-growing part of the European energy industry. The result is a constant tug-of-war between upstream oil and downstream industries, and the balance is shifting in favour of Gazprom. Can the West turn the tables on Russia? Not really, and the Russians know it. But the Russians, too, are tied to the West as it will take many years and enormous effort to open alternative export routes for gas from Western Siberia to reach Japan and China, let alone wait for enough climate change to allow big tankers to take the northern route around Siberia to East Asia.

Yet Europeans are worried, as they should be. Political unrest in Russia, a war of succession between the various Kremlin fractious, secessionist movements in parts of the Russian federation – all of this would inevitably impact on the gas monopoly. After a period of low prices in 1997–98 investment is still lagging behind. Political uncertainty could add to the current reluctance to invest in pipelines and extraction; the Russians were late in embracing LNG technology. Gazprom, rather than welcoming foreign direct investment, has often been hostile to outsiders, its dealings secretive and therefore risky for Western companies who have to operate under the watchful eye of the public press, financial watchdogs and governments.

The limits of power

Moreover, Gazprom's output has been flat for many years, while demand at home – at give-away prices – and abroad is bound to increase. Energy experts expect a 'gas gap' as early as 2010, and prices are likely to rise. But it is not only the instinct to corner the market that drives the Kremlin's gas and oil policies, it is also a question of power. In the process of dismembering Yukos – unpaid taxes were the pretext – and the incorporation of most of its assets into Rosneft, with some help from Western banks, the Kremlin demonstrated brutality in dealing with a Russian company that was not in line with Kremlin policy. But foreign groups have not been immune to strong-arm tactics either. Gazprom has pushed Western companies out of Siberian enterprises, most notably the giant Sakhalin II project, developed by Royal Dutch Shell together with Mitsui and Mitsubishi of Japan. This project involved the LNG technology that the Russians had so far not mastered and was, until recently, the only big operation that did not involve a Russian firm.

In 2006, the Russian authorities cited environmental transgressions in order to exclude the Western companies. Agreements were cancelled that had been concluded in the 1990s, when Russia was down and almost out, and no longer appeared advantageous. But these manoeuvres, pushed through by the Kremlin, created widespread concern about the future. In the West, parallels were seen between the dismemberment of Yukos and Sakhalin II. The London *Economist** cited an old KGB adage: 'Give me the man, and I shall find you the crime.'

The European Union, after having worked on the European Energy Charter for the last fifteen or so years, has not made much headway with the Russian authorities. The Eurocrats of Brussels aim for reciprocity, hoping to repeat the experience of the 1970 and early 1980s when after two price explosions Arab petrodollars were converted into industrial and other investment in the West, thus creating a network of interdependence. Can this kind of strategic deal be achieved with Russia's rulers? Gazprom wishes to acquire an assured stake in downstream industries, while European companies want to invest upstream in

* 16 December 2006

Russia. It sounds like a perfect match, except that it does not work.

The EU, particularly EU president Barroso and German chancellor Angela Merkel want an agreed legal framework to facilitate two-way investment, while the Kremlin wants asset swaps. 'Europe wants openness, Russia wants control.'* The Russians fear that the European dwarfs want to bind the Russian Gulliver through their legal constructions, and resent it. Meanwhile, reciprocity works in Russia's favour. By the end of 2007 Gazprom already had investments in most of the twenty-seven EU countries – including, in Germany's Ruhr area, the first-league football club Schalke 04. Gazprom not only invests in energy-related fields like storage facilities and distribution networks but also goes beyond this. In the Kremlin the EU is ill-understood in its supranational appearance and shared sovereignty, and therefore the Russians, following the time-honoured principle of 'divide and rule', tend to conclude bilateral deals with German, Belgian, French and Italian companies. Thus, Gazprom gains direct access to consumers in the West. Meanwhile, the EU's energy charter, meant to create a legal framework for European investment in the Russian energy sector, is unable to move forward because the Russians refuse to ratify it.

This is a serious conflict of policy: the EU is dependent on Russian natural gas, and Russia needs the steady flow of Western consumption. The Europeans negotiate on rules, the Russians on deals. During the Cold War this difference of approach was taken for granted as immutable. Today, the relationship is different and the EU is trying, without much support from individual states, to export its standards of good behaviour and partnership and tame the Russian bear. The EU wants to extend its version of good governance to Russia, especially to Gazprom, which still looks more like the Gas Ministry of Soviet times than like a global player second to none. Brussels cannot accept the Russian approach to reciprocity without compromising its free-market principles and its norms of industrial governance. The EU treaty forbids discrimination against an investor on the basis of nationality. Banning Gazprom from investing in Western Europe would be hard to push through against the wishes of the individual companies who want to do their own deals with Gazprom. The EU has to insist on competition, fair play and transparency, even in the face of powerful

* Katinka Barysch in the *Financial Times*, 3 September 2007

and Kremlin-connected Gazprom. But how far can it go without causing an open rift? What is happening is a clash of strategies as part of a conflict between industrial civilizations, with natural gas attracting ever higher prices.

The EU is not only facing tough Russian resistance, it is also the big companies at home like E.ON and Gaz de France who oppose the principle of 'unbundling', i.e. opening national networks to competition. The EU Commission cannot allow monopolies to form under its eyes. The rationale, seen from Brussels, is not only lower prices for the consumer but also lower profits for the producer. As long as competing companies use the gas networks, no single player can abuse the market – be it Gaz de France or Gazprom. The outcome is open.

Europe as seen from the control room

Meanwhile, Gazprom continues to develop and enact a continental strategy. The company headquarters, a bold concrete and dark-blue glass tower in the centre of Moscow, with many heavy black premium-class cars from Germany parked in front, commands respect far and wide. Those fortunate enough to have access to the inner sanctum take the lift to the topmost floor. That is where the displays in the control room show the gas pipelines that cover most of the Eurasian landmass, i.e. from the easternmost tip of Siberia to the southern end of the Iberian peninsula and on to North Africa. The display shows, for instance, Algerian gas being transported to Spain and, via Tunisia, to Italy. In all innocence one of the Gazprom directors explains that, to improve Europe's energy security, it might be a good idea to link the Russian pipeline system with the one coming from North Africa; nobody mentioned the word cartel. What is also on display, perhaps prematurely, is the future North Stream pipeline from Russia to Germany through the Baltic Sea. There was also on show a pipeline to be built to the Far East, but Gazprom planners cannot overlook the fact that Chinese companies will soon be unable to pay the prices Gazprom can demand from European consumers.

The sky is not the limit. LNG technology will, before long, work to the advantage of European consumers and bring gas from Qatar to, for example, Britain. And so will alternative energies. It was Putin who said that Russia has to be careful not to raise prices too high, or the premium on alternative energy will increase to tipping point. What is not on display at Gazprom's top floor, of course, is the Nabucco pipeline – the EU-project to allow Central Asian gas to bypass the Russian system – much to the chagrin of Gazprom.

So far, Gazprom is landbound. But one day soon, with help from Norway, Europe, and the US, LNG technology will allow not only the gas producers of Qatar in the Persian Gulf but also Gazprom to free itself from some of its terrestrial restrictions and become an amphibious animal.

When President Putin nominated Dmitri Medvedev, for years the chairman of Gazprom's overseeing board, to be his successor in the Kremlin, the all-Russian share index at the Moscow stock exchange jumped forward, and Gazprom shares gained 2.5 per cent within minutes, quoted at USD 14.25 per share. Whatever the democratic shortcomings of the preceding Duma elections – there were many, some serious – Russian and foreign investors were united in the belief that stability is more important than democracy, that Medvedev would be the best choice available, and that his Western, enlightened views hold a promise for Russia's place in the world. Little did they realize that Medvedev's greatest asset, his liberal charm, is also his greatest weakness, as he surely does not have much control over the FSB networks running the Kremlin and, by implication, most of Russia's power structure. Much as in the recent past, investors see the continuity of the Putin-Medvedev couple, under whatever label, as the guarantee of pro-business price and investment strategies. Medvedev, in the past, was not only Putin's *chef de cabinet* in the presidential administration but, at the same time, his young representative among the Gazprom directors. This personal union was to assure that the national interest – as defined in the Kremlin – would always prevail.

Medvedev, soft spoken, competent and worlds apart from the old Soviet apparatchik, made himself known at the 2007 Davos World Economic Forum with a speech – in retrospect a kind of business card issued to the great and the good – that not only named the chief Russian weaknesses but also the ways and means to tackle them. Among the weaknesses he listed the dangerous dependence on the export of resources and, therefore, on the swings of world markets, the miserable demographic situation, the weak infrastructure, the decline of the educational system and, worst of all, endemic corruption.

Medvedev argued for more openness towards the West, invited Western investment and Western technology but also promised vast investment in education, research and development. He is young enough to think of the world after oil and natural gas. He is also aware that Gazprom's known gas reserves are enough, at current production rates, for almost 180 years. And he must be painfully aware that without very major investment in pipelines, pumping stations and new exploration and extraction huge problems lie ahead – problems not only for Gazprom but for the whole of Russia. As President, the man from Gazprom has a painful agenda to deal with.

The rise of Gazprom over the past decade has been the rise of Russia. Gazprom, going with the tide of energy prices, was the beneficiary not only of a stable business cycle among Western industrialized nations, leading to ever-increasing demand, but also of the rise of China and India and their ever growing thirst for energy in whatever form – and at whatever price. Natural gas, moreover, answers the prayers of Western nations for environmentally compatible energy, thus putting a virtuous premium on Russia's chief commodity.

By land, by sea and everywhere

Throughout Russia, Gazprom is by far the most popular company. In a recent opinion poll one in two Russians named Gazprom as the workplace of their dreams; they may have been thinking less of Siberia's unforgiving winters and mosquito-filled summers and more of the regular pay, the generous benefits, the assured pensions, the prestige, the housing, the hotels and hospitals the company runs, in a tradition from Soviet times. In order to attract the key personnel needed for research and development in Siberia, Gazprom does indeed, on top of high salaries, have to offer incentives otherwise unknown.

Putin's favourite football club is Zenit St Petersburg, who won the national championship in November 2007. Not difficult to guess who the main sponsor might be. Alexei Miller, head of Gazprom, also owns the media conglomerate Gazprom Media. Both *Izvestia* and *Komsomolskaya Pravda*, the two most influential newspapers of the country, are owned by Gazprom Media. *Izvestia*, in earlier times a serious paper, is now part of the popular press, selling juicy but non-political stories after most of the more critical minds have left the paper. *Komsomolskaya*

Pravda likewise would not dream of criticizing people in high places. Most conspicuous in this kind of streamlining is the TV station NTV (Independent TV). Throughout the 1990s the station could be relied upon to ruffle government feathers, but after it was taken over by the gas giant most of the journalists moved to the *New Times* and the *Moscow Times*. Film production, too, is taken care of through NTV-Kino. The internet is not left out, the popular videoportal RuTube (analogous to YouTube) is now also part of Gazprom's omnipresence. Gazprom Media makes sure, meanwhile, that the media are friendly towards Putin and his people. One way or the other: Gazprom is Russia, and Russia is Gazprom.

A state corporation

In the Kremlin's strategy under Putin 'reprivatization' – undoing the privatizations that took place under Yeltsin – has become the guiding principle of economic policy, certainly in the key areas of technology and resources. In this, Gazprom is the leader. Putin, however, in November 2007 reassured German business leaders by saying: 'The development of state corporations is not an end in itself. They were created in order to mark the vectors of development in those areas where private business does not like to be involved. We shall not keep those state corporations for ever. We are not going to develop state capitalism; that is not our way. But without support from the state we will not be able to reconstruct some important segments of the economy.' Putin added, somewhat cryptically, that those state corporations should 'function under free market conditions'.

For the time being and far into the future, Gazprom functions as monopolies function. And some of its pricing policies are visibly inspired by Kremlin policies. The Orange revolution that led to the defeat of the Kremlin's favourite in Ukraine, was followed – after many years of negotiations – by a sharp increase in prices and widespread anxiety all over Gazprom-dependent Europe. At the end of 2005 relations between Russia and Ukraine came to a grinding halt. In the past, Gazprom had supplied Ukraine with natural gas at the rate of USD 50 per 1000 cubic metres – a sweetheart deal by any standard. The rationale was that Ukrainians, faced with the choice between a cold winter and a candidate acceptable to the Kremlin, would instinctively vote for

Victor Yanukovych. But he lost the 2004 elections to Victor Yushchenko.

The rulers in the Kremlin were not amused, accused Western NGOs of meddling in Ukraine's affairs, suspected the CIA of undermining the pro-Russian candidate and feared that the Orange revolution might be a contagious disease in Russia and elsewhere. Gazprom, pretending innocence, suggested a new pricing system 'on a market basis', raising the price to USD 230. When Kiev refused, Gazprom sliced its exports to Ukraine on 1 January 2006–and alarm bells rang all over Europe. Europeans were not only wringing their hands over Ukraine. Given the fact that 80 per cent of Russian natural gas to Europe comes via Ukraine, they also had reason to fear the worst for their own comfort. Russia suddenly stood accused of blackmailing weaker neighbours. Who could tell what would come next?

Energy is destiny

Gazprom's threats to cut off energy supply were in open breach of the European Energy Charter, negotiated and signed by the Russian government though not yet ratified. This contained a non-interruption rule, and failure to comply with such basic international rules of behaviour was bound to raise serious doubts about Gazprom's reliability as a supplier, far beyond the energy dimension.

On 4 January 2006 Moscow and Kiev settled the matter on a compromise base for the next five years. Under the terms of that deal, natural gas from Central Asia – Turkmenistan, Uzbekistan, Kazakhstan – would be transported via the Russian Gazprom net to Europe and sold at a price of USD 50, while Gazprom would feed into the mix at Gazprom's full rate of USD 230. In commercial terms, everything seemed to have been settled amicably. Politically, however, things were more complicated. By securing delivery of Central Asian gas via Russia, Gazprom saw to it that direct deliveries to Europe via the Black Sea and Ukraine would not materialize soon. Moreover, by maintaining its initial demand for USD 230 the Russians signalled what the future pricing situation would be, especially if taking into account the dollar's decline vis-à-vis the Euro. Initially, Gazprom wanted to establish a *droit de regard* over Ukraine for the Kremlin. As it turned out, the crisis gave Russia some leverage over Ukraine through Europe's anxieties.

What looked like a squabble between a powerful monopolist and a poor consumer was in fact a conflict over Ukraine's geopolitical orientation between East and West, and in the last analysis over Russia's ability to restore its geopolitical fortunes. In 2005 and 2006 the Orange revolution had been the spectre haunting Russia, and the stage-managed elections to the state Duma on 2 December 2007 owed much of their bitterness and pettiness to this trauma, second only to the memory of the Soviet implosion. Kremlin leaders had learnt the hard way how suddenly their fortunes could change, and this time around they wanted to be on their guard. Therefore the Kremlin party over-reacted to any democratic expression of criticism, let alone serious opposition to the Kremlin, unsteadily steering between the instinctive desire for full control and the need to save democratic appearances inside Russia and outside. Ever since 2004 the Kremlin saw the Orange revolution as the writing on the wall, justifiably or not. The comeback of the blonde power-lady Yulia Timoshenko in December 2007 only strengthened misgivings in the Kremlin.

In the Soviet past, oil and gas exports to satellite states had served as the Russian equivalent of soft power, and in the final days and weeks of the Soviet system the International Department of the Central Committee, headed by former Soviet ambassador to Germany Valentin Falin, reassured itself that the satellite states would not dare to leave the Soviet camp for fear of being left out in the cold. Energy prices were the Kremlin's long leash, or so the Soviet strategists believed.

After 2004 and especially after those cold winter days at the beginning of 2006, those memories were acutely painful. In the future, would Gazprom, more powerful than ever, at prices higher than ever, be the Kremlin's instrument to punish unwilling neighbours and give a premium to others? The Russians pointed at Western demands for fair, i.e. market-driven, pricing as a precondition for their entry into the World Trade Organization, but they continued to charge different prices to different countries – the highest prices of course to be paid by the rich West Europeans.

Since then, Europeans have had to realize, courtesy of Gazprom, that their access to energy is not only a matter of pipelines and prices, but also of politics and power. The Kremlin in its turn, while using energy as the continuation of strategy by other means, pretends that no such nexus exists. Gazprom is an integral part of the Great Game, and it operates on two levels. One is commercial, creating networks deep into Western Europe and using energy dependence to convert petrodollars into market share on a long-term basis and even with an eye on the post-oil, post-gas economy of the future. The other is political and strategic, reminding the Europeans of their ever-growing dependence on Russian oil and gas, and extracting a political price far beyond what a commercial partnership warrants.

The Kremlin's use of energy to further its global ambitions far beyond the commercial sphere will be a given in international affairs for a long time to come, and European nations had better see to it that their dependence on one source of energy and one kind of supplier is under control. It was at the EU summit at Lahti, towards the end of the Finnish presidency in the second semester of 2006, that the energy question was raised, and how to deal with Putin. The *tour de table* did yield some platitudes about saving energy and promoting alternative fuels but failed to come up with any revolutionary ideas; it was left to the EU's High Representative for Foreign and Security Policy Xavier Solana to say that if the Europeans wanted to be less dependent on Russia the only practical alternative would be to cultivate nuclear energy and start building new power plants. Of course, the presidents and heads of governments only shook their heads at so much realism.

Meanwhile, Gazprom is forging ahead, encouraged and controlled by the Kremlin. No downstream, no upstream – this is how the commercial gas equation is being described at the Gazprom HQ in Moscow. Gazprom holds the monopoly for Russian gas exports and wants to control as much as possible of other, complementary markets. The Ukraine deal of early 2006 is a case in point: Gazprom gained indirect control over Central Asian exports and pipelines. Moreover, Gazprom also wants to link its networks, via Italy's Enel, with the southern pipelines transporting gas from Algeria into Europe. With an eye on LNG and the future of sea transport, Gazprom is even trying to invest in gas fields and transportation systems as far away as Bolivia and Nigeria.

Pursuing a dual strategy of commercial and strategic interests, the Russians want access to distribution networks throughout Western Europe and are willing to concede minority share holdings to Western companies. One such example is the complex relationship of BASF and Gazprom. The day after Medvedev was named by Putin for the succession, the leaders of BASF and their Russian counterparts at Gazprom, assisted by German foreign minister Frank-Walter Stein-meier, celebrated their joint efforts in extracting gas from the vast Yuzhno-Russkoye field in Western Siberia ('From Jamburg to Ham-burg' is the slogan). While celebrating and pushing the start-button in Moscow, thousands of kilometres away and working at −40 degrees Celsius, employees of Severneftegazprom welcomed the first gas from the new field developed in partnership by BASF – through its Kassel-based subsidiary Wintershall – and Gazprom, promising something between 600,000 and one million cubic metres of natural gas. The overall size of that field corresponds roughly to Russia's production throughout 2006. Annual exports to Germany, now at 40 billion cubic metres, could be assured from Yuzhno-Russkoye for a minimum of fifteen years. In 2009 production at the field is planned to rise to an annual 25 billion cubic metres.

Via Wintershall, BASF holds 25 per cent minus one share in Sev-erneftegazprom, who hold the licence to exploit the field. In addition, BASF holds shares without voting rights in the Russian company, assuring the Germans 35 per cent of future profits.

This is the upstream side. In return, on the downstream side Gazprom raised its stake in Wingas, a Wintershall subsidiary selling gas, from 35 to 50 per cent (minus one share). In addition Gazprom has 49 per cent in a Wintershall subsidiary producing oil in Libya. This helps the Russian gas giant in its strategy to seamlessly control the entire value chain from the source to the consumer. At BASF head-quarters in Ludwigshafen this is seen not as a step towards absolute market dominance by Gazprom but as a fair deal between production and distribution.

Meanwhile, E.ON, not having secured a share in the Yuzhno-Russkoye field, is out to find other lucrative business with Gazprom. E.ON is another major player in the energy field in Germany and Europe. There seems to be agreement with Gazprom that certain assets owned by E.ON are open for Gazprom participation. So far, the project comprises natural gas reservoirs in Central and Western Europe (for instance Belgium) and power stations.

All three companies are already cooperating in the Baltic North Stream pipeline, planned to carry an annual volume of 55 billion cubic metres of natural gas from Siberia and, in the not too distant future, from the northern Shtokman field to Western Europe. The Baltic pipeline is bypassing Ukraine and Poland. This means that those countries are not only losing the lucrative transit fees but can also, if the Kremlin so wishes, be cut off from supplies without directly hurting more important customers like, for instance, Germany or France. The Swedish Defence Research Agency, reflecting concern throughout the Scandinavian and Baltic countries, in early 2007 published a report warning that this will divide the EU and increase European dependence on Russia. Poland is anxious, while countries like the Netherlands, so far relying on their own dwindling production from North Sea fields, will be linked to the new pipeline. In the south, Russia has built the Blue Stream pipeline supplying gas to Turkey. Now Gazprom wants to extend the line to Hungary (80 per cent of Hungary's gas comes from Russia) and link up with Italy's system; once in Italy, it is linked to the gas coming from Algeria. At the same time, the EU's Nabucco project, devised to bring Central Asian gas to Europe via the Black Sea and Ukraine, is being sidelined. When the Hungarians, relative newcomers to the EU, were accused of undermining the EU's energy policy, the tart response from Budapest was that you cannot undermine something that does not exist.

Do not irritate the bear

Indeed, while the Europeans cannot agree on a mutually acceptable energy strategy – Germany religiously against nuclear power plants, France religiously for, the rest divided – Europe's dependence on Russian gas is growing, at somewhere between 40 and 50 per cent of overall consumption. Alternatives are expensive, technologically immature or politically incalculable.

Of course Russia's well-being also depends on continuing high prices for oil and gas, and on the ability of Europeans to pay up. But while China gobbles up more and more of global gas and oil, underlining and strengthening Russia's key position, all the efforts invested in the European Energy Charter over the last decade have not strengthened the hands of the Europeans. The equation is ever more in favour of the Russians – and Putin knows this. He is on record as saying that Gazprom is 'a powerful lever of economic and political influence in the world.'

Today's currency of power is energy. The Soviet Union's number one currency of power was military might, and oil and gas, after the first oil price shock in 1973–74, helped to pay for it. It was the sudden fall of oil prices in 1985 – due to the Saudi strategy of pricing the Iranians out of the war with Iraq – that administered the *coup de grâce* to the Soviet system. The shock was repeated in 1997–8 when, once again, the price of a barrel of oil touched USD 10 and remained there for the best part of a year. This has taught the Russians some painful lessons. The Kremlin wants absolute control over Russian energy reserves and production, control over the pipelines conducting the ever more precious stuff through Russia and beyond, whether Rosneft for oil or Gazprom for gas, and long-term contracts with the Europeans to hedge against another sudden fall in oil prices. What could be observed, not so long ago, when Mikhail Khodorkovsky was accused of tax evasion and other assorted misdeeds and the Yukos company was taken over by Kremlin-sponsored competitors, was an object lesson in Russian energy strategy that should not be lost on the West. The meaning was clear: you follow our rules, or else.

Most European governments are careful not to alienate the Russian bear. They would rather join the race to Moscow to obtain special favours. By now, the European Energy Charter, basically meant to bind Russia and make it part of a continent-wide balance of economic power – Russian natural resources v. Western industrial knowhow – has been written off. Instead, the Kremlin seems to aim for a gas OPEC together with Algeria and Iran and, possibly, Qatar. Putin has said: 'It would be a good idea to coordinate our efforts.' Russia, Iran and Qatar hold no less than 60 per cent of the world's known gas reserves. Gazprom has already signed a memorandum of understanding with Algeria to cooperate in gas production. To Europeans the idea of a producer cartel is sold in terms of improved energy security. In fact it would make it even more difficult for the Europeans to find alternative suppliers in bad times or, in good times, serious price competition.

Even at the worst of times in Soviet relations with the West, energy has continued to flow. The sombre warnings by successive US presidents that Europeans trusted the Russians too much and received too much of their energy from Siberia proved to be unfounded. In 1982, at the height of the INF (Intermediate Nuclear Forces) crisis, German industry, backed by both Chancellor Schmidt and Chancellor Kohl, wanted the gas-pipeline deal – and got it in the face of stiff US opposition. Why should today's situation be more alarming?

Predictability: unpredictable

There are significant differences both in philosophy and in the distribution of power. The Soviet system, because it was theory-driven and rigidly administered, was, in spite of all its deficiencies, fairly predictable. Today, Russia's precarious stability is dependent on the continuing high price of oil and gas, and on Mr Putin's continuing control over the apparat and its policies. In the past, the energy relationship between the Soviets and the West stopped at the border. Today's Gazprom, successor to the former energy ministry, reaches out for as large a piece of the Western distributive networks as possible, and aims even further. While in the past Soviet energy policy was run by technocrats, though supervised by the Central Committee's International Department, today the energy business is under the control of ex-KGB types obsessed with money and power. No wonder that people in Europe have a natural apprehension about their homes being heated and their industries supplied by people from whom, to use a well-worn phrase, they would never buy a second-hand car.

The irony was that in Soviet days commercial interests would override political manoeuvring, while today this is an open question. Of course, Russia is dependent on a constant flow of cash from Europe, while Europe is equally dependent on a constant flow of energy from Russia. But, in a recent study from Sweden, fifty-five cut-offs were listed, explicit threats or coercive price rises (such as vis-à-vis Ukraine in January 2006), while only eleven had no political underpinnings.

Underinvestment is another threat to the uninterrupted flow of supplies to the West. The three major Gazprom fields, accounting for three-quarters of production, are rapidly declining at an annual rate of 6 to 7 per cent. Never mind the proven reserves said to last for more than a century at present rates of extraction, the crisis of the 1990s cast a long shadow. Domestic demand is growing at 2 per cent per annum, and the gas infrastructure is creaking, with gas being sold at extremely low prices and mostly wasted, much to the dismay of Gazprom's bosses. Gazprom has indeed invested in pipelines and downstream assets, but development of new sources lags behind and could well become a serious problem, both at home and abroad, from 2010. Even today, Gazprom has to buy from Turkmenistan. There could be more to come.

Can oil go back to USD 10?

Before investing in new fields, Gazprom insists on guarantees concerning prices and quantities from major players in the West, notably Gaz de France, ENI of Italy, VNG in the eastern part of Germany, Wingas and Ruhrgas in the west. Ruhrgas has a 7 per cent share in Gazprom and a seat on the overseeing board. When the gas assets of Yukos came to auction, Gazprom was too careful to take part in the bidding. Instead ENI and ENEL of Italy picked up what was on offer, only to cede it to Gazprom against a foothold in Russian gas and oil fields.

Missionary zeal on the part of the EU for fairness, transparency and mutual interdependence has led the EU to promote the European Energy Charter – but not to go much further. To convert Russia to the ways of the market for energy has proved difficult in the past, and outright impossible at present and well into the future. It will also be difficult, and probably impossible, to prevent European member states from scrambling for oil and gas at favourable conditions granted by Moscow. No EU energy strategy worth its name is in sight. So the EU Commission can do little, but it must be done: unbundle the downstream networks, bring in competition in the face of opposition from E.ON and Gaz de France and others, and bring down prices so that the premium for being on the inside with Gazprom is somewhat reduced. The EU Commission's president Manuel Barroso wants to protect European energy companies against the dominating influence of non-European giants, but the Commission is up against strong headwinds.

Are there alternatives to charming Gazprom? LNG from Africa and Latin America could help to reduce the power of the Russian gas giant over Western markets, but this is an expensive technology, still in its infancy, and requires long-term commitments because of the enormous cost of investment. And the Gazprom explorers are not sleeping.

Obtaining direct access to Central Asian and Caspian gas would be helpful for Europe's diversification of supply, but part of this strategy was already frustrated when, on 4 January 2006, Ukraine signed the deal with Gazprom that would bring gas from Central Asia via the Russian pipeline system to Eastern Europe. On the chessboard of European energy Ukraine was saved, for the time being, from the cold. But the Nabucco project, the EU's strategic pipeline project to bypass Russia, has been seriously downgraded.

Saving energy, developing alternative resources, reconsidering nuclear power – if the West wants to have an equitable relationship not only with Gazprom but with Russia as a political player, the energy equation must change. But whatever new technologies may be about to weigh in, energy will be the most important of the new currencies of power. Gazprom will be the number one player.

9
Power and the people

'Here to lie is to protect the social order, to speak the truth is to destroy the state. Nothing is lacking in Russia, except liberty ... that is to say life.'

Marquis de Custine, *Journey for Our Time*

Imitation is the sincerest form of flattery. The mass rally organized in Moscow in the run-up to the elections on 2 December 2007, to provide a stage for Vladimir Putin, owed more than a little detail to Republican and Democratic convention in pre-election USA. It was widely reported throughout Russia and beyond. The audience in Moscow's Luzhniki sports stadium consisted largely of teenagers; some had daubed their faces in the blue-white-red colours of Russia, while others chanted old Soviet songs and waved banners in front of television cameras, eager to convey a message of strength, vigour and patriotism. The organizers did not even shrink from sending in a girls' band, who chanted that if they wanted a man he would have to be like Putin, strong and decisive. This was, to be sure, anything but Soviet- style heaviness and formality. But it revealed an imaginative approach to staging a symbolic event rooted in former times. The rally was the centrepiece of the campaign, just ten days away from election day. It crowned the most intense election campaign seen since Soviet times – if election is the right word for a referendum organized to secure massive support for the party of power, United Russia, and, even more important, for the Kremlin's incumbent. No other party than United Russia, where power and big business met, had much chance to make an impact. All the others had been harassed in every conceivable way by officialdom, and had been all but denied even a sporting chance.

Putin for president?

Putin marched to the rostrum shaking the hands of the faithful, American style, left and right. Wearing a smart black sports jacket with a turtle-neck pullover underneath, he gave a rousing speech. Before he had come to power, that was the leitmotif, chaos had beset the country, enemies were trying to grab what they could, terrorists were eyeing their targets, the outside world was envious of Russia's rebirth, gas, oil and newly found strength. Ever since, the wisdom, decisiveness and energy of the President had turned the tide – Putin in his speech did not of course dwell on the fact that it was the rising tide of oil and gas at ever higher prices that had carried Russia to its new wealth and standing in the world at large. Putin offered a tonic to a deeply troubled nation not at all sure that the windfall profits were shared equitably or that a new age of prosperity for the masses or of fairness and justice was dawning. 'Together, my friends, we have already done so much,' he told the crowd and, via TV, all of Russia. 'We have strengthened the sovereignty and revived the integrity of Russia. We have revived the power of the law and the supremacy of the constitution. Despite grave losses and sacrifice, thanks to the courage and unity of the people of Russia, the aggression of international terrorism against our Russia has been repelled.'

Stylish TV commercials were underlining the message of newly found power and glory. 'Today we are successful in politics, economics, arts, sciences, sports,' people were told on huge billboards. Prominent TV personalities sang, to the sound of a brass band, in praise of the leadership and, above all others, Putin: 'We have reasons for pride. We enjoy respect and deference. We are citizens of a great country, and we have great victories ahead of us. Putin's plan is a victory for Russia.'

Time and again Putin declared victory. But over what enemy? The greater the danger the greater the saviour. Was Russia going to war? Not really. Russia was not even channelling disproportionate amounts of oil money into arms or the army. The pompous language merely addressed a widespread sense of both pride and paranoia, deeply in-grained in the public mind and ready to be mobilized by the Kremlin.

Pride and paranoia?

Of course this sounds contradictory but it makes sense when compared with the fact that the vast majority of voters had not seen much benefit from the new oil wealth and that the Kremlin is uncertain how to channel the necessary amounts of money into infrastructure, pensions, or wages without setting in train a financial meltdown far beyond the recent two-figure inflation. So the parliamentary elections, instead of addressing painful bread-and-butter questions, were artificially elevated to a celebration of Russia's greatness, a reminder of grave dangers past and present, from inside and from outside, and unspecified promises.

The Putin plan is widely advertised, a road map to the promised land, but without any detail, landmarks or clearly defined goals. Whatever it means, it hints at the fact that Putin and his people want to keep power independent of the controlled risk of elections and that voters are being persuaded to believe that without Putin all their achievements over the last eight years would be lost. The very vagueness of the Putin Plan implies that it is for the long term, a projection far into the future, that its realization needs a strong man, and that this man can be no other than Putin himself – a not-so-hidden sign that Putin will be around to help, direct and, if necessary, play the saviour. During the election campaign he was announced, in no uncertain terms, as the national 'leader'. This is a new terminology that indicates what is in the offing. Not a *voshd*, which would be reminiscent of Stalin, but also not a mere chairman, of whom there were many in Soviet times. Secretary General is also that has had its time. Thus, national 'leader' has become a new word in the Russian language, sounding sufficiently innocent and also open to creative interpretations.

So far, no one in the government or in the United Russia party machinery has bothered to seriously spell out the detail of what is universally acclaimed as the Putin Plan. If people really wanted to know the long and the short of it, a Putin aide joked, they should read all the President's speeches and find out. In fact it would take away the mystery if the plan were displayed and exposed to daylight like a modern-day version of the Gosplan of Soviet times. It is, at best, a roadmap, and only the driver is supposed to know where he is going.

Remaking the past

Putin understands that the post-Soviet spiritual void has to be filled. What he has to offer is a mix of history and religion, of enemies at the gates and enemies within the walls. History, from the ancient Rus to the more acceptable exploits of Stalin, is carefully and selectively reconstructed in schoolbooks and on TV screens to remind Russians of glories past and present: Gagarin without the Gulag. The great national holiday is no longer Red October (7 November 1917, when Lenin ousted the moderates through a coup) but 4 November 1612, marking the end of the time of troubles, dual rule and foreign occupation – in this case by Polish invaders.

The evil spirits of the Soviet past are being exorcised without too much noise. Both the Kremlin's chief ideologist Victor Suslov and Metropolit Cyril emphasized that this day marked 'the greatest historical event in the history of the nation'. A day of unity of the people exceeding in importance even 9 May 1945, the day of triumph in the Great Patriotic War, for four decades the unassailable pinnacle of Russian remembrance and Soviet self-congratulation. The Metropolit stated on TV: 'What happened in the seventeenth century was worse than the events from 1941 to 1945 because in the Great Patriotic War the enemy did not occupy Moscow, Hitler did not set foot in Moscow, the Germans did not destroy the vertical of power, the enemy had not provoked internal struggle which would have paralysed our country. In those distant times everything was different, and that is why they are called the time of troubles.'4 November holds many lessons – not so much about the past but about the future, Putin style.

2007 was the year not only to celebrate the glorious resistance to Polish invaders but also to remember ninety years of the Bolshevik revolution and seventy years of the Great Terror. While the founding myth of Soviet rule was passed over in official silence and only the diehard communists found something to glorify, the memory of Stalin's terror was hardly more visible. There were a few mourners who flocked to the silent dialogue between the Solovietsky-granite boulder in front of the Lubyanka and the resurrected monument to 'Iron Felix'.

Ambiguity lingers on concerning the inheritance of Lenin, his standard statue still present in many a city square across the country, showing the way to a glorious future. Uncertainty surrounds the Russian pantheon, while Russian greatness is promoted as the unifying principle. All the Russian heroes qualify for their new role by triumphing over foreign enemies, like Alexander Nevsky over the Teutonic Knights, Ivan the Terrible over the Tatars, Peter the Great over the Swedes. Stalin in all of this is a great embarrassment – not displayed in stone or bronze but very much present in people's hearts and minds. The Christ Redeemer Cathedral on Red Square in the centre of Moscow and Russia; torn down by Stalin in a brutal act of destruction was recreated, in concrete, under Moscow mayor Yuri Luzhkov, with generous contributions from oligarchs who wanted to be in the good books if not of God Almighty then at least of the mayor. To this day there is no national, as opposed to local, monument to Stalin's – and the NKVD's – horrors, and there is not much chance that there will be one any time soon. The FSB, having risen from the ashes of the KGB, is not likely to press for an agonizing reappraisal.

In the absence of a national consensus on the meaning of seventy years of communist rule, an open and outspoken intellectual discussion will have to wait for a long, long time. Remembering the Great Terror and the Gulag archipelago will remain in the private domain, rather than the public sphere. What has survived is the memory of the victims – even among the New Russians one can suddenly come across the memory of a grandfather who was shot or an uncle who was taken away in the early hours never to be seen again. To ask who the perpetrators were and what they bequeathed to Russia's present and future is not fashionable, and possibly hazardous to people's health. There are books and films. It is not a forbidden discourse. But there is wide consensus, whether victims or victimizers, that it is best to forget. So the trauma lingers on.

Russia today is a country of mixed feelings. But, together with the timeless reassurance offered by religion, visibly embraced by Yeltsin and even more so by Putin, a narrative of Greatness is being celebrated in the form of both great suffering and great triumph. In pre-Revolutionary times the Tsar, the Orthodox Church and the people were united in a Holy Trinity. But this is a thing of the past, as twenty million Muslims within Russia would make it a recipe for disaster if the state were to embrace, wholesale, the Orthodox Church. Kremlin leaders have to manoeuvre carefully, having seen after 1990 that things can fall apart overnight. At present, an uneasy coexistence prevails, but with the numbers of ethnic Russians going down and the numbers of Muslims going up, not much more than uneasy coexistence is to be expected. Putin and his people are not interested in precipitating a showdown.

An empire no more

Nation building or state building? It is a very real dilemma. The ambiguity was born with the new Russia when the Soviet Union went the way of all flesh. Putin and whoever follows in his footsteps will have to avoid ever being forced into a decision which can only produce problems and, in fact, a crisis of state and society. How can one consolidate the state and the nation when there is no congruence or anything close to it? Ethnic and religious diversity, accentuated by the Islamic revival in the south, stands in the way of straightforward political doctrine. Compromises are dictated by reality from within and from without. Therefore the common denominator is rather Greatness than Russianness and, with regard to the present and future, standing together against the enemy.

'Normalization' is the new key term, announced in all directions and all dimensions. It sounds reassuring to most Russians, but what counts as normal is defined from above. This would also serve to bolster the Kremlin's claim to 'sovereign democracy', as Putin calls the particular blend of authoritarianism and public acclaim developed under his presidency.

In this situation holding serious elections could amount to risking the whole blend of authority from above and democracy from below. United Russia, the 'party of power', as it was called, offered the most pragmatic of answers to an impossible question. In fact the December 2007 elections, or rather the confirmation of the party of power by not-so-secret ballot, were characterized by three striking political features.

Saviour of the nation

First, Putin had everybody guessing as to his own plans for the future: anything but a third term. Referring to the constitution and his respect for its letter, he repeated time and again that he would not be available for first manipulating the constitution and then accepting a third term. Was he bluffing? Or was he revealing his innermost feelings and aiming for *otium cum dignitate* (leisure with dignity), as the Romans would have called a retreat from the Forum Romanum and the centre of the state to the margins of power? Putin even went so far as to indicate a certain philosophical weariness with having to nudge the country towards a post-Soviet promised land without being able to effect change at a stroke. At times, he seemed to prefer the presidential palace near Sochi to the Moscow Kremlin, running the presidency and the country from his more convenient southern headquarters. This period of serenity, pretended or genuine, was visibly over when the election campaign began to get under steam. Putin allowed United Russia to adopt him as their 'national leader' and number one without, however, joining the party. A strange ambiguity indeed, suiting a tsar more than a democratic politician. Meanwhile, United Russia was elevated to the rank of party of power.

Second, while Putin carefully marked his distance from all the political parties, even creating another party, Just Russia, – to the left of United Russia, the brutal power struggle behind Kremlin walls, extending into the secretive quarters of the intelligence services and the financial world, seems to have forced his hand, steered him into the thick of the electoral battle and compelled him to throw his hat into the ring. Obviously the balance of power was shifting and threatening to spin out of control. So Putin had to assert his role as the supreme powerbroker. What would have been the alternative? Nobody outside the Kremlin can tell, but the rumour mill produced all kinds of explanations, including an unconcealed struggle between various branches of the intelligence services for the spoils of power.

Third, and most conspicuous, during the run-up to the election the United Russia campaign took on a decidedly nationalistic tone, accusing unspecified foreign forces of scheming against the great motherland and denouncing every opponent as being in the pockets of foreign governments.

The Nasi youth organization of United Russia borrowed phraseology, hymns and marches from the time of their fathers and mothers, who in their own youth had to display fiery Komsomol loyalty. Although last-minute opinion polls indicated that Putin's popularity was well over 60 per cent and that his party would win hands down, the nervous energy invested in the campaign, the suppression of any opposition through the 7 per cent threshold for representation in the state Duma, the extreme entry requirements for admission to the election process, the ban on party alliances, the seizure of leaflets and posters by the police and many imaginative forms of harassment and, on top of everything else, an almost Soviet-style pressure on people not only to go to the voting booth but also to place their mark of approval in the right spot – all this betrayed great nervousness over the real state of affairs and opinion throughout the country. The Kremlin does not trust the Russian people.

To the sound of militant boasting and aggressive rhetoric the police showed an old-style heavy-handedness in controlling the opposition. On 21 November 2007 Garry Kasparov, the former chess world champion, a hero throughout the chess-obsessed Russian lands and, to his credit, leader of the opposition coalition Other Russia, was taken into custody for allegedly organizing, without previous written permission, a demonstration – not such an outrageous thing to do in an election campaign. What he had received from the local authorities was indeed permission to stage a demonstration – though not a march, and certainly not in the direction of the official commission appointed to supervise the flawless progress of the election. Kasparov, world famous, good-looking and a man of conscience, was immediately sentenced to no less than five days in prison, while the damage to Putin's and indeed Russia's reputation in the West was taking on remarkable proportions. Someone on the militia level exceeded their authority, or followed orders from above which did more harm than good.

Throughout the campaign the powers that be did not bother to discuss the arguments of the opposition but simply ignored them or, even worse, denounced them as being an expression of the 'fifth column', siding with the enemy. Putin spoke of *shakals*, the hungry wild dogs of the desert, and accused the liberals of making common cause with foreigners out to destroy Russia and working against the motherland. There was no group strong enough, and outspoken enough, to really take up the challenge from the Kremlin and its auxiliary troops in United Russia. Electioneering was blended with traditional Russian xenophobia. National unity was the order of the day. High prices for milk and bread? Inflation? Corruption, soaring rents and housing prices? The election was a festival of problem avoidance.

We need no opposition

A whiff of 'Who is not for us is against us' was in the air. Friend or foe. There was not much of a third way open to Russian voters. In their despair some of the opposition parties advised protest voters to cast their lot with the communists so that United Russia would at least fail to attain the two-thirds majority. Some in the opposition argued for a 'Russian Pinochet' to save the country from its enemies, weakness and treason. Nationalist hysteria was whipped up and it will stay with Russia and the Russians for a long time to come, even when the excitement of the elections has been forgotten.

Many Russians, long before the election results were announced to confirm the not unexpected triumphal victory of the party of power (64.4 per cent of the popular vote, rounded up to almost 70 per cent when the lesser parties were counted out), made it clear that they thought the charade was not worth bothering to go to the polls. Admirable was the courage of those bloggers who denounced the window-dressing as well as the police brutality, admirable also the willingness to conduct serious debate in cafés and restaurants, and even on private television. But for the common man or woman, fearing for their job or promotion or the kids' scholarship, the base line was more or less: they pretend to play democracy, and we pretend to take them seriously. It must also be added that many voters were sick and tired of instability, that their idea of democracy and liberalism was formed in the Yeltsin years and associated with turmoil, uncertainty, loss of status, vast riches for the few and poverty for the masses. Putin was associated with a return to stability, rising wages, pensions paid and a brighter outlook in life for many. People would still complain about steeply rising prices for groceries, milk and bread. But a vote for Zuganov's dead-end communists or Zhirinovsky's ill-named Liberal Democrats? For those – who would like to promote a more Western, pluralist style of politics – estimates put them at 20 per cent of the electorate, many of them young urban professionals – the SPS and Yabloko offered a losing proposition. Having failed to merge their fortunes in time and unite, they were sure to falter at the 7 per cent threshold and would therefore punch below their weight, which in due course they did.

The campaign for the election of the lower house of the state Duma, once it got under way, was clearly conceived, organized and stage-managed as a hybrid between parliamentary elections and a referendum to keep Putin, whatever his official position, in control. Putin was, right from the start, the central figure. But in what capacity? Voters received little detailed information throughout. The fact that ahead of the elections he designated himself as the party leader of United Russia, while at the same time putting much emphasis on his being above party, left many, in fact all, options open. Even if, towards the end of his second presidential term, he really and truly entertained the idea of withdrawing from public office, this uncertainty did not last long. In the meantime the balance of power in and around the Kremlin, impenetrable though it is between the various intelligence services, the power ministries, the United Russia coalition of oligarchs, and the state bureaucracy, seems to have changed so much and become so precarious that looming danger to the regime must have persuaded him not to give up the role of leader and supreme arbiter. At present and for the foreseeable future, no one but Putin can claim the throne of the overall powerbroker, command respect and keep the peace between the warring factions.

The national leader

The parliamentary election turned referendum on Putin, whatever the masterplan behind it, hinted at a solution to the riddle of who would be the future master of Russia. United Russia chairman Boris Gryzlov was the first to announce that in reality the elections for the 450 members of the state Duma would be a referendum for Putin. All of a sudden, the Russian parliamentary election was a kind of US-style primary. This in turn opened the way to interpret victory for United Russia as a mandate from the people to be creative with the constitution. Even before the election had ended its results were seen as an appeal for a popular campaign to beseech the man in the Kremlin to stay and to add, through a two-thirds majority for United Russia and its loyalists, a little amendment to the constitution in order to allow Putin a third term. Forever the saviour of the nation.

The elections were manipulated in many ways, some brutal, some fanciful, all of them betraying deep-seated anxiety, but they were far from meaningless. In summing up the modus operandi one could say they were, on the whole, half free and half fair. Meanwhile, the result was bound to mean different things to different people. The Kremlin at least had the good taste not to insist on the 99 per cent approval required of the people during Soviet times. But even the comfortable two-thirds majority for United Russia was not obtained, despite so much pressure and propaganda: 64 per cent for United Russia, given the noise and commotion before the elections, was unimpressive and amounted to less than the triumphal victory expected. Nevertheless, the elections for the lower house on 2 December have to be seen as the start of a critical transfer of power in two stages – equal in importance to the electoral victory of Boris Yeltsin as the first democratically elected president of Russia or the elevation of Vladimir Putin in 1999 from being an unknown official in the Kremlin to new tsar.

After the elections to the state Duma the presidential elections of 2 March 2008 were the second part of the process. In the run-up it seemed ever more likely that the combination of the quasi-referendum of December 2007 and the presidential election 100 days after would usher in a new phase of authoritarian democracy in Russia. The announcement of the Putin Plan, intentionally unspecific, meaning all things to all men, allowed the assumption that in the hurly-burly of the future the role of Putin would be significant, and probably central. The elements are all there, formal and informal, but given the turmoil during the autumn of 2007 throughout the state apparat it would be astounding if the future distribution of political and economic power were to be enacted without serious – and visible – conflict at the top. The triangle of power between the state machinery, the intelligence services and the oligarchs is anything but monolithic, the distribution of power and the nature of governance anything but settled. Who gets what, and how much of it, has not yet found a firm and reliable answer. The various groups have irreconcilable differences of outlook, investment opportunities, alliances and modus operandi.

The party of power sees no need for an opposition, except of course the communists as they have to make the bogeyman to show the outside world as well as doubters at home that, whatever the shortcomings of the Putin system, it is, to say the least, the lesser evil. The arguments of political opponents were not discussed but simply ignored. In any society this approach comes at a price, and in Russia too. Former prime minister Mikhail Kasyanov and other opposition personalities predict, if the authoritarian system persists and hardens, social unrest and political upheaval within three years from 2007.

Opposite the mausoleum where the embalmed Soviet Union's founder still waits for communism to save the world, the pre-1914 department store GUM, during Soviet times a drab affair, has been refurbished and attracts people for whom money is no object. Boutiques sell Western luxuries to the New Russians, wives and mistresses alike.

Top: Drifting into insignificance: the Soviet deity showing the way to nowhere. Lenin's statue, once meant to be the Soviet challenge to the old-world Nevsky Prospect, is one of only three surviving public images out of a total of 124 during Soviet times in St Petersburg alone.

Above: Icons for sale at a stationery shop.

Fading memories at the Northern River Port, Moscow. The canal linking Moscow with the Volga river was one of the monumental projects of Soviet modernization, costing the lives of uncounted hundreds of thousands. Opposite the quay, on the other side of the canal, a decommissioned nuclear submarine is awaiting slow death or rejuvenation as a Cold War museum. (Victoria Zhukova)

Power and omnipotence. An Orthodox memorial service aboard
a ship in the Barents Sea for the 118 crew of the ultramodern
nuclear submarine *Kursk*, 24 August 2000. (Associated Press)

Above: Rising cresecent over Kazan. Is this
what Ivan Grozny and his Russian warriors
fought for? (Associated Press)

Right: Not of bread alone. The dissident is
honoured by the tsar: Putin visiting Nobel
laureate Alexander Solzhenitsyn on his 89th
birthday. He died on 3 August 2008.
(Associated Press)

The tutor and his master student.
(Evgeny Tkachenko)

Wanted: civil society

The long-term implications of the election campaign, however genuine or manipulative the process and the outcome may have been, will be twofold. The emergence of civil society throughout Russia, a painful process at the best of times, will be seriously thrown back, and foreign and security policy will continue to intone the shrill sounds of resentment. Civil society was the real loser of those December elections.

It is remarkable that Putin, when naming the weaknesses of today's Russia to Western audiences invariably deplores the absence of civil society – and he is right to do so. It must indeed be doubtful that in today's Russia there is enough independence from state and state organizations to allow for the unfolding of the manners and morals that, throughout history, have tended to accompany and transform the rise of the market society. The path of Russian democracy is punctuated with intimidation of dissenters, even the occasional murder of journalists through traffic accidents, mysterious disappearances or outright assassination.

György Konrád, Hungarian dissident and writer, talks about an anti-political mentality throughout Eastern Europe, where people are tired of the overdose of politics and rhetoric, and there is ample scepticism concerning politicians' character, effectiveness and ability to deliver on their promises.

In Russia, however, things seem to be different. There are many who are tired of politics or given to more pleasurable pursuits, but there is also a growing number of citizens seeking the expression of their values and aspirations. They can be divided.into two camps, activists of both an optimistic-nationalist conviction and those of a more liberal persuasion. Both sides are present in public discourse and engage in tense dialogue. Nasi, the youth wing of United Russia, reflects the proud pro-government and nationalist activism but is now paying the price of having been created from above. There is a deficit of authenticity. Inventing the Putin Youth has misfired.

Meanwhile, there is another variation on the theme of proud nationalism, loyal to the powers that be and on the ascendant throughout Russian society. The majority are well-educated, intelligent and publicity-conscious young technocrats who are out to create a forward-looking Zeitgeist. Meanwhile, the protagonists of the new Russia tend to be conservative in outlook and social orientation. Their philosophy is guided by two principles: nostalgia for the empire and refusal to be part of the West. Self-confidence is back to levels absent for most of the Soviet period. The mineral wealth of Siberia, at present surely the base for Russia's rise, is seen as providing a launchpad for a better future for Russia beyond oil, gas and pipelines.

Beyond democracy: a new public discourse

The political ideal is not Western-style democracy but an enlightened authoritarianism, free of contradictions and in control of its own destiny. The 'vertical of power' – as Putin likes to describe the new geometry for running state and society – is seen as the winning formula, and the new Russians are not afraid to talk of a systemic conflict with the West. They display confidence that their system will ultimately prevail. This new thinking is promoted by a new Russian intelligentsia, organized around think tanks, journals and university seminars, giving shine to Putin's system. The main public TV channels First Channel and Rossiya are used to promote the new thinking about Russia and Russia's destiny in the world. So far, success has crowned their efforts. Opinion polls reveal that most Russians see autocracy as by far the best form of government.

Russia is still in the Hobbesian state. John Locke will have to wait. Wealth and material well-being does not automatically produce a liberal middle class. On 25 November 2007 about 500 demonstrators tried to stage a march on Nevsky Prospekt in the middle of St Petersburg. They called themselves the 'Disagreeing'. A third of the demonstrators were briefly taken into custody by the police. These included a prominent former prime minister, Boris Nemtsov, who was invited in no uncertain terms to sign a record of his conversation with the police. Intimidation works, and many denizens of St Petersburg who otherwise might attend political events and demonstrations feel that discretion is, once again, the better part of valour. The state-controlled media invariably paint such marches in the darkest of colours. The liberals, handicapped and intimidated, lose their public presence and their voice in public discourse.

Few Russians would be willing to agree with British Prime Minister

Winston Churchill's famous statement that democracy is the worst form of government – 'with the possible exception of all others that have been tried from time to time'.

Throughout Russia, democracy has a bad name because it is associated with the economic and financial crisis of the Yeltsin years and the ensuing political trauma. The Kremlin's media, including the various parts of Gazprom's media holding, find it easy to denounce their opponents as 'russophobes', playing on the Russian penchant for self-pity and suspicion. The term 'Western agents', generously applied to anybody less than enthusiastic about Putin's regime, is borrowed from Soviet times and KGB phraseology.

Power and the people – the December 2007 elections suggest that the Kremlin is willing and able to merge them into unity. There is not much room left for political dissent, let alone a material base. Khodorkovsky's fate serves as an unequivocal warning to all those who want to try. The fall from grace of the energy tycoon who challenged the Kremlin and its incumbent is never talked about but always remembered.

As long as oil and gas fire the economy, inflation is curbed and pensions and wages are paid, the memory of the bad old days, whether the last Soviet decade or the Yeltsin years, will be strong enough to buoy the authoritarian system, especially when it allows and encourages bread and circuses, Russian pride and foreign travel. What can clearly be seen, however, is that politics in the future will be more monochrome than in the initial Putin years. Social engineering will help to keep the voters quiet. A lot of social control will ensure a balance between autocracy, there will be the velvet glove over a steely hand, and an occasional, reluctant display of democracy.

The pleasures of doing business with Russia

'What is it to travel to Russia? For one who has his eyes open it is continuous and obstinate work which consists of laboriously distinguishing, at every turn, between two nations in conflict. These two nations are Russia as it is and Russia as it would like to show itself to Europe.'

Marquis de Custine, *Journey for Our Time*

German business is not normally given to displays of public enthusiasm. At the end of 2007, however, the well connected Ost-Ausschuss der Deutschen Wirtschaft, representing most of the German companies active in Russia, made no secret of its endorsement of Putin's choice of successor, of continuity secured and stability promised.

The mood among German companies in Russia is optimistic, a summary assessment reported for the year 2007. Dr Klaus Mangold, chairman and former Daimler-Chrysler member of the board, outlined the results of four opinion polls conducted among the thousands of Germans doing business in Russia, mostly out of Moscow: 'The business climate in Russia has continued to improve, and companies see this trend continuing well into the next year.' 'Seven out of ten companies believe that overall conditions have improved.' Among the reasons given were the rise in purchasing power, the spending mood among Russian consumers and the high quality of the companies' Russian employees.

But there were also the usual caveats. Companies made their optimism conditional on visible progress in reducing red tape, fighting corruption, securing rational and predictable rules for import duties and taxes, harmonization of norms and standards in general and a more positive attitude of government towards medium-sized family-owned companies. In 2006 foreign direct investment from Germany reached a record high. At an accumulated USD 10.1 billion since 1990 Germany at the end of 2007 holds 6.6 per cent of foreign direct investment, ranging behind recycled Russian money from Cyprus and

Luxembourg, energy investment from the Netherlands, and assorted funds from the UK, the latter due to ConocoPhillips and TNK-BP. German investment came not only through large-scale commitments by E.ON and Volkswagen, but also from hundreds and thousands of small and medium-sized companies seeking entry into the rapidly expanding Russian market for everything from capital assets to consumer goods to colourful journals like *Computer World*, *Forbes* or *Newsweek* – the Russian edition. But again, the caveats were serious. One in four companies expected the forthcoming legislation on foreign participation in Russian industries to put a dampener on further investment. Half the companies polled said it would make no difference. One in four expected an improvement through predictable framework conditions.

Never so close

Bypassing the high level of trade before the First World War, the specific conditions of the inter-war years and forty years of Comecon, today's Ost-Ausschuss proudly maintains that never before have Germany and Russia been so close in economic terms. Indeed, Germany is Russia's number one partner for foreign trade, at roughly 10 per cent of Russian exports – mostly hydrocarbons in the form of natural gas and oil from Siberia.

Meanwhile, Russia continues to be the fastest-growing market for German products, primarily machine tools and premium cars. German exports to Russia grew twice as fast as exports to the rest of the world, and from January to October 2007 increased 28 per cent over 2006. At the end of 2007 commercial turnover reached 40,64 billion euros. During the same period, imports from Russia went down by 11.7 per cent in dollar terms, due to the fall of the US dollar against the euro.

This enthusiasm contrasts sharply with impressions which old Russia hands like Anders Aslund from the Carnegie Endowment for Peace brought back from Russia not long before. In the autumn of 2005 Aslund, a paper circulated among the strategic community, had recorded some warning signs: 'The dominant impression for the World Economic Forum Russian Summit was the contrast between the jubilant Western investors, both portfolio and direct investors, and the

Russian businessmen. The Western investors were cheering not only Russia but also Putin, and would have given him a third term by acclamation, if the choice were up to them. The Russian businessmen kept their heads down and displayed a remarkable lack of enthusiasm. Nobody believed in any severe risk of oil curse because the government's macroeconomic policy remains convincing.'

What do Russian businesspeople know that their Western counterparts do not? It may well be that among well-informed Russians the gap between the oil and gas economy and the rest of the economy is indeed disconcerting, and that the cocksure attitude displayed by Kremlin officials at all levels creates an impression of hubris and uncertainty about business and foreign policy, in long-term relations with the West, particularly the US. Aslund again, combining anecdotal evidence with the long view: 'In private conversations, Russian businessmen mentioned both their wonderful profit expansion and the unpleasant political climate which also aggravates the business climate. It is all too striking how big Russian businessmen prefer to stay abroad as much as possible so that they are not called to the Kremlin to be extorted. As a result, many Russian businessmen seem lost. They do not want to invest too much in Russia but to diversify abroad, and they have already done so in the CIS countries. Many do not quite know how to proceed further. Therefore, Russian investment is only rising by some 10 per cent a year when it should increase by 20 to 30 per cent a year.'

Aslund had already observed the decline of the more liberal-minded ministers like deputy prime minister Alexander Zhukov, a Putin loyalist throughout, who announced many reform measures either adopted or in the pipeline – 'but not all that important' – while omitting the vastly increasing role of the state in the resource sector. The minister was visibly uncomfortable when asked about the recent Yukos affair and the ensuing near stagnation of oil production. Aslund said that he 'responded very officially that state companies could also work and that oil production would rise again because of tax changes and investment policies'. German Gref, a star among the Western-oriented liberals, seems to have confounded the visitors from the West by first denouncing the old Russian habit of concentrating resources in state hands and then stating, out of the blue: 'All legislative activity is oriented in that direction.' Aslund's conclusion after the performance of the liberal ministers was: 'They are without power and they swing between public protest and resignation.' German Gref, responsible in the government for industrial modernization, was dismissed in September 2007 only to reappear at the helm of Sberbank, Russia's foremost high street bank.

As to the long-term prospects, Aslund reported that many of the senior managers of big companies were interested in boosting the market value of their companies, planning for IPOs in the years to come. Even the CEO of Rosneft after the acquisition of Yukos assets, seemed to be thinking on the same wavelength. Aslund, notwithstanding the more sombre mood among Moscow's Russian business elite, reassured his readers: 'State ownership, nationalization and Russian isolation do not look like credible threats because the leading operators do want to transform their asset control into money in private international markets. Capitalism is the name of the game ... and capitalism is international. The leading *siloviki* want to get very rich and legalize their assets.'

State companies

In September 2007 the Russian government initiated legislation which is bound to shape state companies, define strategic sectors, make life harder for foreign investors and force foreign companies to think twice before getting involved. It could well be a deterrent for foreign money and expertise – both needed by Russian companies. While the Ost-Ausschuss der Deutschen Wirtschaft, echoing concerns from all over Western countries, warns against re-creating state monopolies and argues for the creative destruction of old monopolies, for open markets and for the transfer of international standards safety regulations and environmental protection, Russian legislation is, by and large, moving in the opposite direction. The creation of state corporations, in the official Russian version, is meant to show the way for various sectors of the economy, provide an impetus for development and make them attractive for business. On 11 December 2007, Putin told business leaders from the Russian Chamber of Commerce and Industry that the Kremlin does not intend to create 'state capitalism', adding: 'We don't plan to keep state corporations the way they are now. After the corporations are stabilized and standing on their own feet it would be good for them to work in the market.' Putin also promised that the government would protect private enterprise and ensure that state corporations 'do not strangle other businesses'.

Putin wants Russia's economy to modernize, and fast. He knows that basing Russia's future solely on natural resources would be profitable in the short term and detrimental in the long term. He wants innovative sectors throughout the economy and has charged Sergei Ivanov, ex-KGB and former minister of defence, with the task of pushing the country into the world of modern technology. That is the bright side. The dark side was visible when Yukos, Russia's most successful energy company, was placed under state control, the assets sold to more docile companies and the CEO jailed in Siberia.

It is the state that wants supreme control over strategic sectors like ship-building (United Shipbuilders), aircraft industries (United Aircraft Holdings), nuclear technology (Rosatom), and nanotechnology (Rosnanotech) – the latter, according to Sergei Ivanov, the 'mega- project of the modern age', generously supported through the national budget.

There is method in this mega-thinking. All important property – much as in the days of the Tsars and the Commissars – should ultimately be seen as merely on loan from the state, that is to say from the Kremlin. The panacea for Russia's largely backward industries is seen in a broad array of techno-holdings with not much competition between them but full government control. Size is what mattered in Soviet times – and the ideology of quantity over quality has not yet died. Whereas Germany's very successful machine-tool industry, including those companies working in the Russian market, is by and large organized in medium-sized companies, many of them family-owned, the Kremlin still believes that bigger is better, even for machine tools.

German doubts

German business, by far the largest foreign community in Moscow, fears that imposing restrictions on foreign participation will seriously impede growth, prosperity and employment. Whether these voices are heard in the Kremlin, after the dismissal and reinstatement of German Gref and other liberals, is another question.

Ost-Ausschuss also fears that investment protection will suffer, that agreements will be broken and foreigners discriminated against. Time and again the Germans demand that bureaucracy be reduced, administrative decisions become more transparent and, indeed, more predictable, and that import rules be relaxed. The word corruption is conspicuous by its absence from polite conversation but ever present in real life.

German industry speaks of 'strategic partnership', leaving everybody guessing what this could mean in practice. There is no level playing field between the Kremlin administration and German organized interests. Instead, there is much wishful thinking. Industry demands political support from Berlin and has set up a 'strategic working group' on economic and financial cooperation, designed to put more pressure on the government in Berlin as well as in Moscow.

How much this is worth, nobody can tell for now. In addition, to secure a large piece of the Olympic business, Ost-Ausschuss has even set up a special working group called Sochi 2014. The Germans are in favour of reciprocity and understand the long-term strategy of many Russian companies to invest abroad, not only to share know-how but also to secure their assets against the secretive strategies of the Kremlin. Most German investors must have taken notice of the notorious *Kommersant* interview with Oleg Shvartsman, reported at length in the London *Financial Times*, with some concern, wondering what that might entail for their own economic future in the treacherous Russian business environment. This is also the reason why foreign investors argue for Russian entry into the World Trade Organization, which should create mutual obligations and restrict the temptations of a command economy. The Russian discrimination against meat imports from Poland and, in parallel, Russian restrictions on Lufthansa overflight rights were anecdotal evidence in 2007 and 2008 for the kind of state intervention Western countries have to fear. Copyright infringements are another sore point, together with increased industrial espionage and a notorious disregard for industrial patents.

A strategic partner of sorts

Behind the official rejoicing in Brussels about Russia being a 'strategic' partner,* there lurks some uneasiness. Russian–EU rela-

---

* Eneko Landaburu EU, DG Relex, House of Lords, November 2007.

tions are doing well. Overall volume of trade rose 29 per cent from 2006 to 2007. At 52 per cent of Russian exports the EU is by far the most important trade partner of Russia, while Russia ranks as number four for the EU. Growth is expected to continue, 'Russia presenting itself as economically strengthened and politically stable', according to a position paper circulated by Ost-Ausschuss der Deutschen Wirtschaft in September 2007. The most important factor is of course the continuously high oil price and, in its wake, the high price of natural gas. But foreign importers also note that private consumption and rising net investment contribute to self-sustained growth, beyond the energy dimension. Russian legislation is seen as more business friendly, as long as the strategic dimension as determined by the Kremlin is respected, and helpful in defining competition and cartels. There seems also to be a growing awareness at the top that small and medium-sized companies deserve some support. Diversification is the guiding principle, and the need to create more intelligent employment beyond energy and the weapons industry.

Anybody entering the inner courtyards of the Kremlin – or the parking lot of Gazprom not far from the Kremlin – cannot fail to be impressed by the number of large black limousines from Germany, most of them Mercedes but also a growing number of BMWs. Outside the Kremlin walls, the smart and glitzy Porsches are conspicuous, with ladies at the steering wheel, driving at high speed. Moscow's streets are saturated with cars, many imported from the West. Kremlin leaders and oligarchs are not alone in their penchant for premium cars. It is a high-priority objective of the Russian government to bring car manufacturers and their complementary industries to Russia. National as well as international companies received aid in order to engage in this area. By 15 September 2007 those special favours had ended, and outsiders as well as insiders are united in clamouring for more. French, Italian and German manufacturers demand that support for Russian car industries should not come at the cost of foreign investors. Indeed, in late 2007 Renault of France and AvtoVAZ – better known as Lada – set up a long-term partnership with both sides holding 50 per cent of the shares.

Investing in Russia

Ernst & Young in 2006 put Russia third in Europe as a recipient of foreign direct investment, but in 2007 it fell back to number six, after France and before the UK. Meanwhile, competitive Russian companies are forging ahead in international markets. Russia's investment corporation Basic Element (one of the largest in the business) acquired a major interest in Magna, Strabag of Austria and Hochtief of Germany. Severstal, a leading steel producer, bought the US giant Rouge Steel as well as the Italian group Lucchini. Evraz Holding took over the steel producer Palini e Bertoli, Gazprom got engaged with ENI of Italy, Wintershall, a subsidiary of BASF, and E.ON, Ruhrgas of Germany, Total of France and Statoil of Norway. Russia's Alfa Group went for the Turkish mobile telephone company Turkcell and is looking at Vodafone and Deutsche Telekom, which is also being wooed by AFK Sistema.

Investment corporations Alfa Group and Renova have put capital into innovative industries, notably nanotechnology in Switzerland and the US. As far as high-tech aviation is concerned, state-controlled Vneshtorgbank acquired – and sold after a short while – a 5 per cent share of EADS, the mother company of Airbus.

The list could be continued. Russia as a place for investment, inbound or outbound, is better than its reputation, but investment is held back by serious doubt about where Russian industrial policy is going, about the security of investment, the reliability of the tax regime and the experience of occasional harassment, omnipresent corruption and the vicissitudes of the legal system. That explains why direct foreign investment develops only slowly, not much compared with the inflows into China's booming industry. It is only very recently that investment from abroad has picked up – much of it Russian money channelled through Cyprus or Luxembourg. In 2007 foreign direct investment into Russia stood at USD 49 billion, according to UNCTAD, up 70 per cent over the previous year.

But the remaining risks are still strong enough to put a damper on foreign enthusiasm. Sovereign risk is no longer the problem, Russia has proved to be a reliable partner. The country has accumulated USD 400 billion in reserves, plus the stabilization fund of well over $150 billion as insurance for a rainy day when the oil price may take a downturn. The more obvious risks are being seen in the conduct of business in Russia; this is what weighs heavily on the ranking of Russian companies. The system of licences and regulations is notoriously obscure, the legal system unpredictable. Not many judges understand the economic intricacies they are called upon to decide, and once a court case has been decided it is uncertain that any decisions will be acted upon.

Concern in Brussels

At the EU growing concern is being expressed while Russian companies continue their shopping spree. Many Russian corporations are taking over capital assets, often the controlling share. While the recycling of petrodollars should be welcomed, the precedent having been set after the first and second oil price shocks in the 1970s and 1980s, the EU Commission is thinking about protecting European energy networks against takeover bids from Russia, notably through Gazprom.

There is indeed a strange contradiction. The Russian economy has been expanding at a rate of 7 per cent per annum since 1999 and shows no signs of weakening. Russia turned from poor debtor to serious creditor. Financial institutions are gaining credibility – some more, some less. But progress is seriously hampered by the absence of a new agreement on partnership and cooperation – there is not even a mandate for negotiations. Notable also was the fall-out from the Kosovo crisis, the US missile defence project in the Czech Republic and in Poland, the removal of a Red Army victory monument from the centre of Estonia's ancient capital Tallinn to its outskirts, etc. In all of this the Kremlin wanted to make its displeasure felt. The interruption of oil supplies via Belarus in early 2007 reminded Western nations of their growing dependence on Russia. It is wishful thinking when Ost-Ausschuss der Deutschen Wirtschaft demands that in future mechanisms between the EU and Russia will have to be developed to prevent any repeat performance.

What has failed to materialize after the end of the Cold War is a sustainable strategic partnership based on confidence and mutual security. While the political climate has become unfriendly, cooperation and partnership can still be found in the economic sphere given that the rulers of Russia today are no longer interested in fighting 'over the soul of mankind', to quote a recent American study on the Cold War by Melvyn P. Leffler, but in material well-being, money and long-term prospects for themselves and their children. The strategic aim for European and US industries must surely be to bring Russia in from the cold and to make the Russian economy conform to the silent standards and passumptions of a rule-based system, first in economic life and then, slowly but surely, in political life as well.

The broad canvas of EU–Russian relations is characterized by the glaring contradiction between economic partnership and political misgivings. Russia is both a close neighbour – sometimes too close for comfort – and a 'strategic partner'. This is how the EU Director-General for External Relations, DG RELEX, in a briefing for the European Commission at the House of Lords recently described the fundamental ambiguity of the relationship. With Brezhnev enlargement the EU inherited a difficult eastern legacy from the times of Eider, Stalin and the former Soviet Union. This affects the relationship with Russia and presents challenges both positive and negative. Moreover, Russia is emerging from what is officially seen – and also felt by the majority of the people – as the economic and political mismanagement of the Yeltsin years, associated with Western democracy and out-of-control capitalism. Eight years into the Putin presidency, the EU was not alone in registering 'a new-found assertiveness on the crest of high energy prices', a situation likely to remain. 'Differentiation from the West is often seen as a definition of that assertiveness.'

The result is usually described as a paradox, but perhaps it is much more the combined effect of imperial nostalgia, unrealistic expectations, everyday bullying and the desire to develop an identity somewhere between the vastness of the Eurasian steppe and the complacency of the Western club. Much as the Canadians resent the role of, as they say, 'the hewers of wood and the drawers of water', Russians after a century of catastrophe, humiliation and disappointment have a need to define for themselves a role in accord with their self-respect and their newly discovered – one-dimensional and therefore fragile – power. The national discourse is not only about material well-being, it is also about the meaning of Russianness, history, civilization, the relationship with Europe, and the mirror image of the US.

This, however, is not where the EU Commission can be very helpful, nor the Western companies seeking business in Russia. While the latter would like to divorce business and democratic values, the EU cannot – and the business community should not. During the Cold War the responsibility of Western companies ended at the Iron Curtain while, in the globalized market place of today, cross-cultural investment is growing all the time and standards of fairness, rule of law, answerability and transparency work across political borders. That is why the EU must be concerned about the cultural and legal underpinnings of trade with Russia or – for that matter – the PRC. This dilemma will not be solved soon. 'EU–Russia trade and investment are booming and our energy interdependence is growing. European business is rushing to the Russian door. There are huge profits to be made on the Russian market, but we have serious differences as regards the political relationship, and in some questions of foreign and security policy.'

Politics still matters

The EU is not liked in the Kremlin, nor is the principle of shared sovereignty accessible to Russian thinking. In the Soviet past, Russian analysts waited for the Western capitalists to go for each others' throats. When this did not happen, a younger generation in IMEMO, at the Institute of Europe and even in the Foreign Ministry began to study the architectural principles of European integration more carefully and found that Comecon could even learn something. But this recognition came late in the day and bore no fruit. Apart from political expediency this is one of the reasons why Kremlin rulers to this day prefer to work with individual countries bilaterally instead of with the EU Commission. The Brussels Commission, in turn, has not been able to summon full and unwavering support for its policies, be it the fight against Russia's boycott of meat from Poland, or the long-term planning and realization of the Nabucco pipeline from Central Asia to Europe, bypassing Russia.

EU member states still strike their own bargains with Russia whenever they can, and they leave the nagging and criticizing of Russia's human rights practices to the EU while concentrating on the business side of the relationship. Thus they play the Russian game of divide and rule. Meanwhile, the EU Commission does not resign itself to an observer role. It voiced its concern before the Duma elections of 2

December 2007 because of the restrictions placed on OSCE observers, and finally decided not to take part in a charade. The Commission also regularly raises concerns on human rights issues such as the limitations on freedom of radio and TV, attacks on journalists, pressure on NGOs and the miserable situation in the northern Caucasus, and they do it on all levels from the summit down to the twice-yearly consultations among human rights experts. It is noted in Brussels that 'sometimes these consultations can degenerate into an exchange of recriminations', as for instance when Putin mentioned that the police practices at the G8 Heiligendamm meeting were no softer than anything happening elsewhere.

Give me the EU telephone number

The Commission is strongest when it deals with economic matters, and weakest when it takes up political issues. This imbalance is clearly reflected in the EU–Russia relationship. EU countries rarely speak with one voice, except in routine matters. Foreign policy is jealously guarded by national governments, but individual governments are not strong enough to impress the Kremlin, while together their common denominator is often weak to the point of being meaningless. Both sides seem to speak past each other. The slow-moving conflict over the future of the Serbian province of Kosovo – independence or far-reaching autonomy – was a striking example. It reached a tipping point when, on 10 December 2007, the UN Security Council failed to agree on the report by former Finnish President Marti Ahtisaari. Before this, a 'troika' commission that brought together Russian and American diplomats and German Ambassador Wolfgang Ischinger worked for a last-minute reconciliation. It failed as expected. The EU Commission does not cut an impressive figure when it appeals to Russia to 'act responsibly'. 'It is not in the interest of Russia itself to stir up tensions there or elsewhere and to continue to speak of "precedent". This may turn against Russia at some point.' Of course, the Commission was aware, long before the UN non-decision, that Russia seeks compensation elsewhere; Putin at Heiligendamm had warned that Kosovo could be the starting point for looking, once again, at the Soviet inheritance elsewhere. He probably meant Transnistria, Abkhazia and South Ossetia, where the Russians still keep troops, some as peacekeepers under blue helmets, some under Russian colours. He also, starting at the Munich Security Conference on 10 February 2007, had distanced Russia from the CFE Treaty in its revised version of 1999, which the West had made conditional on Russia withdrawing most of those soldiers. Only two days after the UN vote on Kosovo Putin formally suspended application of the treaty's provisions, leaving the fate of this important element of confidence- and security-building in limbo.

The Commission, which under the Lisbon Treaty would have been entitled to more than an opinion on foreign policy, indeed a determining role, cannot resolve the dilemma that to influence Russia requires more cohesion than it can muster, while at the same time this is the most challenging test of its foreign policy competence. Middle East, Afghanistan, Iran or Burma: 'Where we share the same ultimate objectives, Russia tends to emphasize differences of approach.'

Can the EU Commission translate economic clout into political leverage? This requires the EU to speak with one voice and Russia to respect this single voice instead of turning to individual European capitals. The EU has to avoid a confrontational tone but, as DG RELEX tries to bridge the gap: 'We need to speak firmly in defence of our interests and thereby to find common ground with Russia.' In an ideal world, this can work. In the real world of 2008, this is more difficult.

EU–Russia: managing differences

Indeed, the EU– Russia relationship is by nature asymmetric, and the diversity of national interests which the EU Commission has to take into account tends to make compromise inevitable; and sometimes it fails altogether. The legal basis for EU–Russian relations is the Partnership and Cooperation Agreement (PCA) signed in 1994, which came into force in 1997. The Russians today claim that it reflects a time of Russian weakness and that is why they are pressing for a thorough revision. A new agreement is being negotiated which would have to take into account Russia's new assertiveness – open-ended. Meanwhile, in 2005 four– 'common spaces', in well-chosen Eurospeak, were defined, together with four 'roadmaps' setting out an ambitious-sounding agenda which, however, basically means talking among the relevant working groups. They range from industrial and regulatory policy to border cooperation (notably Kaliningrad/Königsberg), judicial cooperation, foreign policy, and science and technology. Not much of this hits the headlines, nor is there much reason for it to do so. It is basically the groundwork for a new overall agreement at some time in the future. Parallel to the issue-oriented working groups in 2003 a Permanent Partnership Council was set up to replace the Cooperation Council of the past. This means that EU chiefs and Russian ministers can meet in many sectoral forums, supplementing the two annual summit meetings. But this is all politics. There is no effective forum on a senior official level between expert and ministerial get-togethers. On one level, there is no politics; on the other level, there is only politics.

EU does not rhyme with energy

Energy has become the defining element in EU–Russian relations. It is the paramount concern on both sides, but for different reasons, and EU incoherence is notorious. The European Council has gone for a comprehensive legislative package which, unfortunately, flies in the face of what the Russians want: no 'unbundling'. The effective separation of the networks from energy generation (in Russia) and demand (in Europe) is the aim of the EU Commission, while both Russia's Gazprom and France's Gaz de France and Germany's E.ON are united in keeping things together, in their own hands of course. Whether the early warning mechanism agreed with the Russians will in future take the politics out of the pipelines remains to be seen. So far, the EU Commission has not been able, despite serious attempts by energy commissioner Pielbags, to produce a comprehensive energy concept that includes nuclear power and excludes the competition for Russian favours.

To turn dependence into interdependence is never an easy task, and it is especially difficult at a time of rising energy prices around the globe, reflecting rising demand. It is only with third country suppliers such as Algeria or the Central Asian republics that the EU has been able to seriously negotiate reciprocal agreements regarding trade, transit and investment possibilities. Currently, the EU is trying to convince the Russians that one such new framework agreement should include provisions for transparency, reciprocity, non-discrimination and a level playing field – in other words, the Brussels Eurocrats want to teach the Russian bear a few dancing lessons. What is sadly lacking is EU solidarity, especially in the energy field. All the preaching from president Barroso that a problem for one member state should be a problem for all does not change facts on the ground.

For the EU, Russian WTO accession has a high priority, as the Russians would be bound to conform to general rules. The process is only inching forward, however, with no final date in sight. WTO accession remains a pre-condition for any far-reaching free trade agreement. Once Russia has acceded, the EU would aim for deep and comprehensive economic integration through a new overall agreement. This would, if all went well, include a strong component on energy, aiming at a sustainable balance between the production side and the consumption side.

A grand bargain?

The EU, behind all the detail, the compromises and the frustrations, seems to be developing something amounting to a grand strategy. For any foreseeable future, Europeans will need Russian energy. But the Russians, too, will have a growing interest in creating a level playing field with the high technology of Western industries. They understand that they have to diversify their economy away from sole reliance on energy and weaponry and create a post-oil technology base. This is where the Europeans come in. To quote, once again, from the DG RELEX briefing for the House Lords: 'There are many prizes which can be obtained to our mutual benefit: much closer cooperation, innovation and high technology, outer space, aviation, biotechnology, nano-technology, increased people-to-people contacts with visa freedom as a long-term perspective, substantial increase of tourism, tens of thousands studying in each others' universities. . . . Our difficulty is that we agree on the need to get from A to Z but have great difficulties in getting from A to B to C.'

The EU on its own cannot handle the Russian dossier. It would need much more cooperation from the nation states who are going to profit from any future framework agreement. It would also benefit greatly once Russia meets the conditions for acceptance into the WTO with its code of conduct. Personal networking also has an important role to play, particularly the Association of European Business (AEB). AEB has a membership of 540 companies, all of them from the EU or EFTA (formerly the European Free Trade Association and now the European Economic Space) doing business in Russia, or with Russian partners. It was established in 1995 under the name of the European Business Club. Later, it was renamed and reorganized and is by now the framework organization for EU companies in Russia, parallel to national institutions with similar objectives, such as the British Business Club. It ranks just behind the American Chamber of Commerce in terms of membership numbers and activities. The AEB tries to operate like a think tank for both the EU in Brussels and the authorities in Moscow. This is considerably more than the usual lobbying, and covers fields like energy, banking, tax, copyright and patent law. It is not precisely grassroots work but brings a lot of fundamental issues to the fore.

Better believe in Adam Smith

In the long run, however, the logic of the market is the most important force in creating a common legal and economic space between Russia and the EU Europeans. You don't have to be a Marxist and look at the material foundations of human behaviour. Follow Adam Smith and trust in the rules of enlightened egotism. Much as the rough and tumble of the early Industrial Revolution gave way to a more equitable system in Britain and Europe, and much as robber barons in the US eventually made their peace with the law and the rest of society, there is a good chance that the new ruling class of oligarchs and *siloviki* will sooner or later understand that to secure their ill-gotten gains they have to be part of a rule-based system. Moreover, Western companies wanting to do business with their Russian counterparts have to make sure that the more unappetizing elements of many of Russia's big companies are being eradicated and that the rule of law prevails. They don't want to be robbed, burn their hands or risk their reputation at home – under, for instance, the watchful eye of the Securities and Exchange Commission of the US. There is broad convergence.

Today Russia's markets are underregulated and overregulated at the same time, burdened by corruption and red tape in any conceivable combination. After centuries of tsars and commissars, improvement will take time, but also pressure from outside. It is the civilizing influence of advanced global capitalism that can convert robber barons into regular guys, and responsible players who will force them, sooner or later, to conform to rules made in the global market place.

II

In search of a foreign policy

'The Kremlin is not just a palace like any other, it is a complete city, and this city is the very heart of Moscow; it serves as the frontier of two parts of the world, the East and the West. The Old World and the Modern World are present there. Under the successors of Genghis Khan, Asia stamped on the earth and out of it came the Kremlin.'
Marquis de Custine, *Journey for Our Time*

Russia, to modify what US Secretary of State Dean Acheson famously said about Great Britain, fifteen years after the Second World War, 'has lost an empire and not yet found a role'.

In Russia the domestic foundations of a new global role, markedly different from the failed aspirations of the Soviet empire, are being re-designed. No longer Soviet power but the Russian federation is being praised, a halfway house between an overblown nation state and a continental empire, in uneasy cohabitation with a restive Muslim population. In economic terms, everything so far is based on oil wealth and the building of powerful, though in many respects inefficient state concerns comprising industries designated by the Kremlin as strategic. The outside world would be well advised to understand both the brutal power accumulated and the brittle nature of the power structure on top. There are some golden fortresses in Moscow, St Petersburg and elsewhere throughout the Russian federation, but beneath the proud towers the foundations are unstable.

Defining the international environment

The population base is probably the foremost long-term concern of Kremlin leaders, to be reconstructed and strengthened. The demographic challenge, for Russia more serious than for the rest of Europe, is seriously undermining recruitment in the army and other employment sectors, particularly natural sciences. It is also a threat to the homogeneity of the Russian federation. Rarely spoken of in public, it is an ever-present concern, the modern Russian equivalent of France's *'Jamais en parler, toujours en penser'*, referring to Alsace-Lorraine: always think of it, never speak of it.

The Iron Curtain provided a symmetry of friend and foe, without many grey zones in between. This is, after the disillusionment of the 1990s, still a point of departure in public discourse, East versus West, with Russia pretty much alone, and Putin at Munich must have been aware that, while raising eyebrows in the world at large, he was winning at home. By contrast, democracy in Russia is associated with weakness and intrusions by the West into the Russian sphere of influence. Domestic support and foreign policy orientation correspond.

Today one out of two Russians believes that during Soviet times the international situation was more favourable to Russia, stable and reliable – the misery of Afghanistan being conveniently forgotten. Only one in twenty Russians would name the time of Yeltsin as being good for Russia's international standing. To produce a sense of direction, it helps to have a foreign enemy. When, however, Putin refers to the enemy, people are given to understand that it is, without always being specifically named, the United States of America that dropped the first atom bomb in anger, poisoned Vietnam and is, above all, envious of the rise and glory of the motherland.

Europe by contrast is liked, to some extent admired and certainly not feared. Four out of five Russians admit to positive emotions about Europe and Europeanness. This should not, however, be taken as a final farewell to Russia's Asian vocation. One out of two Russians asserts that Russia was never of Europe or in Europe, and should therefore do everything to cultivate Russian traditions and Russian values. In terms of global players, Europe and the various European countries are not big enough to be deemed worthy of the enemy image: what power can an assemblage of twenty-seven states wield? What sovereignty can be exercised by a Commission that is the servant of twenty-seven masters big and small?

In search of enemies

Big powers need big enemies, and superpowers deserve a superpower on the other side. The greater the enemy, the greater the glory of standing up to him. Only America qualifies, for better or for worse, as a worthy antagonist. But while the US is part of the new Great Game, Britain, yesterday's great power, serves as the focus of Kremlin wrath. The bitterness seems to have started with oligarch Berezovsky narrowly escaping, with most of his money, Russian rough justice and receiving British citizenship. The Litvinenko murder in 2006 created acrimony and uncertainty. It was meant to remain a perfect enigma and a threat to any future defector. But it pointed the finger at unidentified agents who can obtain polonium-210, certainly a deadly poison not to be bought in the drugstore round the corner but available only to state agencies. The Russians refused to hand over the main suspect, Andrei Lugovoy, and added insult to injury by first harassing British embassy personnel in every conceivable way and then forcing the British Council to close down its operations, especially language teaching in St Petersburg and Yekaterinburg. This was an unfriendly act by any standard and sent a message of some significance: we do not care about the outside world.

The creation of a new identity from the top down is both a substitute for Soviet ideology, too absurd to resurrect, and the domestic reflection of an ongoing quest to define Russia's place in the world and its posture among the great powers of today and tomorrow. Russia is being presented to its denizens as the new promised land. The West, a model to be emulated during the early Yeltsin years, has lost its shine among both the people and the policy-makers.

China is too alien, too threatening, too vast to be an alternative model – notwithstanding the positive noises accompanying every meeting of the Shanghai Cooperation Organization, joint military manoeuvres with China's People's Liberation Army and the growing sales of technology and military hardware. To most Russians, the generals included, China is a brooding presence and too close for comfort. Rumour has it that more than five million Chinese have settled in Siberia, not much less than the remaining Russians. In Moscow's foreign policy think tanks China is praised as a potential ally against the US, but in cultural terms China is worlds apart. When Russians consider countries to travel to, or settle in, their thoughts turn to Italy, Spain or the peaceful villages around the lakes of Upper Bavaria, or the mild climate of Baden-Baden in the Upper Rhine valley. When Russians look for cultural role models, they choose Italian fashion,

French cuisine, German cars and Japanese electronic toys. China is an ally not of choice, but of necessity.

For the time being, China serves as a counterweight to the dominance of the United States but, as they say, only a diamond is forever. The Kremlin's rulers must surely be aware of the unlimited potential for conflict over Siberia and the Far East: all the people and no resources on the Chinese side, all the resources and no people on the Russian side of the divide. The Shanghai Cooperation Organization, bridging the gap, serves both sides, but in the long run Russians will look to Europe and the US to find their elective affinities.

Even after the loss of most of Central Asia, Ukraine and White Russia, the Kremlin still rules over a country of vast proportions, its more than eighty different entities stretching across eleven time zones from Kaliningrad Oblast in the west to Vladivostok in the Far East, bordering on the Pacific, the White Sea in the north, the Baltic Sea and the Black Sea, a country of vast Eurasian dimension and ambiguity. It is indeed a continent in all but name, with brutal contradictions not only in climate and demography but also in geopolitical terms. There exist vast differences between Russia west of the Urals and Russia east of the Urals, and thanks to China's ever-growing presence and mounting pressure they are bound to become more marked with time.

Pragmatism of power

The West should not expect a coherent foreign policy on the part of Russia. There is a basic philosophy, but no comprehensive system of thought, as in the time of the world revolution, only a multitude of political influences, manoeuvres and methods, and the usual divide between short-term convenience and long-term strategy. And anyway, given Russia's diversity in time and space, why should Russian foreign policy be any more coherent than that of the US? Even during Soviet times, Moscow would act in one direction today, in the opposite direction tomorrow, uninhibited by too much theory.

Under Bush 'Together where we can, alone where we must' was forged into the slogan, rather frightening for the Europeans and many others around the globe: 'Allies, not alliances.' World order courtesy of the United States? Yes, up to a point. Non-proliferation of weapons of mass destruction is a strategic dimension where the US, like it or not, still has to cooperate and even invite others to do the heavy diplomatic lifting. But for the rest, America wants to go it alone. If it is not isolationism that is beckoning, the name of the game is certainly unilateralism.

Why should Russia be more cooperative? Or more predictable? And why should the Kremlin be blamed for mirror-imaging much of America's newly invented splendid isolation? A 'lonely wolf', this is how Kremlin insiders describe, in a metaphor both heroic and frightening, the role they ascribe to Russia in the early twenty-first century. As long as the wolf does not succumb to self-pity and aggression, is well fed, morally reassured and happy with itself, and in control of ever-increasing oil income, the Kremlin can afford such a policy. But to have no friends comes at a price.

Challenges

The geopolitical challenges are indeed as vast and as contradictory as the Russian landmass. Moreover, their imperial past has bequeathed to Russians an inheritance of huge, almost uncontrollable problems. They range from the ominous presence of China, with ten times the population of the Russian federation, rising and rising over the Eastern perimeter fence at the rivers Amur and Ussuri, to the southern regions under the white peaks of the Caucasus mountains. For many centuries, the Tsar's generals viewed these southern expanses with concern as the empire's soft underbelly, threatened by British imperial expansion and, in more recent times, by US big business looking for natural resources.

For the time being and well into the future the most pressing threat, however, comes from the cohorts, assassins and, in the not too distant future, weapons of mass destruction sent out by militant Islam: this is a fear that hates to give its name. Putin avoids referring to militant Islam when talking about the dangers of terrorism, but from Afghanistan to the trauma of the Chechen wars and the terror scenarios that have unfolded since, Russians are very much aware of a looming threat. This was, after all, the psychology that helped Putin turn around the electorate in 1999 and win his first presidential term. There is more political mileage in the fear of radical Islam – but it has to be handled with care.

In the south-east, there is Turkey, and many a church spire built in the nineteenth century in Moscow, St Petersburg and elsewhere shows the crosses of Russian Orthodoxy piercing the crescent moon of Islam to celebrate victories past and future. Turkey, although a Nato member of long standing, is for Russia more and more a partner, whether it be as a consumer of Russian energy or a contractor for large-scale building. Turkey's secular model of state and society also helps to reassure the Kremlin about the future of Muslims holding a passport adorned with the double-headed eagle.

And, most important of all, there is Europe and, beyond Europe, the United States of America, the latter so vast and so powerful that for Russia the Far West and the Far East almost coincide. For Russia and the Russians, the sun rises over America and the sun sets over America. This is not just symbolism. Cold War or no, Russia compares itself not with China or India, nor with Europe, but exclusively with the United States.

While this approach, by implication, affords Russia the status of superpower, especially in the UN dimension and in strategic arms control, other dimensions are patently absent from the equation. America's military has what Russians do not have, the capacity to project power worldwide. The US rules the waves, Russia, from the battle of Tsushima lost against the Japanese to the explosion of the *Kursk*, has always failed in the maritime power game and is not likely to catch up soon. Iraq, the Russians console themselves, is slowly and inexorably becoming America's Afghanistan – but not quite. There may well be an Iraq legacy, much as Vietnam left deep scars on America's body and soul, but it will not be the beginning of the end of US superpower – as Afghanistan, twenty years ago, was for Russia. Today Russia can just about compete in the nuclear dimension, but not in terms of conventional power, cyberspace or maritime presence across the Seven Seas.

In today's world, however, other elements of US expertise count for even more. While America's 'soft power'* reaches far beyond America's hard power, winning the proverbial 'hearts and minds', Russia after the Soviet Union has little to offer in terms of soft power. America's industrial capacity, research and development are

* Josef Nye

the envy of many Russians, the standard by which to measure their own progress and the target of unrelenting industrial espionage. The US currency is still the benchmark of value, but Russians are beginning to have second thoughts, reading into the decline of the US currency a message of secular decline. Empowered by oil and gas, they consider extricating themselves from the sinking USS *Greenback*, putting their faith into the freely convertible rouble and keeping major savings in euros – though certainly not in Chinese renmimbi.

'Does America need a foreign policy?' Henry Kissinger famously asked. It was no surprise that the Doctor came out with a book prescribing medication based on balance of power, cooperation and compensation, alliances and containment of major adversaries. Russia, too, needs a foreign policy, but does Russia have one? Russians do not mind very much that Russia is, by and large, a country without friends as long as Russia wields a veto over great matters of global concern or lesser matters within its sphere of interest, territorial or political. In today's world, one could imagine Kremlin leaders secretly citing to themselves Lord Palmerston's words 150 years ago in the House of Commons: 'We have no eternal allies and we have no perpetual enemies. Our interests are eternal and perpetual, and those interests it is our duty to follow.'

New chessboard, old rules

Russia's policy-makers today claim an almost boundless measure of freedom of manoeuvre and sovereignty. This has vast practical implications, worlds apart from the Soviet orthodoxy which combined unlimited geopolitical ambition with the idea of a Marxist-Leninist 'Third Rome'. It is much closer to tsarist aspirations for a place at the head table, control of warm seaports and strategic sea lanes like the Dardanelles or the Baltic approaches; most of Germany in the nineteenth century lived *sous l'oeil des Russes*, and so did the Balkans and much of Scandinavia. Russians also tend to remember fondly the informal veto in world affairs that they wielded before and after the Vienna Congress of 1814–15, not unlike today's veto power in the UN.

Today, there is not much of an overriding doctrine beyond the pragmatism of oil and gas and the wish to translate eight years of windfall profits into a dominant position in the globalizing world of industry and finance, national self-respect and an acceptable idea of history past, present and future. There is a love-hate relationship with the US, a kind of cold marriage, forever strained but unlikely to end in divorce. The idea in Berlin and elsewhere that the quarrelling couple needs counselling, and that the Germans are called upon to provide friendly advice and mediation, is not of the real world. Russians and Americans know each other's telephone numbers well enough, be it in the situation centres in Moscow and Washington, in anti-terror departments at the CIA and the FSB, or in those exclusive clubs concerned with non-proliferation.

Both sides still have important principles in common, and they share large parts of their risk assessment. They want to defend the present structure of the UN Security Council, regardless of other nations' desire to take a seat at the High Table; they do not wish to admit new members to the nuclear club; they have an ambitious understanding of their own sphere of influence; and they fear the weapons and warriors of asymmetric warfare at home and abroad – while both sides tend to trespass, from time to time, into territory designated by the other side off limits. The Russians do resent interference by the West in the CIS and what they term the 'near abroad', and they are not impressed by the argument that any such interference is sanctified by democracy and liberal economics.

Too close for comfort is not only a rule to be observed in everyday life but also an important, though unspecified, part of the code of conduct between today's great powers. This is a matter of territorial disputes, when US ships come close to Russia's coastal waters and the twelve-mile zone, or Russian 'Bear' bombers on patrol cross, unannounced, into British airspace. All of this happened in the course of 2007. But coming too close is also a question of meddling in each other's domestic affairs. US preaching about human rights and democratic values is suspected, by the Russians, as being subversive and part of a major attempt to undermine the present regime through all kinds of NGOs, foundations, publications and, ultimately, colour revolutions, from Ukraine in the west to Georgia in the south.

On the American side there is no real equivalent; the Russians are mostly not taken seriously as a powerful adversary, either in the Balkans, the Caucasus – especially Georgia – or throughout Central Asia. This is not only irritating for the Russians, it is also positively dangerous as it can lead to strategic misunderstanding concerning the value each side ascribes to its assets or what it sees as a vital interest.

We do not like Nato

The accession of Poland and the three Baltic states to Nato after 1994 is a case in point, and it has never been forgiven in Moscow. After the implosion of the Soviet empire and the inclusion of Germany's eastern provinces in Nato, military and diplomatic experts in the West had suggested that 'Partnership for Peace' (PfP) might be a wise answer to a pressing problem, allowing the Russians to save face while giving enough warmth to the countries coming in from the cold. But Bill Clinton wanted reelection in 1994, and in crucial states of the American Midwest the Polish vote could mean victory or defeat. US domestic pressure at election time put the issue of Polish accession to Nato high on the US agenda. This was followed, inevitably, by more enlargement until the three Baltic states had been incorporated. Nato experts, in a display of black humour, called the exercise 'a bad idea whose time has come'. The Russians still feel that, after the 'Two plus Four' agreement in 1990 had suggested that the Oder river would be the future eastern border of the Western alliance, the West has cheated.

The game is nothing but a modernized version of spheres of influence which, of course, need to be defended, whether they are defined in territorial or in value terms, or both. It is here that dangerous entanglements are most likely to occur. Ukraine's Orange revolution is a case in point and, more especially, that fine line inside Ukraine that divides Russian speakers from Ukrainian speakers, and predominantly Russian sympathies from Western sympathies. The attempt in late 2005 and early 2006 to put pressure on Ukraine through a rise in gas prices and the future North Stream gas pipeline circumventing Ukrainian territory has backfired. Georgia, too, is a case in point, especially Georgia's breakaway province of Abkhazia, with Russian troops still present, or nearby South Ossetia. Or Moldova, where 500,000 Russians in what is called Transnistria are protected by Russia's 14th Army, comprising approximately 1500 troops.

On the global chessboard, Putin linked three issues which, on the face of it, are not connected: the Kosovo conflict, the Conventional Forces in Europe (CFE) Treaty and the US proposal to build a radar site for missile defence against Iran in the Czech Republic and deploy ten anti-missile missiles in Poland. After a while, the Russians developed second thoughts concerning missile defence. They realized that, once Iran was in possession of nuclear warheads and could combine them with medium- and long-range missiles, Russian territory would be much closer to the danger than European, let alone US. So instead of staging another missile crisis as in the early 1980s over Intermediate Nuclear Forces (INF), Russian diplomats offered the Americans a disused radar site in Azerbaijan, thus taking the steam out of West European protests against the US project. One of the controversial issues was taken off the chessboard at least for a while. The Russians are unsure whether to oppose or cooperate – and so are the Americans – while most Europeans have a foreboding of confrontation.

Remember the Congress of Vienna

The absence of a grand design, tsarist or Soviet or post-Soviet, does not, however, mean that there is not a certain traditional methodology or approach at work and a set of rules more akin to nineteenth-century diplomatic practice than to the ideologically fraught competition that dominated the world scene after Lenin's promise of world peace through world revolution in 1917 and Wilson's promise of world peace through democracy in 1918. The basic principles are based on the concept of state power, sovereignty, equilibrium and the idea of a zero sum game between the players. If one side wins a promise or a province, other players in the game are entitled to compensation of equivalent value – whether Western foreign offices like it or not, understand it or not, follow it or not. The basic metaphor is a never-ending game of chess, not the high-tension high-risk drama of poker. Therefore springing a surprise on the other side is generally seen as dysfunctional and dangerous: the sin of adventurism, in Soviet speak. Predictability counts as a virtue, trust as an asset, personal relations as a channel of influence and a source of prestige.

Another principle important to understand as a key to Kremlin thinking is that big countries count for more than small ones who have, when asked, to sign on the dotted line or look for protection from further afield. The instinct for multilateralism driving most European countries and embodied in the EU's Common Foreign and Security (CFSP) or even its Common Security and Defence Policy is something the Russians refuse to take seriously – not unlike the Americans. Whenever possible they choose the bilateral route, especially when and where they are in the stronger position: gas for Germany, Italy, Hungary or any other recipient is not negotiated with Brussels Euro-crats but with individual countries. The asymmetry is striking – and mostly successful.

Spheres of influence, while even the term is anathema to Western thinking, are seen as a reality in international affairs. For the Kremlin the CIS is not a makeshift halfway house but a claim to pre-eminence, whether governments in Kiev or Almaty like it or not. Those spheres of influence must be respected, and the term 'near abroad' was invented, after the fall of the Soviet Union, as the equivalent of the French *chasse gardée*. Its undefined nature invites trespassing and misunderstanding but it also keeps up a certain pressure on those who feel they might, willingly or unwillingly, be included.

The Western equivalent of the 'near abroad' is not only the tangible prospect of EU enlargement with all its accompanying money transfers, subsidies and other blessings, or a Nato Mem-bership Action Plan. The Russians also feel unnerved by the open-ended mission to spread democratic values, to support democratic reform, to observe via the OSCE what goes on in elections, and to finance all kinds of NGOs. For Bolsheviks of the old school this looks like outright espionage and subversion, while the Kremlin of modern times also shows signs of nervousness. But up to a point Kremlin leaders are willing to accept moral sensitivities in countries like Germany that do not wish to be seen in too close an embrace with the Russian bear.

Summitry, experienced practitioners of diplomacy warn, should only be used when the principals are called upon to make a decision, not merely as a photo opportunity. Otherwise it invites grave mis-conceptions like George W. Bush's observation, after his first meeting with Putin: 'I have looked into his eyes and I have seen his soul.' Whatever the US president saw, there was many an occasion for Bush to doubt the wisdom of this remark later. But in today's world leaders understand the benefits of being part of the PR circus and they know well that TV footage showing them in serious conversation with other world leaders brings prestige and popularity, hope and reassurance, signalling to onlookers at Heiligendamm, Kennebunkport or Sochi that the great and the good are holding the globe's future in their hands. Whether in Paris, Berlin or Moscow, this is an irresistible tool of self-aggrandizement – though not necessarily an instrument to keep the world in balance.

The methodology behind Russian foreign policy would be almost incomprehensible to Soviet diplomats of the Gromyko – 'Mr Niet' – school. But it would be immediately recognizable for practitioners from the time of Prince Gortchakov, Bismarck and Disraeli. In the summer of 1878, new borders were drawn across the Balkans, spheres of influence delineated, the small countries told to behave, to sign and to keep silent; a shooting war between the major powers was avoided, for the time being, and the concert of Europe saved, by Bismarck the 'honest broker'.

Today, the underlying methodology is fairly traditional, with some overriding concerns forcing the big powers together; this is no longer the spectre of communist revolution, now defunct, but the North–South divide, terrorism and the proliferation of weapons of mass destruction. But what about the substance and the strategic long-term guidelines determining Kremlin policy? Is there something like a discernible theory behind all of this? Something that would make the motives of Kremlin leaders more predictable and, somehow, more manageable?

Damn my principles

The heirs to the Soviet system might well be expected, true to their theoretical upbringing, to follow a predetermined course in order to avoid serious contradictions and impasses. But if so, the inherent logic is difficult to discern. In fact there is reason to doubt even the existence of a foreign policy masterplan. Under the overall imperative of the national interest – which, however, is not free of contradictions when spelt out and translated into realities on the ground – it is a system of trial and error, driven more by domestic needs than by any grand strategy in the international arena.

There is, though, one overriding leitmotif expressed time and again. If, as Putin told *Time* magazine in early December 2007, 'one country starts to dictate an agenda in international affairs, this will not meet with understanding but rather resistance'. There was no need to name the United States of America, which was in for a few lessons in diplomacy: 'Today's world requires that we use other methods and instruments to communicate with one another, and other ways to fight against today's threats. ... We need to negotiate and find compromises. The ability to compromise is not just a diplomatic formality you reach with a partner. Rather it is respect for their legitimate interests.'

The containment of North Korea and its nuclear installations, effected after long negotiations around a six-pointed table with China in the chair, US and Russia co-chairing, Japan and South Korea footing the bill, is cited as an instance of successful crisis management and a model for future collaboration. Unrequited admiration for the sole surviving superpower is what lurks behind most Russian protestations.

Chess being the favourite national pastime, the layout of Russian strategy today, tomorrow and far into the future can be compared to the careful, risk-averse combinations an experienced player is contemplating, always watchful of his opponent's movements, expecting the worst. The backdrop, however, is a philosophy of old-fashioned power politics. The ideologically saturated rules of Cold War times have mostly been relegated to the archives. Fundamentally, a country's foreign policy is shaped by forces beyond the control of politicians: climate, size, resources, population, neighbours – the Kremlin after the Cold War being no exception. Russia today, leaving aside the vast expanse of the Russian landmass, is more of a normal country than it was throughout the Soviet period, the foreign policies of the Kremlin – using the Foreign Ministry as a subservient institution – driven by immediate needs, short-term combinations and personal preferences. But there are certain ground rules for the formulation of the foreign policy agenda, defined by the domestic power structure as much as by the long-term idea of how to shape what the Kremlin likes to call the 'near abroad', relations with major powers like the United States and the PRC, and power - blocs like the European Union.

New era of confrontation?

The nearest thing to a theory to come out of Moscow in recent months was published by Sergei Karaganov, not a new name in the Kremlin's corridors of power, in fact a former adviser to Yeltsin and, in more recent years, to Putin. Karaganov also figures as the Director of the Europe Institute of the Academy of Sciences and dean at the State University for Economics in Moscow. He would not publish something completely objectionable to the Kremlin. In fact his ideas fit in very well with what the world has seen in recent months, especially since Putin voiced his anger at the Munich Security Conference in February 2007. In Moscow Karaganov is respected as an authority on the West in general, the US and the bilateral security equation in particular. What he wrote in a Russian periodical that is being published under his supervision and, in an abbreviated version, in the *International Herald Tribune* in May 2007 sounded like the theoretical underpinning three months after that Munich outburst.

Was Karaganov's message directed at the Americans, or the Europeans? Publishing it in the op-ed pages of the *International Herald Tribune* would have been strange if it was directed exclusively at the Europeans. Perhaps the message to the Europeans contained another, hidden message to the Americans: if you don't play with us, we can play with the Europeans, one by one or all together, just as conveniently. And if you play hardball, the Europeans will get nervous, and we will be nice to them, and you will be the odd man out. The Romans referred to this kind of approach as *divide et impera* – divide and rule.

Karaganov, for starters, wondered why the state of Russian–EU relations was so poor. 'Misunderstandings and detail,' he mused, 'push aside major matters of common interest.' Was it not vital to prevent the wider dissemination of weapons of mass destruction together, or at a minimum contain their proliferation? Or take the fight against terror 'which, after the inevitable American retreat from Iraq will be even worse and indeed mushroom'? Last but not least it was paramount to deal with Islamic extremism – the Russians think of Chechnya and millions of Muslims throughout their southern provinces: to deactivate, to block, or to fight.

After that introduction to world affairs Karaganov came to the hard core of commonality: 'There is, on top of everything else, a common though unspoken concern, and that is the management of the United States of America. The objective must be to persuade this important country to give up its ruinous unilateralism and return to a policy of effective leadership in a multilateral framework.' The Europeans should side with Moscow for the purpose of reminding the US of the rules of the game – and of the limits of power. Of course, a seasoned Kremlin adviser tends to understand very well, especially after the Chirac–Schröder imbroglio with the US over Iraq, that the Europeans, if they side with Moscow, would fall apart between pro-American and anti-American tendencies and, before long, paralyse each other. In a multipolar world Russia would be the main beneficiary. Oil, gas, pipelines and, in the foreseeable future, liquefied natural gas are strong arguments for a historic compromise.

Energy is seen as the main strength of Russia, and also the main weakness of Europe. Russia as a supplier, Karaganov argued, is interested in moderately high prices, while the Europeans want moderately low prices: 'This conflict could have been solved if both sides had a common, overriding strategy.' That means not only a long-term predictable and equitable price – Putin quoted USD 50 in September 2006. For Russia it means above all downstream participation in distribution networks, for the Europeans co-ownership and partial control of Russian production. This, Karaganov concluded, had been the hard core of what Putin had offered, but the Europeans refused and, instead, accused Russia of energy imperialism. The oil offer was followed by the long list of Russian grievances, from the EU's support for Ukraine's Orange revolution in 2004 – indeed for the Kremlin leaders a traumatic experience – to its sympathy with the national independence of Moldova, Georgia and Azerbaijan, and on to the removal of the bronze Red Army soldier from the centre of Tallinn to the outskirts of the Estonian capital.

Those are the 'misunderstandings and details' that were irritating for Karaganov and the Kremlin. Meanwhile, he came back to grand strategy concerns: Russia and Europe are united in the secular decline of their position in the world at large. Russia has to cope with the rise of China and of militant Islam, while Europe's international standing is suffering 'due to the incompetence of the small states'. In military matters and in energy policy Europe, Karaganov insisted, does not count for much.

What follows from all of this? The long-term advice from the Kremlin is unequivocal: 'A Russia–EU alliance may not conform to today's political correctness. But it offers so many advantages to both sides that it will surely be back, one day, on the table.' The Atlantic Alliance? Karaganov would have no regrets over its demise. Russia would win where the Soviet Union lost: the Great Game for Europe's future.

Soon after, in a more substantial paper Karaganov talked of what he termed the NEC: 'the New Era of Confrontation'. It sounded like a position paper for the Kremlin's master and was in fact a variation upon the theme Putin had pronounced in Munich in early February, but couched in more academic language and in systematic order. A long list of the West's sins was produced, with the US again in the dock. Meanwhile, the Europeans, after the departure of Germany's Schröder and France's Chirac, were not granted attenuating circumstances. In fact from Nato enlargement towards Eastern Europe to Ukraine's Orange revolution of 2004, from the US anti-missile project in the Czech Republic and Poland to the unilateral sponsorship of Kosovo's separation from Serbia – hardly an item irritating the Russians was left out.

Was NEC the announcement of a new Cold War? Karaganov and whoever else helped in preparing that memo took a more balanced view, remembering that throughout the rest of the world Russia has few friends, and some of those of doubtful reputation and value. Surely the honeymoon of the early 1990s is over. But the Europeans are by far Russia's number one partner for imports and exports, and the strategic relationship with the US is indispensable for bestowing on Russia the coveted status of the other world power. To what extent a future relationship with the US would be based on antagonism, to what extent on partnership would be decided case by case, without sentimentality or grace. But maintaining the non-proliferation regime in working order (including keeping Iran away from bomb-grade enrichment of uranium) is surely among the essentials common to both powers. Russian entry into the World Trade Organization would be difficult to achieve against a US veto, and the same would apply to OECD membership. Altogether, Karaganov understands a few important things: on the one hand the Russian regime needs a foreign enemy to maintain discipline at home; a little diplomatic deterrence cannot do much harm but will earn respect. On the other hand, from the preservation of the non-proliferation regime to cyber security and the fight against Islamic militancy, Russia and the West have strategic and overriding interests in common, and another arms competition as in the past would be costly, wasteful and destructive – most of all for Russia. So the NEC will stop short of a new Cold War. But the West should prepare for, from time to time, resentful rhetoric, displays of military-industrial prowess, and the occasional spell of cold weather from the East.

Status quo or Russia resurgent?

The overriding question, for Europeans as much as for the rest of the world, is about Russia's long-term Grand Strategy. Is there a repeating pattern which would correspond to something like a grand design, administered and executed from within the Kremlin? And, if so, what would be, for better or worse, the distinctive elements? Cold War or no, after the hopes and illusions of the 1990s had vanished, and the United States turned from a policy of balance and respect for Russia to a concept of hegemony and disregard, there is still 'the West'. Even where 'the West' is deeply divided, seen from Moscow it is still a defining concept.

Russia resurgent: the question for the West is whether the new, post-Soviet Russia sees itself as a status quo power or as a force for revolutionary change – and will act accordingly. What is abundantly clear, before Putin threw down the gauntlet at the Munich Security Conference in February 2007, and even more so afterwards, that the time is past when Russia came, cap in hand, and asked for loans.

Russia's leaders and the vast majority of the Russian people do not wish to relive the past, not Stalin's brutal regime, not the modest civility after, not the 'leaden years' of Brezhnev, and not the phased breakdown that followed. The year One in the modern Russian calendar is when the oil price began to rise; when the rouble came back to life and mutated into a convertible hard currency; when, after a calamitous pause, pensions and salaries began to be paid. No wonder that Putin, the man who happened to preside over the Russian economic miracle, is seen as the man of destiny, saviour of the nation and guarantor of a modest, hitherto unknown measure of happiness.

Russians count their new era as beginning in 1999–2000, and there are plenty of reasons to do so, not least the widely shared assumption that the new era is fragile, that too much depends on the steady flow of oil and gas and continuing high prices, and that, between Western democracy and Russian authoritarianism everything is still in flux. In many respects Russia is still caught in the past. That the legacy must be overcome is precisely where the Russian people and their leaders seem to agree. This needs, among other things, a fair amount of working together with Western countries, not least the US. The new era of limited and controlled confrontation is as much a reality as the need to cooperate on overriding concerns. 'The earth is flat' – Thomas Friedman argues with some conviction. That means that, inevitably, what unites Russia and the West is more important than what divides them. Too much is at stake for Russia, just as for other big players in the Great Game.

Russia today is no longer out to collect all of the Slavic soil and soul in its own hands, nor is Russia any longer in the business of world revolution. The Russia of today is not a revolutionary power, nor is it content to leave things as they are. If there is a long-term, sustainable strategy it has two main aspects, one old-fashioned, one ultra-modern. The modern one means control of energy resources, pipelines and LNG technologies worldwide, possibly forming, in spite of many protestations to the contrary, a kind of Gas OPEC. The more traditional one is to create dependence, protect investment, secure friendly governments and put soldiers, if possible, on both sides of the border.

Pipeline politics

The most dynamic dimension of Russian foreign policy is not foreign policy at all – at least not within the established 'Westphalian system' (Robert Cooper) of states, sovereignty and equilibrium. It is a new kind of trans-imperialism based on control of enough oil and gas to determine much of what happens in the world market, and on the availability of enough funds to create a global system. This helps to keep prices stable and, even more important, to hedge against the kind of crises that made the oil price crash twice, in the mid-1980s and again in 1997–98.

Gazprom, the state monopoly, is the most important instrument of this strategy. The home base for Gazprom, however, is weaker than it looks. Investment has been low, in fact insufficient to keep current levels of extraction beyond 2010. Foreign companies like Royal Dutch Shell and BP have been shown the door out of Eastern Siberia so that Gazprom can gain full control in Sakhalin II and get rid of the production-sharing agreements of the 1990s – Russia's equivalent to the 'unequal treaties' which the Chinese never tire of complaining about. But while Gazprom is congratulating itself on achieving 100 per cent control, the technology imported from Western companies in exchange for energy is almost impossible to replace.

Furthermore, domestic consumption continues to grow and does so at giveaway prices – for Gazprom directors it must be torture to observe how much costly gas, instead of being sold for dollars worldwide, is just being wasted because domestic prices are low, individual consumption cannot be accounted for, and opening windows is still the preferred method of regulating temperature at home. But raising gas prices in the face of public discontent, when inflation is driving up the price of foodstuffs, is not something the Kremlin wants to try.

The dynamic side of Russian foreign policy is to a large extent about oil and gas, increasingly in the form of LNG. Energy is part and parcel of a post-modern grand strategy that has grown out of Soviet energy policies ever since the first oil crunch after 1973, has experienced ups and downs, and is now being used to provide reassurance to the Kremlin as much as to the nation at large.

Moscow's rulers have done everything possible to control pipelines far beyond their own turf – not unlike the Chinese or, for that matter, the United States. The US-sponsored and part-financed Baku-Ceyhan oil-pipeline, following the same logic, was built at the same time as the older Russian systems, bypassing the northern slopes of the Caucasus en route to Novorossiysk on the Black Sea, were growing more and more ramshackle due not only to the wars in Chechnya and trouble in nearby Daghestan but also as the natural result of neglect and inefficiency.

The new Great Game is not about forward-based Cossack regiments, nor is it about T 34 tanks or SS 20 'mirved' missiles but about oil, gas, and pipelines. The Kremlin, far from reconstructing the overstretched Soviet Union of the past, instead wants to control the natural resources of Central Asia and also the downstream consumer markets. Only a few weeks after having secured the South Stream project with Turkey and Italy – and, possibly, Serbia – another agreement was signed, this time on the supply side, with the presidents of Turkmenistan, Uzbekistan and Kazakhstan, all of those countries having vast amounts of gas to sell from their landlocked fields and, if possible, into different directions, to China for instance, or to Iran. The Kremlin strategy is to make sure that pipelines are under Russian control. While Gazprom creates facts on the ground, EU summits can continue to recite pious wishes for European energy independence. Only a few weeks after the contracts with Austria's OMV, Italy, Bulgaria and Turkey had been signed, Gazprom clinched a deal with the Serbian gas and oil monopoly, closing the gap between the Balkans and the Adriatic Sea and Italy – and possibly Algeria. This strategic move cost Gazprom no more than what the *Financial Times* called a 'bargain price' (26 January 2008) in return for guaranteeing Belgrade a key role in shipping gas to Western Europe and handsome fees (€200 million per annum) for transit. In the financial auction for Serbian political loyalties the European Union, anxious to protect Kosovo's precarious independence, had wooed Belgrade by waiving some of the stiff entry conditions to the EU and offering a substantial stabilization package. But Gazprom, bidding on behalf of the Kremlin, outsmarted the Brussels eurocrats. It was the looming Kosovo question that secured for Russia Inc. both a powerful political presence and a controlling stake in south-eastern Europe's energy future.

Gazprom, aka the all-powerful ministry of gas technology of Soviet times, has found its new incarnation as a state monopoly, and more often than not it is difficult to decide whether a certain strategy is business-based or a political move. Where the Soviets feared to tread, Gazprom goes global, much as the Chinese do, and no less than the US. Concessions in Bolivia, for instance, were added to Gazprom's portfolio in the second half of 2007.

Another scramble for Africa

This, however, was not enough. In 2008 the New Year was greeted with a mega-deal: 'Gazprom plans Africa gas grab' was how the *Financial Times* revealed a Russian bid for Nigeria's vast reserves on 5 January 2008. Gazprom was offering to invest in energy infrastructure in return for the chance to develop some of the biggest gas deposits of the world. In 2007, Putin had written to Nigeria's leader Umaru Yar'Adua, in power since April of that year, to seek energy cooperation. What Russia offered seems to have overwhelmed the Nigerians. 'Mind boggling,' as one of the Nigerian officials close to the deal admitted. 'They are ready to beat the Chinese, the Indians and the Americans.' In this list of global players, with Russia in pole position, the Europeans were not even mentioned. Gazprom happily confirmed that a deal was on its way: 'We made a decision to go global in terms of acquiring assets and developing strategy outside Russia. Africa is one of our priorities.'

In the recent past, Nigerian energy had been dominated by Royal Dutch Shell, Chevron and Exxon from the US. They concentrated mostly on oil, Nigeria being Africa's biggest producer of crude. Growing demand for natural gas and the capacity to cool it down to liquid status and transport it safely have changed the equation. The Russians seem to have recognized that gas production was under-performing, and taken their chance. With Gazprom and the Chinese state monopolies bidding against each other, the market turns in the direction of state-backed companies challenging Western rivals. What Gazprom proposes is to win gas exploration blocs and, in return, approval to build LNG plants. In 2006, the lion's share of Nigerian LNG still went to Spain and France (7.10 and 4.23 billion cubic metres respectively). The US had a meagre 10 per cent share, just ahead of Turkey, with all others far behind. Over the past five years, Western companies had invested USD 5 billion in LNG, yielding a revenue of USD 9 billion.

The move into Africa is not without risk for Gazprom, and it will demand deep pockets. Because multinationals, together with the state-owned NNPC, already control most of the gas fields operating, Gazprom will have to take a gamble and go into the costly and uncertain business of exploration. If that proves too costly, they will concentrate on capturing the gas that comes with the oil, normally burnt in a singularly wasteful process called flaring (environmentalists estimate that about half of the world's gas production is thus burnt away). The Russians are in for a huge challenge, both from the hostile nature of the terrain and the climate and from the enduring social and political violence in the Niger Delta, where most of the resources are. But they would not go in if they weren't sure that the gamble will pay both in energy terms and in political influence. A new scramble for Africa, more than a hundred years after the first one, is under way. Gazprom's move is an unprecedented foray into the global competition for African energy assets. In military terms it would be recognized as a bold pincer movement.

A great power

It is foolish for policy advisers and politicians in the West to deny that Russia is a great power or that its influence continues to grow. For each concession Russia makes, whether over Kosovo or over arms control, the Kremlin quotes a price.

Putin became president in 2000 when Russia's foreign reserves were down to USD 8.5 billion. Today Russia's economy is the world's eighth largest, and foreign reserves are at close to USD 500 billion. It is no longer the Warsaw Pact's tanks that are threatening European security, but the ever growing dependence on oil, gas and pipelines from Russia, the inability to come up with a coherent and sustainable energy strategy, and the fear of 'sovereign funds' gobbling up with their petroroubles ever larger chunks of European industry. The currencies of power have changed. The methodology of power has become more civilized, but the essence of power is still the same. Nowhere is this better understood than in the Kremlin.

What the spookocracy in the corridors of power fails to understand is the fact that the biggest threat to Russia's future is not foreign enemies but the combination of various factors, all domestic in nature: the looming demographic crisis, the absence of long-term confidence in the leadership, the weakness of the industrial sector still relying almost exclusively on natural resources, the universal corruption and the stifling of transparency, free press, and answerability in the public domain; in short the severe shortcomings of the political culture. What does all of this tell us about the future actions of Russia? Russia's objectives and performance in the world cannot be divorced from the rules of the game at home.

A U-turn back to the Soviet Union is as unlikely as an enthusiastic conversion to West European or American ways and means. The West's best hopes were expressed by Dmitri Trenin in his essay 'Getting Russia Right' (2007) : 'Russia is probably not going to join the West, but it is on a long march to become Western, "European", and capitalist, even if not for a long while democratic. I mean European in terms of civilization rather than part of the European Union, and gradually more Western than pro-Western (or pro-American). Russia will matter in the foreseeable future, and that is why it is important to read it right.' The outcome will depend on Russia and Russian power elites, first and foremost. But it also depends on the West and on the kind of competition the West manages to put up. If it is, as it should be, the overriding objective to turn the face of Russia and the Russians towards the West, then the presumption must surely be that the transatlantic system gets its own act together, that Western capitalism does not fall apart, that governments and central banks manage their economic and financial affairs with competence, that Western welfare states do not succumb to their inherent weaknesses, mountains of debt and infla-tionary pressures and that Western leaders find the right balance in managing Russia. Neither an enemy nor a friend. Russia is still in the process of redefining itself and, by implication, its relations with the West.

Russia Inc.

Sometimes, when the outside world seems to be addressed it is really the Russian people who are the recipients. 'Our pilots have been grounded for too long. They are happy to start a new life' – this is how President Putin launched the ex-Soviet strategic bomber fleet once again into world-spanning patrols suspended after the end of the great confrontation and the collapse of the Soviet Union, due as much to lack of funds as to the absence of the enemy. The opening of another base on Syria's Mediterranean coast, the long-term lease dating back to Soviet times, had preceded the flying orders. When it comes to selling military hardware the need for defence contractors to make money often comes into conflict with the more diplomatic strategies of the Kremlin and Russian long-term security. Selling advanced anti-air weaponry to Syria is bad enough, but selling the same materiel to Iran, in addition to fourth-generation fighter bombers, is positively dangerous – certainly in the eyes of those in the Moscow General Staff charged with thinking about the long term.

The planting of the Russian flag with the double-headed eagle on the bottom of the polar seabed in late summer 2007, as close to the North Pole as possible, was a grandiose gesture, claiming that Russia's continental shelf – with whatever subterranean treasures it might contain – extends all the way to the pole.

All of this should be taken seriously, not as a return to the Cold War stand-off but as a signal, to Russians as much as to the rest of the world, that Russia claims great power rank, second only to the US, and is back in business. Behind all the boasting and showing off, the truth is, as Dmitri Trenin put it, 'Russia's business is Russia itself.' Power and property are, ironically more than anywhere in the West, one and the same. This is also underlined by the fact, reassuring up to a point, that the people who run Russia are also the people who own much of Russia. Post-imperial Russia on its way to becoming a nation state drums up greatness and Russian nationalism, but it is among the least ideological countries of the world, with plenty of natural resources to export but no ideology to match. The true values are capital assets at home and, preferably, abroad, beyond the reach of the FSB and the sniffer dogs of the tax police. Russia Inc. is doing well while expanding markets, controlling the flow of oil and gas, and acquiring shares in whatever lies downstream.

While in Soviet days antagonism to the bitter end was the founding formula and co-existence imposed upon Soviet ideologues only in later days under the grim shadow of intercontinental ballistic missiles and nuclear warheads, today the relationship is seen as competitive rather than antagonistic. Russia's leaders are not recreating the Soviet Union. 'We made this mistake once,' Sergei Ivanov said, when still defence minister, only half jokingly. Globalization, with China and India rising and their insatiable appetite for raw materials growing, has dealt Russian leaders a hand of cards that is sure to help them through the next thirty or more years and allow them to expand their one-dimensional economy into a science-based post-industrial economy. This is the grand strategy in which the West is assigned an important, in fact essential, more as a partner than as an antagonist. China, for a long time to come, will sell growing quantities of low-tech goods to Russia, as to the US. But capital goods, especially machine tools fitted with cutting-edge technology, and also the more sophisticated technical toys and luxury goods which the Moscow and St Petersburg elites cherish, can only come from Western countries.

Time for a grand strategy

Putin and his people want to rebuild Russia as a great power, with global reach – and with Gazprom's recent excursions, after Central Asia, into Latin America and Central Africa, there is more to come – and they understand their strengths and weaknesses very well. Where Russian tanks never rolled, Gazprom is now doing business, acquiring market share and aiming for monopolies – just as faithful communists had been told, in the old days, about the wicked ways of capitalists cultivating worldwide monopolies.

Obviously, there is much reason for the West to watch and worry. But there is even more reason for the West to get its act together and cheer up, welcome Russia back among the living and to define the areas where strengths are complementary and interests converge. There is no guarantee against serious rivalry over territory, loyalties and markets, from the Balkans and Eastern Europe to the Greater Middle East and beyond. This should be handled in troikas – Kosovo – or quartets – the Middle East, hopefully with more success than in the recent past. Going back to the UN is also an important option to minimize friction and, if crisis occurs, to keep talking and negotiating and avoid confrontation.

The one great premise that Western politicians have to understand is that Russia's foreign policy thinking comes mostly from the nineteenth century. America's was formed in the twentieth century, 'the American century', while Europe's is based on a vision of never never land in the twenty-first century. That makes talking over each other, especially at summit meetings, from Heiligendamm to Kennebunkport, a time-consuming exercise, fraught with misunderstanding and resentment.

A country without friends

Russia the lone wolf – this is not a reassuring metaphor for the West, nor is it a viable strategy for Russia. Developing something like a joint Russia strategy throughout those countries who see themselves as the New West as opposed to the New Russia will take time, and it will – and should – stop short of any kind of neo-containment. This is something that cannot work and would be divisive for Europe and the US.

Cultivating relations with Russia will be a long-term, difficult and sometimes painful effort for the West, but it is as unavoidable as it is promising, and it is in the long-term interest also of Russia and the Russians.

The strange marriage of pride and paranoia, so characteristic of Russian diplomacy from the tsars right down to the present, will persist. The West will have to get used to – and will have to manage – a more aggressive tone and, possibly, the rough substance of Russian political discourse both at home and abroad. Authoritarian democracy needs the image of the ruthless, wily enemy. Meanwhile, the evil forces outside also legitimize toughness and roughness in dealing with dissent and opposition at home. The 2007 election campaign, as well as the presidential campaign to follow, were not an aberration. They were orchestrated in order to make people forget their material complaints, a concerted effort to add fuel to the flames of the new Russian nationalism. What all of this means for Russia's domestic situation as well as for Russia's relations with the outside world, especially with the West, is not difficult to predict. The forecast is for more strong-arm tactics at home, more power struggles at the top, and a rough climate in international affairs.

What began at the Munich Security Conference 2007, when Putin said goodbye to Mr Nice Guy and took off the kidgloves, has turned out to be a two-pronged manoeuvre: not only an opening shot in the new contest with the West but also the first act in a drama orchestrated by the Kremlin for the benefit of the domestic audience. Russian foreign policy and the Kremlin's domestic power base are, for better and for worse, intimately connected, in fact inseparable. The West should not expect a mellowing of the Kremlin's confrontational tone without prior softening of domestic authoritarianism. Or, the other way round, the outside world should not expect the domestic toughness to soften without a climate of détente in international affairs. The domestic scene and the international performance are intimately connected, in fact inseparable. Therefore it is an illusion among many practitioners in the West that they can do business without paying attention to the wider political context. This did in fact work at the time of the Soviet Union, when Russia was both an existential threat and a reliable supplier of gas and oil, but the juxtaposition of democratic values and economic interests cannot work in an environment where mergers and acquisitions are being negotiated on a daily basis and where share swaps between major companies are a feature of everyday life. The democratic rules of the game include, after human rights, transparency, openness and the rule of law.

For the time being the Kremlin, buoyed by high prices for energy and other strategic resources, is not afraid to preside over a country without friends. By and large, however, those who walk the Kremlin's corridors of power are nothing if not realists. They will be careful not to become the victims of their own rhetoric when it comes to existential issues. They have acquired, in practice more than in theory, a keen and crisis-hardened sense of the national interest – such as preserving the core of the non-proliferation system, nuclear parity with the US both in arms build-ups and in arms control, protecting Russia against southern terrorism, keeping China at a safe distance, and cultivating the constructive ambiguity with European nations and more especially the European Union as the most important and, for the time being, almost exclusive market for oil and gas. The availability, in the foreseeable future, of LNG and much more flexible transport facilities may change the equation. But, by and large, Russia will be guided by what the ruling class defines as the national interest in the broadest sense of the term, from the domestic equilibrium to what the Soviets used to call the 'correlation of forces' in the world at large, beyond Russia's borders and sphere of influence. If the Europeans in all of this feel they are getting a rough deal, they have nobody to blame but themselves for as long as they are punching below their weight.

Cold War relations with the Soviet Union were much tougher, it should be remembered, but also much simpler. Relations with today's Russia will see good times and bad times. For a long time to come Russia will not be a Western style democracy. But Russia will go through election cycles. The leaders will need monsters to blame and enemies to identify, much as Western leaders from time to time feel tempted to do. But in an unforgiving world both sides will ultimately converge on a number of important objectives which they have in common, overriding security concerns and common challenges. There is also a healthy base in expanding business, cross-border investment and cultural exchange. Based on more recent experience it is fair to assume that with time, patience and, if necessary, some plain speaking, a code of conduct will emerge helping both sides to manage their relations reasonably and profitably – though surely not without major differences.

No need to get hot under the collar

Russia joined the Council of Europe in the mid-1990s, signing up to a catalogue of civilized behaviour and political restraint. It was meant to be a confidence- and security-building measure. It was also a standard against which Yeltsin's Russia wanted to be judged. Meanwhile, Russia's leaders and the high priests of European values are unhappy with each other, and accusations of bad behaviour are flying in all directions. Throughout the West it should not be forgotten that Russia is only in the year 17 of liberty, that the country comes from a difficult home and has not had a happy youth. With time, and under the civilizing influence of market forces, democratic virtues like the rule of law, transparency and answerability may make themselves felt and transform society, slowly and steadily, as they have transformed the wilder excesses of capitalism throughout the West – in fact constituting the West.

In all of this, cross-border investment will help, because Russian companies will continue to need know-how and foreign direct investment while Western companies engaging with their Russian counterparts will have to live under the watchful eyes of the American SEC (Securities and Exchange Commission) or the German BaFin (Bundesaufsichtsamt für das Finanzwesen), and nobody in his right mind wants to run foul of those venerable institutions. The same is true when it comes to the major Western stock exchanges, whether New York, Chicago, London or Frankfurt. They have their own ways, irreverent and brutal, to punish anybody, big or small, who disobeys the rules. While toning down public criticism of Russia, it may well prove to be more effective to draw Russian attention to the fine print in the Western club rules. At the time of the Soviet Union the Iron Curtain separated two different worlds, and business could be conducted irrespective of Soviet repression, and kept very much insulated. Today this would be a dangerous illusion. The internet, global TV and travel produce an interconnected universe of information, almost impossible to control. More important still, the interdependence of world capital markets does indeed impose rules and regulations upon

Russia that are impossible to shut out and likely to unfold revolutionary powers of transformation. Western business, while often downplaying the human rights rhetoric of political leaders, must be aware of the moral basis for business in an interconnected universe.

Cultural exchange among the academic elite, journalists and managers ought to be encouraged. The harassment inflicted by the FSB on the Russian operation of the British Council in the early days of 2008 is counterproductive by any standard, Russian or otherwise. The 'lone wolf' theory of Russia in the world may be good for Nasi enthusiasts but it is bad for the projection of soft power. It is impossible to play to the gallery and whip up Russian xenophobia, and at the same time attract investment and investors from outside. Sooner or later Russia's modern leaders will have to overcome the authoritarianism inherent in the FSB and open doors and windows. The Soviet Union left no civil infrastructure behind. Paying lip-service to the virtues of civil society will not do in the long run. Reality must change.

Meanwhile, there is plenty of room for cooperation. What both sides share is the need for stability. This starts with an imperative to join forces in the struggle against climate change – though Russian official policy seems not to mind the prospect of a milder climate in Siberia and elsewhere. There is the old arms control agenda from the Cold War and a new one from the time thereafter. The old one comprises the Test Ban Treaty, the various strategic arms limitation treaties, the Non-Proliferation Treaty and the additional watchdog bureaucracy in Vienna, the International Atomic Energy Agency. The IAEA is, however, also part of the new challenges. Not only because there are more proliferators, some like North Korea and Iran active and others waiting in the wings. But there is also the growing need, all over the globe, for more nuclear energy and the enriched uranium to fuel it. To control this peaceful proliferation without allowing any military aspirants to play foul is a gigantic task requiring the greatest attention of the two original superpowers, and their close cooperation.

Transport systems will have to be redesigned to save energy and make use of those northern passages hitherto covered by ice and soon accessible as a result of global warming. Piracy in its traditional form as well as in combination with modern terrorism is another threat requiring joint surveillance, exchange of data and joint defences.

Offshore drilling for gas and oil, whoever owns the seabed, will be another effort in which Russia will need cooperation from abroad, especially from Norway. Otherwise the Russian dream of Shtokman riches from under the Polar Circle will remain a dream for a long time to come. This is only part of the grand bargain to be developed between Russia and the West: energy from Russia; technology from the West in the form of machine tools, information technology, avionics and nanotechnology. Russia, for all its petrodollars, has an enormous need for technology imports from Europe and the US. From road-bulding to housing, from electricity grids to superfast telecommunications, Russia is far behind its needs and its possibilities – and behind the people's expectations.

Russia and the West

The question remains: is there still a political agenda, a system of thought, a pattern of interests, a global vision constituting the West? The answer is no when defined in terms of the Cold War: the organizing principle was containment of the Soviet Union, and with the Soviet Union the organizing principle has gone too. The answer is also yes when defined in terms of soft power and political culture, open society and the right to the pursuit of happiness.

But where is the moral and political place of Russia in all of this, now and in the foreseeable future? Russia has gone through one or two burnouts, and this can be seen in the body language of the older generation, in the massive exodus of elites, and the conditioned reflex of the security services to take control. Russia, in spite of appearances, goes back to its roots – this could be one answer, and both the *siloviki* in the Kremlin and the weakness of civil society could be cited as proof, together with the burden of history and the age-old instinct of Russians to define themselves in defiance of Europe and the US.

There is also another answer, however, and it holds out more hope for Russia and its neighbours far and wide. No return to the leaden years of Brezhnev or the brutal suppression under Stalin and Lenin. Russia is reinventing itself, and the vast natural resources of Siberia at rising world market prices are a chance both to create firm financial ground and to compete with Western countries. Of course Moscow will not soon accept the European Union as a major player in its own right on the world scene but will try, whenever possible, the bilateral track. And Moscow will, whenever possible, try to enhance differences across Europe and between Europeans and Americans. This is nine-teenth-century great power diplomacy played out in an early twenty-first-century environment – and that is why it cannot be the winning strategy. The interdependence of highly industrialized countries in terms of global challenges is too vast, the punishment for unilateralism too severe, the lure of the West throughout the Russian population is far greater than anything China has to offer. The idea in Moscow that a systemic conflict is developing between on one side countries combining capitalism and authoritarianism and on the other side countries opting for liberal capitalism is academic, because it ignores the geopolitics of Asia in general, and Siberia in particular.

Ever since Russia became part of the power play of Europe, i.e. more than three hundred years ago, for all its exceptionalism Russia has been a European power with a vast Asian hinterland. 'Europe our common house' was, in Gorbachev's time, less of a propaganda slogan and more of a vision. Today the democratic subtext of this vision has faded, but the material base has grown. Russia and the countries of Europe, Russia and the US will, whether they like it or not, share a common destiny.

12

Epilogue: the making of a president

*'Do not reproach me for my contradictions. I perceived them without
wishing to avoid them, for they exist in the things that I describe – let
this be said once and for all. How can I give you a true idea of what
I am describing without contradicting myself at every word?'*

Marquis de Custine, *Journey for Our Time*

Britain's Prime Minister Winston Churchill once described viewing
the Kremlin's political machinations as like watching a fight among
bulldogs under a carpet; outsiders hear plenty of growling but have
few clues about the outcome until the victor emerges. Soviet times or
no, the analogy was present in the minds of those who tried to make
sense of the twists and turns – and surprises – ultimately leading to
the nomination of Dmitri Medvedev by the incumbent president to be
his successor – with the Russian electorate offered the chance to cast –
or withhold – a vote on 2 March 2008. In the case of Dmitry Medvedev,
once he had been anointed in mid-December 2007 by Putin, public
consent was less of a drama. Medvedev, when running for election,
was in a one-horse race. Putin's backing virtually assured Medvedev of
the chief prize. In addition the Kremlin made sure, through applying
gentle and not so gentle pressure by the police and the internal intelligence services that the media were restrained and that no outsider
had much of a chance in the run-up to the electoral contest.

In fact the elections were stage-managed but not manufactured.
Russian imaginations were hardly set alight. Apart from Medvedev,
the other candidates on the ballot paper were communist and nationalist has-beens and a little known liberal who praised Medvedev. There
were no serious competitors; those who were on the list only served
the purpose of underlining the reasonableness of the Kremlin's official
candidate. A few weeks before the elections Mikhail Kasianov, until
2004 Putin's reform-minded prime minister and the best hope for
Russia's marginalized liberals, had been barred from taking part on a
formality: the authorities insisted that some signatures on his list were

forged. Kasyanov spoke of a 'coordinated campaign of pressure'. To preserve a façade of public enthusiasm the Kremlin put pressure on people to go and cast their vote, thus underlining the popular character of the elections. In the end, Medvedev collected close to 70 per cent of the vote – a far cry from the hollow 99 per cent usually announced after Soviet 'elections'. The pessimistic interpretation is that the elections were a demonstration of Kremlin control over hearts and minds. The optimistic interpretation would be that Russia is in transition, that 'administered democracy', as the Kremlin coined the phrase, is better than no democracy and that at least the basic principle of democratic legitimacy had been upheld. Only time will tell which interpretation carries more truth.

But stating that the elections did not spring any surprises is not to say that what comes after the election in terms of policies and personalities will be a foregone conclusion. Putin himself, when asked about becoming prime minister, had answered: 'Quite a realistic proposal.' But to Russians and non-Russians alike the idea of having the Tsarevitch in the Kremlin and the Tsar in the White House sounds unlikely, and is indeed fraught with uncertainty. The last thing Russians want is to put at risk the precious stability they have gained over the last eight or so years. The newfound well-being is mostly a function of soaring oil prices. But in the imagination of most Russians it is, above all, a product of Putin's statesmanship. Dual rule? For most Russians this would herald a new time of troubles.

Who is Mr Medvedev?

Medvedev himself seems to have felt this unspoken question when, immediately after thanking the President for his nomination he added that, surely, once elected, he would need advice and support from Vladimir Putin. Was this an excessive measure of humility, or the indication of an early deal to step down after a while and make room for the predecessor to be his own successor? Or, most likely, was it simply an indication that even the masters of the Kremlin were not sure of what would come next? Before and after the election, the opaque nature of Russian politics keeps Russians guessing – and the rest of the world too.

The battle for the presidency could have been cut short by the incumbent himself had he followed earlier suggestions from United Russia activists simply to manufacture a two-thirds majority in the Duma, change the letter of the constitution – perfectly legal if a two-thirds majority so wishes – and allow himself a third term, possibly of long duration. This would have answered the universal call for stability, prevented any scramble to succeed the incumbent and answered the question on everybody's mind as to what the former president would do after leaving the innermost sanctum of the Kremlin: not leave the Kremlin.

Throughout 2007, speculation about who would succeed Putin as president concentrated on two candidates: Dmitri Medvedev and Sergei Ivanov. In early summer 2007 Ivanov was promoted from defence minister to first deputy prime minister with responsibility for setting up Russia's future industrial policy – nanotechnology capturing much imagination and most of the funds – creating national champions, inviting foreign direct investment and know-how but also for keeping foreigners away from the keys of industrial power.

Medvedev, a jurist by training, once leapt to Putin's defence when he was under investigation in St Petersburg for some shady real estate transactions. Easy-going, soft-spoken and elegant in appearance – the *Boston Globe* newspaper named him best-dressed politician, and with style – Medvedev is well versed in the world economy and seems to understand Russia's role in it. At the Davos World Economic Forum in February 2007 he pronounced every article of the liberal credo. Medvedev also set himself apart from Putin by insisting that he believed in democracy without any specifications – distancing himself from Putin's Russian-style 'sovereign democracy' – and that he ultimately believed in the regulatory power of the markets over the wisdom of the state bureaucracy. This should not be taken as a flirtation with rebellion but as an indication that Medvedev could be more than his master's voice. His experience in addressing the paramount needs of people across the country must have informed him about the real state of the country beyond the deceptive glitter of Moscow and St Petersburg. In Davos he spoke about the need to diversify the economy, to restore run-down infrastructure, to develop human capital. He knows that this cannot be done by fiat, and that it will take time and a lot of energy, not to mention serious cooperation with the West. He mentioned the danger in Russia's one-dimensional dependence on energy production and energy prices. On the scourge of corruption he was as brutally outspoken as Putin – and as bewildered as Putin. In all of this, the decline of the Russian population, and what to do about it, will be his greatest worry.

Surely, Medvedev presented himself not as a Eurasian ideologue but as a Western-type businessman. If Davos man had had a say in the Kremlin's appointments policy here was the man who seemed to share his language and his pro-business philosophy, wearing elegant suits flown in from Berlin and English shirts, soft spoken and intelligent, with pleasant manners, liking heavy metal and presenting the civilized, European face of post-Soviet Russia. Had a vote been taken at Davos, Medvedev would have won hands down.

But what carried the day at Davos needed a Russian translation, and Medvedev gave it, a fortnight before he was to be elected president, at Krasnoyarsk, a well-to-do city in the very heart of Siberia, not far from Novosibirsk. There he outlined what in the West would pass as an election; he shied away from precise commitments but indicated the general direction for Russia, provided always that world energy markets would continue to fuel for Russia's economic miracle. He talked about the 'Four Is': Infrastructure, Innovation, Investment, Institutions. While it took Medveder forty-five minutes to outline his programme, Putin took away the limelight by holding, live on national TV, a four-hour presidential press conference – his last one, for the time being. Medvedev, most likely, was not amused.

What Medvedev outlined was the translation of public wealth into private welfare. Pensions should be doubled. Private property should be protected – 'we will support free enterprise' – and the conservation of the environment should be inscribed into the constitution. His programme could best be described as a social market economy. *Wohlstand für alle* – Ludwig Erhard's famously effective formula has found, at long last, a Russian echo: well-being for all and sundry, and respect for mother nature.

Medvedev poses as a pragmatist. Vis-à-vis a nation deeply tired of big ideas, he does not waste his time on ideologies. His family background is middle-class, a techno-elite with liberal leanings. He poses as a technocrat, above party and politicking. Does he have a national vision? Even less so than Putin: 'Each nation should have multiple ideas and objectives which bring people together sharing the same state, the same country.' He presents himself as open to a pluralism of ideas and social concepts. 'We do not have to reinvent anything of importance. The basic values have long been pronounced. What matters is to adapt them to Russia's present and future.' Will he have the courage and the power to reduce the role of the intelligence services and the police while opening Russia to liberal market forces? In the 1990s privatization gained a bad name, making many poor and few rich. The early years of the twenty-first century have seen a reverse movement, towards state corporations, national champions and sovereign wealth funds. Medvedev will have to face not only the losers of the past two decades but also the winners. His challenge will be to turn the windfall profits from oil and gas into the basis of a future middle-class society and, in order to turn theory into practice, to find allies for all of this, both at home and abroad.

The making of a president

'Dima' Medvedev had been, ever since Putin had returned from his Dresden assignment to St Petersburg in 1989, a loyal assistant and adviser, more than ten years his junior. In the mid-1990s he had followed Putin to Moscow and into the Kremlin. When Putin was anointed by the ailing Yeltsin to be the future president, Medvedev organized – and won – the dicey 1999–2000 election campaign.

In recent years, combining the key dossiers of public welfare with supreme control of Gazprom made him central to Putin's programme. Although Putin's chosen successor, he is unlikely to be the absolute master of the Kremlin. The Kremlin administration is a spookocracy, and Medvedev, while the nominal master, comes from a different tribe. So far, his role was to be the moon to Putin's sun. What made him attractive to Putin as a potential successor is also his greatest weakness: he lacks traction with the power ministries (Interior, Emergencies, Defence, Foreign Affairs).

Medvedev's tenure will be a continuation of Putin's policies, and Putin, in whatever incarnation, will continue to be for some time the ultimate authority. To the Moscow White House, where the Premier resides, he will take with him his enormous popularity and influence, and it will last for a year or two. Within this period he will have finally to determine what kind of future he envisages for himself. Kremlin or no, Putin is able to redesign the organization of government in his favour without much difficulty and keep the levers of power – most of them.

United Russia will wave anything through the state Duma if and when Putin so decides. Just how thorough a revision of the power structure Putin will want to make depends on whether he is considering a renewed bid for the presidency in 2012 – or at any time before. Questions remain: can Putin be safe and content in a second-rate position? And can the wielders of power in Moscow live comfortably with a split leadership? And what about the Russian people: can they imagine supreme power residing anywhere but in the Kremlin's hallowed halls?

Putin will probably remain Russia's voice for high politics, world affairs and the occasional confrontation with the West and he will be able and willing to make foreign policy an instrument to shape the domestic power structure. Medvedev will embody reliability and be a partner for big business. When he was named successor to Putin the Russian share index jumped forward. But he will also need to be the man to grasp the nettle and be serious about Russia's ailments old and new.

The implications of Dmitry Medvedev

So what are, finally, the foreign policy implications of Dmitri Medvedev? The short answer is: more of the same, but *sotto voce*.

The long answer has to start from inside Russia and take into account the country's vast strengths and its equally vast weaknesses, and the power structure at the top. Medvedev and Putin will need each other. Medvedev needs Putin because otherwise he would be alone among the wolves, a king without a country, moving the levers of power without much effect, not feared and therefore not followed. This is the reason why, when nominated by Putin in mid-December 2007, Medvedev responded, almost in a reflex, that he would need Putin as a tutor and, please, Putin should be prime minister.

But Putin, too, needs a non-threatening, reassuring successor with proven loyalty. Not only in a formal way, the incumbent of the Kremlin sooner or later invariably acquiring the magic of Russia's centre and the mantle of the Tsar, but also in political reality to protect Putin from a backlash by all those whom the president from St Petersburg bypassed, removed or pushed aside, and the many powerful men who have an axe to grind with yesterday's power-holder. Will Putin conform to the role of Number Two in the Russian hierarchy? Or will he signal a comeback to the Kremlin's gilded halls, power and prestige, thus pulling the rug from under his successor's feet? When asked whether he would hang a picture of Medvedev in the White House, Putin's answer was, cryptically: 'I have known Dima for so many years, I do not need a picture of him.' If this was a joke, it was an ambiguous one.

So the question invariably arises: will Dmitri Medvedev be his own man? And, if he can manage to emancipate himself from Putin's powerful presence as well as from the spookocracy around the Kremlin, what policies will he stand for? Everything is still in flux and the world may see what Russians fear most: an uneasy competition for power at the top. In the public mind this is associated with a new time of troubles, while the one thing all Russians, high and low, have come to crave is: stability, stability, stability. They have had too much trouble over the last hundred years, and the economic implosion, just nine years ago at the time of writing, when oil was at ten dollars and the Russian economy down and out, is still fresh in everybody's mind. Compare the fall of the Soviet Union, the melt-down of the economy and run-away inflation with Weimar Germany, and then you realize what the stakes were a few years ago, and what could have happened but, mercifully, did not. Medvedev takes over at a time when Russia has 500 billion petrodollars in its state coffers. This is the upside, and one can observe the conspicuous glitz and unashamed glitter in the heart of Moscow and St Petersburg and even in Western Siberia in the oil-town of Khanty-Mansiysk – just as in Paris, Munich, London and Cannes, Baden-Baden or wherever the rich and beautiful of the inter-national jet set mingle.

But there is a downside, too, and it is serious. Russia's economy is a one-dimensional giant, based exclusively on high prices for oil and natural gas. Apart from natural resources and robust weaponry there is little that Russia has to offer on the world markets. At home, every-thing from fresh fruit to computers has to be imported. Foreign com-panies are only just beginning to set up shop in Russia, still wary of corruption, unpredictable tax regimes and extortion.

Moreover, if the last few years of rising oil revenue presented a window of opportunity, the Kremlin has failed to make the best possible use of it and reform the country from top to bottom. There is no judicial system deserving the name; Medvedev himself spoke about the 'legal nihilism' haunting the country. This is one of the crucial differences compared with India and even China. Corruption, a Russian disease through the centuries, is worse than ever before, and even Putin had to admit that he and his administration have failed to curb it. Most of the infrastructure is decrepit, including some of the older pipelines, suffering from underinvestment and negligence. Trains are moving slowly in order to move at all. Most of the internal air travel binding the vast Russian lands together is done by Ilyushin bombers fitted with rows of seats, many of the planes older than the pilots who fly them. Four out of ten villages, according to Putin, have neither running water nor electricity. Poverty is widespread, although salaries and pensions are at long last being paid, and rising. But inflation and public unrest – as in 2005 – loom large over an economy based on natural resources. The science-based economy of the future is far away, but it is precisely the promised land that Medvedev, as Putin before him, wants to reach. For this, the West is needed, both in terms of know-how and foreign direct investment.

Russia's national interest

What foreign policy to expect, and what role for Russia in the world? This is a question not only about Medvedev but even more about the Russian establishment, including the Russian Orthodox Church, and, moreover, a question about the geopolitical challenges and aspirations of Russia. But, the tsar being the tsar, the question is not unjustified as to what long-term vision Medvedev will promote. And what place for Russia in the world? Wedded to the status quo or out to reverse, no longer through tanks and missiles, but through oil, gas, LNG and pipelines, the setbacks experienced by the empire that is no more but still looms like a giant shadow over the minds of many Russians? Does Medvedev share Putin's oft-quoted view that the fall of the Soviet Union was one of the great disasters of the twentieth century?

Medvedev states, philosophically, that empires come and go but what matters is the enduring national interest. He means Russia, not the shadows of the Soviet Union. He will have to pay much more attention to the CIS countries, with Ukraine wanting to move closer to the EU and even Nato, and the Central Asian oil and gas states trying to avoid, after shedding their old Soviet dependence, a new dependence on Gazprom and Rosneft. The Kremlin will have to be more business-minded and less imperial in outlook and appearance. And there are also the frozen conflicts of South Ossetia, Abkazia, Nagorno-Karabakh and Transnistria to attend to that the Kremlin cannot control, nor anybody else. Medvedev will not be a walkover for anybody inside or outside. Putin, when talking to German Chancellor Merkel on International Women's Day in 2007, warned the West against underestimating Medvedev: 'He does not have to prove his liberal credentials but I can tell you that he is as much a Russian patriot – in the good sense – as I am. I do not think that our partners will find him any easier to deal with. He will stand up most actively for the Russian federation's interests on the international stage.' Medvedev will turn his attention to improving the 'lone wolf' image of Russia sported by his predecessor. But as far as substance is concerned he cannot afford to give anything away – nor will he.

In short, the outside world should not expect much change, and certainly not a U-turn, but keep in mind what Churchill, in describing Russia as 'a riddle inside an enigma, shrouded in a mystery', said in conclusion: 'The only key is the national interest.' So what is, finally, Russia's national interest? First and foremost to be, once again, a great power with global reach, making sure that no important matter close to Russia's new borders or anywhere around the globe is decided or settled against Russia. Kosovo's unilateral declaration of independence in early 2008 is a case in point, which the Kremlin will not soon forgive or forget. Russian 'greatness' also implies that other powers should keep a respectful distance. This should be taken as a warning to Nato Councils preparing a Membership Action Plan for Ukraine in the near future and thinking about doing the same on behalf of Georgia. If the Europeans do not have the stomach for serious confrontation they should think again. Even the Americans must reflect on whether the soup is worth the calories. In a world troubled by climate change, weapons of mass destruction, terrorism, organized crime, failed states and, possibly, cyber war, they surely have more important business to attend to, such as containing Iran's nuclear ambitions or keeping North Korea in the box. Russia, too, will want to preserve the

Non-Proliferation Treaty of 1968, nuclear pre-eminence and the Russian place among the world powers. China and Russia have suggested to Washington a treaty to keep outer space off limits for military installations and equipment, so far without takers.

In the long run, Russia's national interest will force Russia to mend fences with the Europeans and with the new administration in Washington. Climate change, terrorism, Islamic jihad, cyber space, drugs, organized crime – all of the above force Russia into concerted action with the Atlantic nations, and vice versa. A long-term sustainable relationship, however, rests on the assumption that Europeans and Americans slow down the race to the Kremlin in order to obtain special favours. Most importantly, the self-fulfilling prophecy of mutual enmity has got to stop. It is too perilous to be pursued, and it can end in tears.

Dmitri Medvedev in all of this is not only an heir to Putin and to Russia's troubled past. He wants to go down in history as a great reformer. On 14 February, at Krasnoyarsk en route to the presidential elections, he began his address by quoting Catherine the Great: 'Liberty is the soul of everything, without it everything is dead. I want everybody to bow under the law but not as a slave.' Medvedev is the man to pronounce that freedom is better than slavery, that democracy is a productive force, that modern societies need to combine freedom and the rule of law and, finally and foremost, that the fundamental interests of Russia and the West are mutually compatible and, in fact, mostly complementary. The rest is, from time to time, a little intelligent conflict management.

POSTSCRIPT

War brings things to light that otherwise remain obscure. The five-day war in the southern foothills of the Caucasus is no exception. Russia has drawn a red line to be respected not only by a small neighbour, but also by the Europeans and by the imperial power from beyond the sea. Russia plays according to age-old rules. What is at stake is not so much the affiliation of the little border districts long controversial between Georgia and Russia. The paramount objective is to keep Nato and the US at a distance. You must protect your periphery and, if possible, position your soldiers on both sides of the fence; and expect compensation (in the Caucasus, for example) when you have lost something elsewhere (in the Balkans, for example). Politics is seen as a zero-sum game, and is not for the faint-hearted. Sending in the military is the continuation of political intercourse by other means. Before the West gets red under the collar, it would be wise to reconsider the path to South Ossetia.

Russian assertiveness in the 'Near Abroad' is a prelude, and more, no doubt, is to come. After the Georgian leadership got out of control and sent in the tanks, the West was not going to allow itself to be dragged into a real war, nor will Russia take more than a calculable risk. In between, however, there are at least a handful of frozen conflicts in Russia and around Russia, most notably the Crimean Peninsula – now part of Ukraine – that can be unfrozen at any time. Much as the Jugo-succession is still sending tremors across the Eurasian continent, the Soviet succession has not yet found a trust-inspiring form. Legality and legitimacy are at odds in many places. But from now on Russia will insist on a decisive say over the Soviet succession, well beyond today's Russian borders. This implies conflict and crisis and, possibly, even military confrontation. Russia under Putin has put the West on notice.

The August 2008 crisis casts a long shadow. But it is not too early to pose the question as to who are the winners and who are the losers.

On the losing side the Georgian president figures prominently. He failed to settle the problem of those breakaway territories of Abchasia and South Ossetia that Georgia had inherited from the Soviet Union. He has also compromised, probably for a long time to come, the chances of Georgia becoming an associate member of the two foremost Western clubs, EU and Nato. If the US, seconded by the Eastern Europeans, presses for membership, Washington risks a severe crisis within the Atlantic Alliance, with Germany and France unwilling to alienate Russia and compromise their energy supply as well as their promising trading position.

On the losing side too, while the US elections were on, is Barack Obama. The dynamics of the election campaign have changed in favour of the Republican frontrunner John McCain who, when it comes to Russia, has firmly established himself as a hardliner.

The European Union is also among the losers. Once again, the Kremlin has pursued a traditional divide-and-rule strategy. In strategic crisis management, Europe is essentially unable to translate economic clout into political negotiating power. It was a favourable coincidence that when the crisis broke French President Nicolas Sarkozy held the rotating presidency of the European Council, bringing to the table the combined might of France and the EU. But by and large the EU has not had much of an impact. The EU's 'Nabucco' project through Georgia, the southern alternative to Gazprom's virtual pipeline monopoly for natural gas flowing in the direction of European consumers which bypasses Russia, has declined in credibility. Its very feasibility, now that the physical risks have becom apparent, is now in jeopardy.

Nor can the US be counted among the winners. Not only was the State Department – according to Secretary of State Condoleezza Rice – unable to restrain the Georgian leaders in the run up to the ill-chosen military intervention; the Russians also demonstrated to the US the limits of their control over faraway places. If in the future the US carries on regardless and pursues Nato membership for Georgia and Ukraine, it risks rendering the Atlantic Alliance hollow and over-stretched, or entering into a serious and fundamental conflict with a resurgent and assertive Russia – or both. If the US pushes for a Membership Action Plan for either Georgia or Ukraine – or both – they are upping the ante. In that case Ukraine, an unstable political proposition by any standard, will be under severe strain and could break apart, with uncontrollable repercussions throughout Europe and beyond.

Moreover, all of the important issues pending with Russia, from containment of Iran to control of the drugs-and-weapons bazaar, from climate change to mass migrations, will be much more difficult to negotiate, let alone bring to a satisfactory conclusion. In the wider geopolitical context, Russia's Chinese and even Iranian options will be strengthened; instead of the European and transatlantic option implicit in Medvedev's proposal from early July 2008, in Berlin and elsewhere, about a future security system from Vancouver to Vladivostock – and not to Beijing.

Russia, too, is a loser, in spite of appearances. When the bad news about tanks rolling into South Ossetia broke in Moscow, the all-Russian stock exchange took a dive and billions were lost. Russia's economy, being built on gas, oil and pipelines, urgently need Western imports, investment, and know how. They will be much slower to materialize in the foreseeable future. Political risk has increased, and every investor is questioning the security of investment and the reliability of the overall investment climate. Western countries, especially Italy, France, and Germany, will continue to export and invest, but with greater circumspection.

The drama in the Caucasus will not only impact on international affairs. It will also be a defining moment for the domestic set-up, much as the coup of 1993 or the dismemberment of Yukos in 2003. On the Russian side the winner is clearly Dmitri Medvedev, but he is also the loser. His popularity ratings shot up, much as Putin's ratings received a boost eight years earlier when, through the war in Chechnya, he rallied patriotic sentiment, fear of Islam and frustration and changed the political landscape in his favour. Medvedev has gained in domestic prestige and foreign policy clout. But what happened to Mr Nice Guy? Medvedev the reformer and moderniser of Russia, the man of the great national projects, has lost his shine and much of his credibility while Putin has demonstrated to the world that the time of Russian weakness is over, that there are red lines which Russia wants respected, and that Russia is able to exert a quid pro quo for the West's success in carving out of Balkan turmoil the statelet of Kosovo. Whatever the merits of the Kosovo-South Ossetia-Abchasia comparison in international law and political legitimacy, the Kremlin rulers were able to give substance to their early warning: if Kosovo goes its way, South Ossetia and Abchasia might follow, but in the opposite direction. Perhaps there is more to come following a somewhat similar script.

But Russia has to be careful in assessing the damage, including the damage to its own national interest. Support from its Central Asian friends was slow in coming. The Chinese signalled open disapproval. The impact on all those inside Russia dreaming of self-determination is not difficult to guess. The wider repercussions across the whole of Asia will become clearer as time goes by.

There is no need to look for a repeat performance of the Cold War. At best what could and should be restored is a healthy respect for the other side, its instincts and its needs, including face-saving, inspired by nuclear weapons and resulting not only in the vast and complex arms-control architecture but also in a sense of global responsibility. Moreover, ever since the dual crisis over Berlin and Cuba in 1958-1962, an exercise in brinkmanship if ever there was one, both super-powers were united in an informal but effective cartel of war avoidance. This also included respecting security distances and zones of influence.

Today, a new Great Game is taking shape. The new rules, however, are not fixed. The new players are inexperienced, ignoring at their own peril – and at everybody else's peril – the rules so painfully learned at the time of the great confrontation. The so-called 'post-cold-war' period has come to an end. A new era of limited confrontation has begun. Confrontation and competition, but also cooperation in an uncertain mix, are on the agenda. US neo-containment meets Russia's imperial instincts and uncertainties. Where does the US democracy mission find its limits? And where does Russia's Near Abroad end? Maybe at the border posts. Maybe where Russians live, many on the other side of those posts. Two uncertain giants are moving in uncertain directions, sure of where to draw the red lines which the other side must not cross, but unsure about self-restraint and that brutal discipline which, at the time of the Cold War, nuclear weapons imposed on those in power.

Will the Europeans pull themselves together and finally, in the face of mounting danger, translate economic power into international muscle? This is hard to believe, given the recent experience when Europeans where faced with the Caucasus imbroglio: the East Europeans firmly on the side of the US, the West Europeans including

227

Germany trying desperately to steer clear of a new Cold War. All in all, the Europeans, without a coherent energy strategy or a concept of how to deal with a resurgent Russia, did not cut a dashing figure. Those differences, today still in the early stages, could well develop into a serious rupture – almost irrespective of the future course of Nato enlargement.

The stand-off between the superpowers of the Cold War taught them a harsh lesson: negotiate, or perish. The drama in the Caucasus also holds some lessons. But so far it is doubtful that those involved are willing to understand what is at stake.

APPENDIX

Births and deaths in Russia 1960–2004

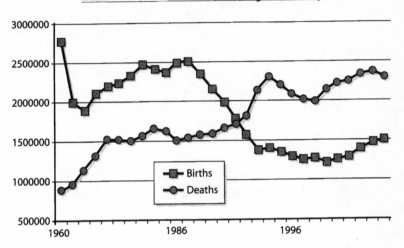

Nationalities

Structure of nationalities in Russia (2002)

Nationalities (% of total population)	2002
Russians	79%
Tatars	3%
Ukranians	2%
Baschkiry	1%
Chuwashy	1%
Checheny	0.9%
Armeny	0.7%
Mordwa	0.5%
Awary	0.5%
Belarusy	0.5%
Kasachs	0.4%
Udmurty	0.4%
Azerbajdschani	0.4%
Mari	0.4%
Germans	0.4%
Kabardiny	0.3%
Osetiny	0.3%
Darginy	0.3%
Burjaty	0.3%
Jakuty	0.3%
Kumyky	0.3%
Ingushy	0.3%
Lesginy	0.2%

Migration in the Russian Federation

	2006	
		per 10,000 population
Migration - total		
Incoming	2,118,068	148,7
Outgoing	1,989,752	139,7
Migration balance	+ 128,316	+ 9,0

Migration from CIS-States into the Russian Federation

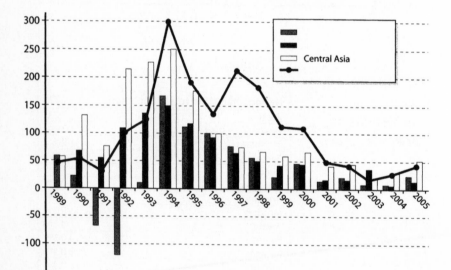

The Demographics of Russia

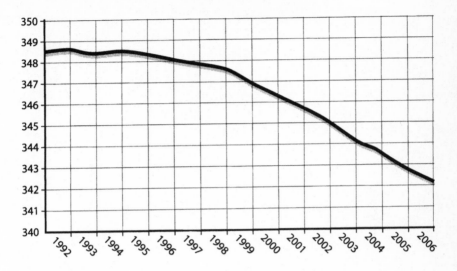

Oil Prices, 1994–March 2008

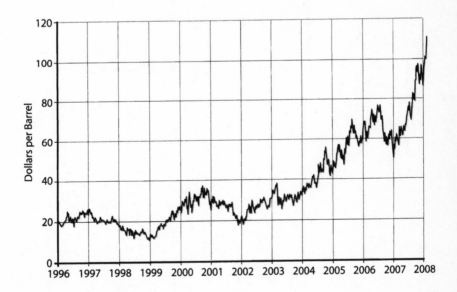

BIBLIOGRAPHY

Epigraphs from Marquis de Custine: *Journey for Our Time: the Journals of the Marquis de Custine*. Russia 1839. Phoenix London 2001 (first published Arthur Barker Ltd 1953).

Books

Adomeit, Hannes: *Die Sowjetmacht in internationalen Krisen und Konflikten*. Verhaltenmuster, Handlungsprinzipien, Bestimtnungsfaktoren. Reihe Internationale Politik und Sicherheit. Baden-Baden 1983.

Altrichter, Helmut: *Kleine Geschichte der Sowjetunion 1917–1991*. München 1993.

Aron, Leon: *Yeltsin: A Revolutionary Life*. London 2000

Baker, Peter; Glassner, Susan: *Kremlin Rising: Vladimir Putin's Russia and the End of Revolution*. New York 2005.

Barysh, Katinka: *The EU and Russia: Strategic Partnership or Squabbling Neighbours*. London: Centre for European Reform 2006.

Beschloss, Michael R.; Talbott, Strobe: *At the Highest Levels: the Inside History of the End of the Cold War*. Boston 1993.

Brown, Archie; Shevtsova, Lilia: *Gorbachev, Yeltsin, and Putin: Political Leadership in Russia's Transition*. Brookings Institution 2001.

Conze, Eckart; Schlie, Ulrich; Seubert, Harald (Hg.): *Geschichte zwischen Wissenschaft und Politik*. Festschrift für Michael Stürmer zum 65. Geburtstag. SWP, Baden-Baden 2003.

Erffa, Wolfgang von: *Das Vermächtnis des Eisernen Emirs: Afghanistans Schicksal*. Böblingen 1989.

Finon, Dominique: *Russia and the 'Gas OPEC': Real or Perceived Threat?* Ifri, Electronic Collection Russie. Nei.Visions. 2007.

Friedman, Thomas: *The World is Flat: a brief history of the globalized world in the 21st century*. London 2005.

Goldfarb, Alex; Litvinenko, Marina: *Death of a Dissident: the Poisoning of Alexander Litvinenko and the Return of the KGB*. New York 2007.

Gratchev, Andrei: *L'Histoire Vraie de la Fin de l'URSS: Le Naufrage de Gorbachev*. Editions du Rocher 1992.

Grotzky, Johannes: *Herausforderung Sowjetunion: Eine Weltmacht sucht ihren Weg*. München 1991.

Hoffman, David E.: *The Oligarchs: Wealth and Power in the New Russia*. 2001

Horvath, Robert: *The legacy of Soviet dissent*. London 2005.

Jack, Andrew: *Inside Putin's Russia*. London 2004.

Kennedy, Paul: *The Rise and Fall of the Great Powers: Economic Change and Military Conflict from 1500 to 2000*. New York 1987.

Kissinger, Henry. *Diplomacy*. New York 1994.

Korinman, Michel; Laughland, John (Eds.): *Russia: a New Cold War?* Vallentin Mitchell Publishers 2008.

Kotkin, Stephen: *Russia under Putin: Democracy or Dictatorship?* Washington DC 2007.

Leffler, Melvyn P.: *For the Soul of Mankind: the United States, the Soviet Union, and the Cold War*. New York 2007.

Levgold, Robert (Ed.): *Russia's Foreign Policy in the Twentieth Century and the Shadow of the Past*. New York 2007.

Luks, Leonid: *Zwei Gesichter des Totalitarismus: Bolschewismus und Nationalismus im Vergleich*. Köln 2007.

Lyne, Roderic; Talbott, Strobe; Watanabe, Koji: Task Force Report to the Trilateral Commission: *Engaging with Russia: The Next Phase*. Trilateral Commission, June 30, 2006.

The Military Balance 2007. IISS London 2007.

Nerlich, Uwe (Ed.) *Die Einhegung sowjetischer Macht. Kontrolliertes militärisches Gleichgewicht als Bedingung europäischer Sicherheit*. SWP, Reihe Internationale Politik und Sicherheit. Baden-Baden 1982.

Nerlich, Uwe; Thomson, James A. (Eds.): *Das Verhältnis zur Sowjetunion: Zur politischen Strategie der Vereinigten Staaten und der Bundesrepublik Deutschland*. Reihe Internationale Politik und Sicherheit. Baden-Baden 1986.

Politkovskaya, Anna: *Putin's Russia: Life in a Failing Democracy*. London 2007.

Pravda, Alex (Ed.): *Leading Russia: Putin in Perspective*. Oxford 2005.

Rahr, Alexander: *Wladimir Putin: Der 'Deutsche' im Kreml*. München 2000.

—: *Russland gibt Gas*. München 2008.

Russia in Global Affairs, Vol. 3, No. 3. July–September 2005.

Sakwa, Richard: *Putin: Russia's Choice*. London 2003.

Scholl-Latour, Peter: *Russland im Zangengriff: Putins Imperium zwischen NATO, China und Islam*. München 2006.

Segbers, Klaus; De Spiegeleire, Stephan (Eds.): *Post-Soviet Puzzles: Mapping the Political Economy of the Former Soviet Union*. Vol. I: *Against the Background of the Former Soviet Union*. SWP, Aktuelle Materialien zur Internationalen Politik. Baden-Baden 1995.

— (Eds.): *Post-Soviet Puzzles: Mapping the Political Economy of the Former Soviet Union*. Vol. II: *Emerging Geopolitical and Territorial Units: Theories, Methods and Case Studies*. SWP, Aktuelle Materialien zur Internationalen Politik. Baden-Baden 1995.

— (Eds.): *Post-Soviet Puzzles: Mapping the Political Economy of the Former Soviet Union*. Vol. III: *Emerging Societal Actors – Economic, Social and Political*

Interests: Theories, Methods and Case Studies. SWP, Aktuelle Materialien zur Internationalen Politik. Baden-Baden 1995.

— (Eds.): *Post-Soviet Puzzles: Mapping the Political Economy of the Former Soviet Union.* Vol. IV: *The Emancipation of Society as a Reaction to Systemic Change: Survival, Adoption to New Rules and Ethnopolitical Conflicts.* SWP, Aktuelle Materialien zur Internationalen Politik. Baden-Baden 1995.

Shevtsova, Lilia: *Putin's Russia.* Washington DC 2003.

—: *Russia – Lost in Transition: The Yeltsin and Putin Legacies.* Washington DC 2007.

Smith, Kathleen E.: *Mythmaking in the New Russia: Politics and Memory during the Yeltsin Era.* Ithaca, London 2002.

Stern, Jonathan: *The Future of Russian Gas and Gazprom.* Oxford 2005.

Stürmer, Michael: *Die Kunst des Gleichgewichts: Europa in einer Welt ohne Mitte.* Berlin, München 2001.

—: *Welt ohne Weltordungt: Wer wird die Erde erben?* 2te Auflage, Hamburg 2007.

Talbott, Strobe: *The Russia Hand.* New York 2002.

Trenin, Dmitri: *Getting Russia Right.* Washington DC 2007

—: *The End of Eurasia.* Washington DC 2002.

Trenin, Dmitri; Miller, Steven (Eds.): *The Russian Military: Power and Policy.* The MIT Press 2004.

Volkogonov, Dmitri: *Autopsy of an Empire: the Seven Leaders who built the Soviet regime.* New York [u.a.] 1998.

Yergin, Daniel: *The Prize: the Epic Quest for Oil, Money and Power.* New York 1991.

Articles

Baran, Zeyno: 'EU Energy Security: Time to End Russian Leverage'. *The Washington Quarterly* (Autumn 2007).

Blackwill, Robert D.: 'The Three Rs: Rivalry, Russia, Ran'. *The National Interest* (Jan.–Feb. 2008).

Bremmer, Ian; Charap, Samuel: 'The Siloviki in Putin's Russia: Who They Are and What They Want'. *The Washington Quarterly* (Winter 2007).

Interview with Vladimir Putin in *Time:* //Kremlin.ru (19 December 2007).

Karaganov, Sergei: 'Imperialism of the Fittest'. *The National Interest,* no. 80 (Summer 2005).

Mankoff, Jeffrey: 'Russia and the West: Taking the Longer View'. *The Washington Quarterly* (Spring 2007).

McFaul, Michael; Stoner-Weiss, Kathryn: 'The Myth of the Authoritarian Model: How Putin's Crackdown Holds Russia Back'. *Foreign Affairs* (January/February 2008).

'Pipedreams'. *Economist* (24 January 2008).

Primakov, Yevgeny: 'Turning Back over the Atlantic'. *International Affairs: A*

Russian Journal of World Politics, Diplomacy and International Relations, no. 6 (2002).

Rahr, Alexander: 'Germany and Russia: a Special Relationship'. *The Washington Quarterly* (Spring 2007).

Riley, Alan; Umbach, Frank: 'Out of Gas'. *Internationale Politik* (Spring 2007).

Trenin, Dmitri: 'Russia Redefines itself and its Relations with the West'. *The Washington Quarterly* (Spring 2007).

Wallander, Celeste A.: 'Russian Transimperialism and its Implications'. *The Washington Quarterly* (Spring 2007).

Papers

Adomeit, Hannes: 'Putins Westpolitik: ein Schritt vorwärts, zwei Schritte zurück'. SWP-Studie. Berlin 2005.

Allin, Dana H. et al: 'Repairing the Damage: Possibilities and Limits of Transatlantic Consensus'. ADELPHI Paper 389. IISS London 2007.

Aslund, Anders: 'Russia's Challenges as Chair of the G8: Policy Briefs in International Economics' (March 2006).

Association of European Business in the Russian Federation. Position Paper, Autumn 2007. Moscow 2007.

Cohen, Ariel: 'The Coming US–Russian Train Wreck: Is Israel Caught in the Middle?', Jerusalem Issue Brief, Institute for Contemporary Affairs founded jointly at the Jerusalem Center for Public Affairs with the Wechsler Family Foundation, Vol. 7, No. 18 (October 2007).

Council on Foreign and Defence Policy (Moscow): 'A Strategy for Russia – Agenda for the President' (2000).

Dannreuther, Roland: 'Creating New States in Central Asia'. ADELPHI Paper 288. IISS London (March 1994).

Das Schwarze Meer zwischen der EU und Russland: Sicherheit, Energie, Demokratie'. Bergedorfer Gesprächskreis / Odessa. 134. Bergedorfer Protokoll. Hamburg 2007.

De Nevers, Renee: 'The Soviet Union and Eastern Europe: the End of an Era'. ADELPHI Papers. IISS London (March 1990).

Energy Information Administration, Department of Energy: 'Russia'. Washington (April 2007).

European Council on Foreign Relations: 'A Power Audit of EU–Russia Relations. Paper Policy. ECFR November 2007.

European Round Table of Industrialists: 'Seizing the Opportunity: Taking the EU–Russia Relationship to the Next Level' (May 2006).

EU, RELEX Briefing for meeting with members of the House of Lords (22 November 2007).

'Europäische Politik in Zentralasien.' Bergedorfer Gesprächskreis / Astana. 137. Bergedorfer Protokoll. Hamburg 2007.

Gelb, Bernard A.: 'Russian Oil and Gas Challenges'. CRS Report for Congress 2006.

Lambeth, Benjamin S.: 'Is Soviet Defense Policy Becoming Civilianized?' RAND, National Defense Research Institute. August 1990. Santa Monica 1990.

Lynch, Dov: 'Russia faces Europe'. Chaillot Papers 60. (May 2003).

—: 'What Russia sees?' Chaillot Paper 74. (January 2005).

Mirtimer, Edward: 'European Security after the Cold War'. ADELPHI Paper 271. IISS London (Summer 1992).

Müller, Freidemann; Ott, Susanne (Eds.): 'Energy and the Environment in Central and Eastern Europe: a Cliff-Hanger with Differences'. SWP – S 414. Ebenhausen 1996.

Nerlich, Uwe: 'Das atlantische Bündnis am Scheideweg: mögliche politische und militärische Funktionen in einem sich verädndernden Europa'. SWP, Ebenhausen. (July 1990).

—: 'Nukleare Waffen und ihre Kontrolle nach dem Ende des Kalten Krieges'. SWP – S 399 (June 1995).

OECD: 'Regulatory Reform in Russia'. 2005.

Ost-Ausschuss der Deutschen Wirtschaft: 'Deutschland und Russland: Strategische Partner mit Zukunft: Positionspapier zu den deutsch-russischen Wirtschaftsbeziehungen' (September 2007).

—: 'Gute Noten für russisches Geschäftsklima 2008: Investitionen in Höhe von über 1 Milliarde Euro von deutschen Firmen in Russland geplant'. Pressemitteilung des Ost-Ausschusses. Berlin (20 December 2007).

Rumer, Eugene B.: 'Russian Foreign Policy beyond Putin'. ADELPHI Paper 390 (October 2007).

'Russian Intelligence'. International Edition. (22 November 2007).

'Russian Military Policy and Strategy', ed. by Forsström, Pentti, Mikkola, Erko. National Defence College Helsinki 2004.

'Russland und der Westen: Chancen für eine neue Partnerschaft'. Bergedorfer Gesprächskreis / Potsdam /Berlin. 131. Bergedorfer Protokoll. Hamburg 2005.

Schwabecher, Heinrich: 'Die Situation der russischen Streitkräfte: Analysen & Argumente'. Konrad-Adenauer-Stiftung September 2007.

'Strategic Survey 2004–2005: an evaluation and forecast of world affairs'. IISS 2005.

Vektor Russlands. 'Erwägungen über den Weg der Entwicklung Russlands'. Centre of Social-Conservative Policy. St Petersburg 2007.

Voas, Jeanette: 'Soviet Attitudes towards Ballistic Missile Defence and the ABM Treaty'. ADELPHI Papers 255. IISS London (Winter 1990).

Weitz, Richard: 'Revitalizing US–Russian Security Cooperation'. ADELPHI Paper 377. IISS 2005.

'Wirtschaftspartner in Europa: Deutschland – Russland'. Daten, Fakten, Information. 7th edition 2007.

World Bank, Moscow Office: Russian Economic Report No. 12 (April 2006).

INDEX